A Concise

GREEK-ENGLISH DICTIONARY

of the

NEW TESTAMENT

Prepared by

BARCLAY M. NEWMAN, JR.

DEUTSCHE BIBELGESELLSCHAFT
UNITED BIBLE SOCIETIES

Orders may be placed with the

German Bible Society
P. O. Box 81 03 40
D-70520 Stuttgart

www.scholarly-bibles.com

Greek-English Dictionary of the New Testament

© 1993 Deutsche Bibelgesellschaft/German Bible Society, Stuttgart
  1971 United Bible Societies

Printed in Germany by C. H. Beck, Nördlingen

ISBN 978-3-438-06008-2

PREFACE

This dictionary has been designed for use in conjunction with the United Bible Societies' Greek New Testament. It is distinctive, for rather than listing the various meanings of words on the basis of traditional etymological methods which follow logico-historical principles, the different meanings are arranged according to their usage in the New Testament, so that the more central and frequent meanings are given first and the secondary or peripheral meanings follow. Moreover, the meanings are given in present-day English, rather than in accord with traditional ecclesiastical terminology.

Other important features of the dictionary include the following: (1) conciseness, (2) coverage of the total vocabulary contained in both text and apparatus of the United Bible Societies' Greek New Testament, (3) the listing and identification of irregular and unusual verb forms both under the primary entry of the verb and in alphabetical order throughout the dictionary, and (4) cross references from all place-names to the maps that are bound with the dictionary.

Unless otherwise qualified, all verb forms, except infinitives and participles, are cited in the present, indicative, active, first person, singular; infinitives are generally cited in their present, active forms, and participles in the present, active, nominative, masculine, singular. In all cases where the inclusion of forms as separate entries would place them in alphabetical proximity to the primary entry of the word in question, they have been listed only under the primary entry.

With a deep sense of indebtedness and gratitude, special acknowledgment is made to Dorothy G. Axelroth, Bruce M. Metzger, Harold K. Moulton, Karen G. Munson, and Erroll F. Rhodes, whose careful criticism and wise counsel contributed immeasurably toward the preparation of this dictionary.

BARCLAY M. NEWMAN, JR.

ABBREVIATIONS USED IN THIS DICTIONARY

NEW TESTAMENT BOOKS

Mt	Matthew	1, 2 Th	1, 2 Thessalonians
Mk	Mark	1, 2 Tm	1, 2 Timothy
Lk	Luke	Tt	Titus
Jn	John	Phm	Philemon
Ac	Acts	He	Hebrews
Ro	Romans	Jas	James
1, 2 Cor	1, 2 Corinthians	1, 2 Pe	1, 2 Peter
Ga	Galatians	1, 2, 3 Jn	1, 2, 3 John
Eph	Ephesians	Jd	Jude
Php	Philippians	Re	Revelation
Col	Colossians		

OTHER ABBREVIATIONS

acc.	accusative case	m	masculine
act.	active	masc.	masculine (in reference to verbal forms, to avoid confusion with middle)
adj.	adjective		
adv.	adverb		
alt.	alternative	midd.	middle
aor.	aorist	mng.	meaning
cf.	compare	n	neuter
comp.	comparative	neut.	neuter (in reference to verbal forms. to avoid confusion with nominative)
conj.	conjunction		
dat.	dative case		
demon.	demonstrative		
e g.	for example	nom.	nominative
etc.	and so forth	NT	New Testament
f	feminine	obj.	object
f, ff	following	opt.	optative
tem.	feminine (in reference to verbal forms, to avoid confusion with future)	OT	Old Testament
		pass.	passive
		pers.	person
fut.	future	pf.	perfect
gen.	genitive case	pl.	plural
i. e.	that is	plpf.	pluperfect
impers.	impersonal	prep.	preposition
impf.	imperfect	pres.	present
impv.	imperative	pro.	pronoun
ind.	indicative	ptc.	participle
inf.	infinitive	sg.	singular
interj.	interjection	sp.	spelling
interrog	interrogative	subj.	subjunctive, subject
intrans.	intransitive	superl.	superlative
lit.	literally	trans.	transitive

Geographical place names are keyed to the maps appearing on the end sheets of *The Greek New Testament*. The first figure, in bold type, indicates the map number; the following letter and figure indicate the location of the place name on the map.

A

α *alpha* (first letter of the Greek alphabet); *first* (in titles of NT writings)

Ἀαρών m *Aaron*

Ἀβαδδών m *Abaddon, Destroyer* (Hebrew name of a demon transliterated into Greek)

ἀβαρής, ές *of no* (financial) *burden*

αββα m *Father* (of address to God) (Aramaic word)

Ἄβελ m *Abel*

Ἀβιά m *Abijah:* (1) person in the genealogy of Jesus (Mt 1.7); (2) founder of a tribe of priests (Lk 1.5)

Ἀβιαθάρ m *Abiathar* (Mk 2.26)

Ἀβιληνή, ῆς f *Abilene* (2 E–1)

Ἀβιούδ m *Abiud* (Mt 1.13)

Ἀβραάμ m *Abraham*

ἄβυσσος, ου f *abyss; the home of demons and evil spirits; the world of the dead* (Ro 10.7)

Ἄγαβος, ου m *Agabus* (Ac 11.28; 21.10)

ἀγαγεῖν aor. inf. of **ἄγω**

ἀγαθοεργέω *do good; be generous with one's possessions*

ἀγαθοποιέω *do good, help; live uprightly, do what is right or good*

ἀγαθοποιῖα, ας f *doing good* or *right*

ἀγαθοποιός, οῦ m *one who does what is good* or *right*

ἀγαθός, ή, όν *good; useful, satisfactory for one's (its) purpose, fitting, beneficial; sound* (of trees)*, fertile* (of soil)*, happy* (of days); in a moral sense *upright, just; kind, generous; clear* (of conscience); *perfect, inherently good* (of God); τὸ ἀγαθόν *the good, what is good; what is right* or *upright; what is beneficial* or *advantageous;* τὰ ἀγαθά *goods, possessions; good things* (Lk 16.25); *good deeds* (Jn 5.29)

ἀγαθουργέω (contracted form of **ἀγαθοεργέω**) *do good, show kindness*

ἀγαθωσύνη, ης f *goodness;* perhaps *generosity*

ἀγαλλίασις, εως f *extreme joy* or *gladness*

ἀγαλλιάω *be extremely joyful* or *glad*

ἄγαμος, ου f and m *unmarried, single*

ἀγανακτέω *be indignant* or *angry*

ἀγανάκτησις, εως f *indignation*

ἀγαπάω *love* (primarily of

Christian love); *show* or *prove one's love; long for, desire, place first in one's affections*

ἀγάπη, ης f *love* (primarily of Christian love); *concern, interest; sacred meal shared by the early Church* (Jd 12)

ἀγαπητός, ή, όν *beloved, dear-(est); only*

Ἀγάρ f *Hagar* (Ga 4.24, 25)

ἀγγαρεύω *force, press into service*

ἀγγεῖον, ου n *container, vessel*

ἀγγελία, ας f *message, news; command*

ἀγγέλλω *tell*

ἄγγελος, ου m *angel; messenger, one who is sent*

ἄγγος, ους n *container* (for a catch of fish)

ἀγέλη, ης f *herd* (of pigs)

ἀγενεαλόγητος, ον *without (record of) lineage*

ἀγενής, ές *insignificant, inferior*

ἀγιάζω *set apart as sacred to God; make holy, consecrate; regard as sacred; purify, cleanse*

ἁγιασμός, οῦ m *consecration, dedication, sanctification, holiness*

ἅγιος, α, ον *set apart to or by God, consecrated; holy, morally pure, upright;* οἱ ἅγιοι *God's people;* τὸ ἅ. or τὰ ἅ. *the sanctuary* (He 9.1, 25;

13.11); superl. ἁγιώτατος *most sacred* (Jd 20)

ἁγιότης, ητος f *holiness, moral purity; pure motive*

ἁγιωσύνη, ης f *holiness; consecration*

ἀγκάλη, ης f *arm*

ἄγκιστρον, ου n *fishhook*

ἄγκυρα, ας f *anchor*

ἄγναφος, ον *new, unshrunken*

ἁγνεία, ας f *moral purity; chastity*

ἁγνίζω *purify, cleanse*

ἁγνισμός, οῦ m *purification* (ritual)

ἀγνοέω *be ignorant; fail to understand; disregard; perhaps sin in ignorance* (He 5.2)

ἀγνόημα, τος n *a sin committed through ignorance*

ἄγνοια, ας f *ignorance, unawareness; perhaps sin*

ἁγνός, ή, όν *pure, holy; chaste; innocent*

ἁγνότης, ητος f *purity, sincerity*

ἁγνῶς adv. *with pure motive*

ἀγνωσία, ας f *lack of spiritual perception; ignorant talk* (1 Pe 2.15)

ἄγνωστος, ον *unknown*

ἀγορά, ᾶς f *market place*

ἀγοράζω *buy; redeem, ransom*

ἀγοραῖος, ου m *loafer* (who frequents the market place); *court session* (held in ἀγορά, the center of public life);

ἀ. ἄγονται the courts are open (Ac 19.38)

ἄγρα, ας f catch (of fish)

ἀγράμματος, ον uneducated (perhaps = lacking formal rabbinic training)

ἀγραυλέω be or live out of doors

ἀγρεύω trap, catch off guard

ἀγριέλαιος, ου f wild olive tree

ἄγριος, α, ον wild

Ἀγρίππας, α m Agrippa: (1) Herod Agrippa I (Ac 12.1ff); (2) Herod Agrippa II (Ac 25.26)

ἀγρός, οῦ m field; farm; country side

ἀγρυπνέω be alert; watch over

ἀγρυπνία, ας f sleeplessness

ἄγω (aor. ἤγαγον, inf. ἀγα-γεῖν; aor. pass. ἤχθην; fut. pass. ἀχθήσομαι) lead, bring; go; τρίτην ταύτην ἡμέραν ἄγει this is the third day (Lk 24.21); ἄγονται ἀγοραῖοι see under ἀγο-ραῖος (Ac 19.38); ἄγε νῦν now listen, just a moment (Jas 4.13; 5.1)

ἀγωγή, ῆς f manner of life, conduct

ἀγών, ῶνος m struggle, fight; opposition; concern; race (He 12.1)

ἀγωνία, ας f agony, anguish

ἀγωνίζομαι struggle, fight; do one's best; compete (of athletic contests)

Ἀδάμ m Adam

ἀδάπανος, ον free of charge

Ἀδδί m Addi (Lk 3.28)

ἀδελφή, ῆς f sister; fellow believer

ἀδελφός, οῦ m brother; fellow believer; fellow countryman, fellowman

ἀδελφότης, ητος f brother-hood (of believers)

ἄδηλος, ον unmarked; indistinct

ἀδηλότης, ητος f uncertainty

ἀδήλως adv. without a goal in mind

ἀδημονέω be distressed or troubled

ᾅδης, ου m Hades, the world of the dead; death; perhaps hell, the place of final punishment

ἀδιάκριτος, ον without prejudice or favoritism

ἀδιάλειπτος, ον endless, constant

ἀδιαλείπτως adv. constantly, always

ἀδικέω wrong, treat unjustly, harm; do wrong or evil; be in the wrong, be guilty (Ac 25.11)

ἀδίκημα, τος n crime; sin, wrong

ἀδικία, ας f wrongdoing, evil, sin; injustice

ἄδικος, ον evil, sinful; dishonest, unjust; (judge who is) an unbeliever (1 Cor 6.1)

ἀδίκως adv. unjustly

'Αδμίν m *Admin* (Lk 3.33)

ἀδόκιμος, ον *failing to meet the test, disqualified; worthless; corrupted* (mind)

ἄδολος, ον *without admixture, pure*

'Αδραμυττηνός, ή, όν *Adramyttium* (4 E–2)

'Αδρίας, ου m *Adriatic Sea* (4 B–2)

ἀδρότης, ητος f *generous amount*

ἀδυνατεῖ impers. *it is impossible*

ἀδύνατος, ον *impossible* (τὸ ἀ. τοῦ νόμου *what the law could not do* Ro 8.3); *weak; crippled* (Ac 14.8)

ἀδυσβάστακτος, ον *not difficult to bear*

ἄδω *sing*

ἀεί adv. *always, constantly*

ἀετός, οῦ m *eagle; vulture*

ἄζυμος, ον *without yeast, unleavened;* τὰ ἄζυμα *Jewish Feast of Unleavened Bread*

'Αζώρ m *Azor* (Mt 1.13, 14)

"Αζωτος, ου f *Azotus,* (2 A–6), *Ashdod of OT* (1 A–6)

ἀήρ, έρος m *air; ethereal region above the earth, space* (Eph 2.2)

ἀθανασία, ας f *immortality*

ἀθέμιτος, ον *forbidden; disgusting* (of idolatry)

ἄθεος, ον *without God*

ἄθεσμος, ον *morally corrupt, lawless*

ἀθετέω *reject, refuse, ignore;*

make invalid, set aside; break (1 Tm 5.12)

ἀθέτησις, εως f *nullification* (of a commandment); *removal* (of sin)

'Αθῆναι, ῶν f *Athens* (3 A–1, 4 D–3)

'Αθηναῖος, α, ον *Athenian*

ἀθλέω *compete* (in an athletic contest)

ἄθλησις, εως f *difficult struggle*

ἀθροίζω *gather together*

ἀθυμέω *become discouraged or disheartened*

ἀθῷος, ον *guiltless, innocent*

αἴγειος, α, ον *of a goat*

αἰγιαλός, οῦ m *beach, shore*

Αἰγύπτιος, α, ον *Egyptian*

Αἴγυπτος, ου f *Egypt* (3 B–4, 4 F–5)

ἀΐδιος, ον *eternal, everlasting*

αἰδώς, οῦς f *propriety, modesty*

Αἰθίοψ, οπος m *Ethiopian*

αἷμα, τος n *blood; death; murder;* σὰρξ καὶ αἷμα *man, human nature;* ἐξ αἱμάτων *through human procreation* (Jn 1.13)

αἱματεκχυσία, ας f *shedding of blood*

αἱμορροέω *suffer a chronic bleeding*

Αἰνέας, ου m *Aeneas* (Ac 9.33, 34)

αἴνεσις, εως f *praise, adoration*

αἰνέω *praise*

αἴνιγμα, τος n *dim* or *obscure image*

αἶνος, ου m *praise*

Αἰνών f *Aenon* (2 C–4)

αἱρέομαι (aor. **εἱλάμην**, ptc. **ἑλόμενος**) *choose, prefer; decide*

αἵρεσις, εως f *religious party; division, faction; false party or teaching*

αἱρετίζω *choose; appoint*

αἱρετικός, ή, όν *causing divisions*

αἴρω (fut. 3 sg. **ἀρεῖ**; aor. **ἦρα**, inf. **ἆραι**; pf. **ἦρκα**; pf. pass. **ἦρμαι**; aor. pass. **ἤρθην**; fut. pass. **ἀρθήσομαι**) *take, take up; take away, remove* (αἴ. ἐκ τοῦ μέσου *set aside* Col 2.14); *carry; sweep away* (of a flood); *raise* (of one's voice); *take over, conquer* (Jn 11.48); *kill* (Jn 19.15); αἴ. τὴν ψυχήν *keep in suspense* (Jn 10.24)

αἰσθάνομαι *perceive the meaning of, understand*

αἴσθησις, εως f *insight, judgment*

αἰσθητήριον, ου n *power of discernment*

αἰσχροκερδής, ές *greedy for material gain*

αἰσχροκερδῶς adv. *with greediness for material gain*

αἰσχρολογία, ας f *obscene speech*

αἰσχρός, ά, όν *disgraceful, shameful; dishonest*

αἰσχρότης, ητος f *indecent behavior*

αἰσχύνη, ης f *shame, disgrace; shameful deed* (Jd 13)

αἰσχύνομαι *be ashamed; be made ashamed*

αἰτέω *ask, request; require, demand*

αἴτημα, τος n *request; demand*

αἰτία, ας f *reason, cause; accusation, charge; guilt, wrong; relationship* (Mt 19.10)

αἴτιον, ου n *guilt; cause, reason* (αἴ. θανάτου *deserving the death penalty* Lk 23.22)

αἴτιος, ου m *cause, source*

αἰτίωμα, τος n *charge, accusation*

αἰφνίδιος, ον *sudden; unexpected*

αἰχμαλωσία, ας f *captivity; group of captives* (Eph 4.8)

αἰχμαλωτεύω *capture, take prisoner*

αἰχμαλωτίζω *make captive* or *prisoner* (αἰ. πᾶν νόημα εἰς τὴν ὑπακοήν *make every thought obedient* 2 Cor 10.5); *get control of, make prey of* (2 Tm 3.6)

αἰχμάλωτος, ου m *captive, prisoner*

αἰών, ῶνος m *age; world order; eternity* (ἀπ' αἰ. or πρὸ αἰ. *from the beginning*; εἰς αἰ. *and the strengthened* form εἰς τοὺς αἰ. τῶν αἰ. always, forever); Aeon (personified as an evil force); existence, the present life (Mt 13.22; Mk 4.19)

αἰώνιος, ον eternal (of quality rather than of time); unending, everlasting, for all time

ἀκαθαρσία, ας f impurity, immorality; impure motive (1 Th 2.3); filth, rottenness (Mt 23.27)

ἀκάθαρτος, ον unclean, defiling; without relationship to God (1 Cor 7.14)

ἀκαιρέομαι be without opportunity

ἀκαίρως adv. when the time is not right

ἄκακος, ον innocent; unsuspecting

ἄκανθα, ης f thorn-plant

ἀκάνθινος, η, ον of thorns, thorny

ἄκαρπος, ον barren, unfruitful; useless

ἀκατάγνωστος, ον above criticism

ἀκατακάλυπτος, ον uncovered

ἀκατάκριτος, ον without trial by law; uncondemned

ἀκατάλυτος, ον indestructible, without end

ἀκατάπαυστος, ον unceasing, insatiable

ἀκαταστασία, ας f disorder; insurrection (Lk 21.9); maltreatment by mob violence (2 Cor 6.5)

ἀκατάστατος, ον unstable; uncontrollable (tongue)

'Ακελδαμάχ Akeldama (mng. in Aramaic field of blood)

ἀκέραιος, ον innocent, guileless, pure

ἀκήκοα pf. of ἀκούω

ἀκλινής, ές without wavering, firmly

ἀκμάζω become ripe, ripen

ἀκμήν adv. still, even now

ἀκοή, ῆς f report, news, preaching; ear(s); hearing, listening; ἀκοῇ ἀκούσετε surely you will hear (Mt 13.14; Ac 28.26)

ἀκοίμητος, ον sleepless, unresting

ἀκολουθέω follow, accompany; be a disciple

ἀκούω (pf. ἀκήκοα; aor. pass. ptc. ἀκουσθείς) hear; receive news of; give heed to; understand; recover one's hearing; give a judicial hearing (Jn 7.51; Ac 25.22)

ἀκρασία, ας f self-indulgence; lack of self-control

ἀκρατής, ές lacking self-control, violent

ἄκρατος, ον undiluted, full strength

ἀκρίβεια, ας f strictness, exactness

ἀκριβής, ές strict (ἀκριβέστατος strictest Ac 26.5)

ἀκριβόω ascertain, find out

ἀκριβῶς adv. accurately; with care

ἀκρίς, ίδος f *locust, grasshopper*

ἀκροατήριον, ου n *audience hall*

ἀκροατής, οῦ m *a hearer*

ἀκροβυστία, ας f *uncircumcision* (often of non-Jews); ἀκροβυστίαν ἔχω *be a Gentile* (Ac 11.3)

ἀκρογωνιαῖος, α, ον *cornerstone, keystone*

ἀκροθίνιον, ου n *spoils, plunder*

ἄκρον, ου n *boundary, extreme limits; tip* (Lk 16.24); *top* (He 11.21)

'Ακύλας acc. αν m *Aquila*

ἀκυρόω *cancel; disregard*

ἀκωλύτως adv. *unhindered*

ἄκων adv. *unwillingly*

ἀλάβαστρον, ου n *alabaster jar*

ἀλαζονεία, ας f *pride, arrogance*

ἀλαζών, όνος m *arrogant boaster*

ἀλαλάζω *wail loudly; clang*

ἀλάλητος, ον *that cannot be expressed in words*

ἄλαλος, ον *unable to speak, dumb*

ἅλας, ατος n *salt*

ἀλείφω *anoint*

ἀλεκτοροφωνία, ας f *before dawn* (lit. *cockcrow*, the watch from midnight to 3 a.m.)

ἀλέκτωρ, ορος m *rooster, cock*

'Αλεξανδρεύς, έως m *an Alexandrian*

'Αλεξανδρῖνος, η, ον *of Alexandria* (4 F–5)

'Αλέξανδρος, ου m *Alexander:* (1) son of Simon (Mk 15.21); (2) a member of the high-priestly family (Ac 4.6); (3) a Jew of Ephesus (Ac 19.33); (4) opponent(s) of Paul (1 Tm 1.20; 2 Tm 4.14)

ἄλευρον, ου n *wheat flour*

ἀλήθεια, ας f *truth, truthfulness; reality;* ἐπ᾽ ἀ. or ἐν ἀ. often *truly, to be sure;* ἀληθείᾳ *with right motives* (Php 1.18)

ἀληθεύω *speak the truth; be honest*

ἀληθής, ές *true, truthful, honest; real, genuine*

ἀληθινός, ή, όν *real, genuine; true; dependable*

ἀλήθω *grind* (of grain)

ἀληθῶς adv. *truly, in truth, actually, surely*

ἁλιεύς, έως m *fisherman*

ἁλιεύω *fish*

ἁλίζω *salt; restore flavor* (to salt)

ἀλίσγημα, τος n *defilement*

ἁλισθήσομαι alt. fut. pass. of ἁλίζω

ἀλλά conj. *but, rather, on the contrary;* with καί, γε καί, ἤ, or οὐδέ *adds emphasis or contrast; not only this but also* (2 Cor 7.11) ἀλλάσσω (fut. pass. ἀλλαγήσομαι) change, alter; transform; exchange (Ro 1.23)

ἀλλαχόθεν adv. at another place; by another way

ἀλλαχοῦ adv. elsewhere

ἀλληγορέω speak (of) allegorically

ἀλληλουϊά praise the Lord, hallelujah

ἀλλήλων, οις, ους reciprocal pro. one another, each other; ἐν ἀ. mutual (Ro 1.12)

ἀλλογενής, οῦς m foreigner

ἅλλομαι (aor. ἡλάμην) leap; well up (of water)

ἄλλος, η, ο another, other (ἄλλος . . . ἄλλος one . . . another); more, additional

ἀλλοτριεπίσκοπος, ου m busybody, one who interferes in another's affairs, troublemaker

ἀλλότριος, α, ον belonging to another; another, the other; foreigner, enemy (He 11.34); stranger (Jn 10.5)

ἀλλόφυλος, ον foreign (of non-Jews)

ἄλλως adv. otherwise; τὰ ἄ. ἔχοντα deeds that are different (1 Tm 5.25)

Ἀλμεί m Almi (Lk 3.33)

ἀλοάω thresh

ἄλογος, ον unreasoning, wild (of animals); unreasonable

ἀλόη, ης f aloes (aromatic tree sap used for a burial ointment)

ἅλς, ἁλός m salt

ἁλυκός, ή, όν salty

ἀλυπότερος, α, ον relieved of sorrow or anxiety

ἅλυσις, εως f chain; imprisonment

ἀλυσιτελής, ές of no advantage or help

ἄλφα n alpha; beginning, first

Ἀλφαῖος, ου m Alphaeus: (1) father of James (Mt 10.3); (2) father of Levi (Mk 2.14)

ἅλων, ος f threshing floor; what is threshed (of grain)

ἀλώπηξ, εκος f fox

ἅλωσις, εως f capture, capturing

ἅμα: (1) adv. at the same time, together; (2) prep. with dat. together with (ἅμα πρωΐ early in the morning Mt 20.1)

ἀμαθής, ές ignorant

ἀμαράντινος, η, ον unfading

ἀμάραντος, ον unfading, permanent

ἁμαρτάνω (aor. ἥμαρτον [often ἁμαρτησ- in moods other than the ind.]; pf. ἡμάρτηκα) sin, commit a sin, do wrong

ἁμάρτημα, τος n sin; sinful deed

ἁμαρτία, ας f sin (ἔχω ἁ. be sinful); περὶ ἁ. often sin offering ἀμάρτυρος, ον *without evidence or witness*

ἁμαρτωλός, όν *sinful; sinner*

ἄμαχος, ον *peaceable, peaceful*

ἀμάω *mow*

ἀμέθυστος, ου f *amethyst* (a semiprecious stone, usually purple or violet in color)

ἀμελέω *disregard, neglect, reject*

ἄμεμπτος, ον *blameless, faultless*

ἀμέμπτως adv. *blamelessly*

ἀμέριμνος, ον *free from worry or anxiety;* ὑμᾶς ἀ. ποιήσομεν *we will keep you out of trouble* (Mt 28.14)

ἀμετάθετος, ον *unchangeable;* τὸ ἀ. *unchangeableness*

ἀμετακίνητος, ον *immovable, steadfast*

ἀμεταμέλητος, ον *free from regret; irrevocable* (Ro 11.29)

ἀμετανόητος, ον *unrepentant, obstinate*

ἄμετρος, ον *immeasurable, unmeasured* (εἰς τὰ ἄ. *beyond limits* 2 Cor 10.13, 15)

ἀμήν *amen* (of prayer); *truly, indeed*

ἀμήτωρ, ορος *without (record of) a mother*

ἀμίαντος, ον *pure, undefiled, unstained*

Ἀμιναδάβ m *Amminadab* (Mt 1.4; Lk 3.33)

ἄμμος, ου f *sand; seashore* (Re 12.18)

ἀμνός, οῦ m *lamb*

ἀμοιβή, ῆς f *repayment*

ἄμπελος, ου f *grapevine*

ἀμπελουργός, οῦ m *vinedresser, gardener*

ἀμπελών, ῶνος m *vineyard*

Ἀμπλιᾶτος, ου m *Ampliatus* (Ro 16.8)

ἀμύνομαι *come to help*

ἀμφιάζω *clothe, array*

ἀμφιβάλλω *cast a fishnet*

ἀμφίβληστρον, ου n *casting-net for fishing*

ἀμφιέννυμι (pf. pass. ἠμφίεσμαι) *clothe, dress*

Ἀμφίπολις, εως f *Amphipolis* (4 D–2)

ἄμφοδον, ου n *street*

ἀμφότεροι, αι, α *both; all*

ἀμώμητος, ον *blameless, faultless*

ἄμωμον, ου n *spice* (from India)

ἄμωμος, ον *faultless; without blemish*

Ἀμών m *Amon* (Mt 1.10)

Ἀμώς m *Amos:* (1) father of Mattathias (Lk 3.25); (2) father of Josiah (Mt 1.10)

ἄν *particle indicating contingency in certain constructions*

ἀνά *prep. used distributively with acc. each, each one, apiece;* ἀνὰ δύο *two by two* (Lk 10.1); ἀνὰ πεντήκοντα *in groups of fifty* (Lk 9.14); ἀνὰ μέσον cf. μέσον

ἀναβαθμός, οῦ m *(flight of) steps*

ἀναβαίνω (aor. ἀνέβην; pf. ἀναβέβηκα) go up, come up, ascend; grow; go aboard (of ships); arise (Lk 24.38); enter, occur to (1 Cor 2.9)

ἀναβάλλομαι (aor. ἀνεβαλόμην) postpone (ἀ. αὐτούς he brought their hearing to a close, he adjourned their trial Ac 24.22)

ἀναβιβάζω draw or drag (nets ashore)

ἀναβλέπω look up; regain one's sight; be or become able to see

ἀνάβλεψις, εως f restoration of sight

ἀναβοάω cry out

ἀναβολή, ῆς f delay (ἀ. μηδεμίαν ποιησάμενος without losing any time Ac 25.17)

ἀνάγαιον, ου n upstairs room

ἀναγγέλλω (fut. ἀναγγελῶ; aor. ἀνήγγειλα, inf. ἀναγγεῖλαι; aor. pass. ἀνηγγέλην) tell, proclaim; report, inform; preach

ἀναγεννάω give new birth or life to

ἀναγινώσκω (aor. ἀνέγνων, inf. ἀναγνῶναι, ptc. ἀναγνούς; aor. pass. inf. ἀναγνωσθῆναι) read; read in public worship

ἀναγκάζω force, compel; urge, insist

ἀναγκαῖος, α, ον necessary; urgent, pressing; close (of friends)

ἀναγκαστῶς adv. under compulsion

ἀνάγκη, ης f distress, trouble; necessity, constraint, compulsion; ἐξ ἀ. under compulsion, out of a sense of duty (2 Cor 9.7), necessarily (He 7.12); κατὰ ἀ. by means of compulsion (Phm 14)

ἀναγνωρίζομαι make oneself known (to someone) again

ἀνάγνωσις, εως f reading (in public)

ἀνάγω (aor. ἀνήγαγον; aor. pass. ἀνήχθην, inf. ἀναχθῆναι) lead or bring up; bring (of offerings); bring before (Ac 12.4); midd. or pass. set sail

ἀναδείκνυμι (aor. ἀνέδειξα) appoint; show clearly

ἀνάδειξις, εως f public appearance (of an event effected by divine action or decree)

ἀναδέχομαι receive; welcome

ἀναδίδωμι (aor. ptc. ἀναδούς) deliver

ἀναζάω come back to life; come to life (of sin)

ἀναζητέω search after, look for

ἀναζώννυμι (aor. midd. ptc. ἀναζωσάμενος) bind up; ἀ. τὰς ὀσφύας τῆς διανοίας make one's mind ready (1 Pe 1.13)

ἀναζωπυρέω stir into flame, rekindle

ἀναθάλλω (aor. ἀνέθαλον) revive

ἀνάθεμα, τος n cursed, under the curse of God; ἀναθέματι ἀνεθεματίσαμεν we are bound by a solemn vow (Ac 23.14)

ἀναθεματίζω curse, invoke a curse on oneself; bind by a solemn vow

ἀναθεωρέω observe closely; reflect upon

ἀνάθημα, τος n votive gift, offering

ἀναίδεια, ας f shameless persistence

ἀναίρεσις, εως f killing, murder

ἀναιρέω (fut. ἀνελῶ, 3 sg. ἀνελεῖ; aor. ἀνεῖλα, subj. ἀνέλω, inf. ἀνελεῖν, opt. 3 sg. ἀνέλοι; aor. pass. ἀνῃρέθην) do away with, kill, destroy; condemn to death (Ac 26.10); annul, abolish (He 10.9); midd. adopt (Ac 7.21)

ἀναίτιος, ον not guilty, innocent

ἀνακαθίζω sit up

ἀνακαινίζω renew, restore

ἀνακαινόω renew, remake

ἀνακαίνωσις, εως f renewal

ἀνακαλύπτω unveil, uncover

ἀνακάμπτω return; turn back

ἀνάκειμαι be seated at table; be a dinner guest

ἀνακεφαλαιόω sum up; unite, bring together

ἀνακλίνω seat at table; put to bed (Lk 2.7); pass. sit at table; sit down

ἀνακράζω cry out, shout

ἀνακρίνω (aor. pass. ἀνεκρίθην) question, examine (study of Scripture Ac 17.11); judge, evaluate; sit in judgment on, call to account

ἀνάκρισις, εως f preliminary hearing, investigation

ἀνακυλίω roll away

ἀνακύπτω straighten up; stand up; look up

ἀναλαμβάνω (aor. ἀνέλαβον; aor. pass. ἀνελήμφθην) take up; take, carry; pick up, get (2 Tm 4.11); take aboard (Ac 20.13, 14)

ἀνάλημψις, εως f taking up, ascension; perhaps death

ἀναλίσκω and ἀναλόω (fut. 3 sg. ἀναλώσει; aor. ἀνήλωσα, opt. 3 sg. ἀναλοῖ; aor. pass. ἀνηλώθην) consume, destroy

ἀναλογία, ας f proportion (κατὰ τὴν ἀ. according to Ro 12.6)

ἀναλογίζομαι consider closely, think of, compare

ἀναλοῖ aor. opt. 3 sg. of ἀναλίσκω

ἄναλος, ον without salt, insipid

ἀναλόω cf. ἀναλίσκω

ἀνάλυσις, εως f departure; death

ἀναλύω come back, return home; depart (i.e. die Php 1.23)

ἀναλώσει fut. 3 sg. of ἀναλίσκω
ἀναμάρτητος, ον sinless, innocent
ἀναμένω wait expectantly
ἀναμιμνήσκω (fut. ἀναμ-
νήσω; aor. pass. ἀνεμ-
νήσθην) remind; pass. re-
member
ἀνάμνησις, εως f reminder,
remembrance (εἰς τὴν ἐμὴν
ἀ. in memory of me)
ἀνανεόω renew
ἀνανήφω regain one's senses
(ἀ. ἐκ regain one's senses
and escape 2 Tm 2.26)
Ἀνανίας, ου m Ananias:
(1) husband of Sapphira;
(2) disciple at Damascus;
(3) Jewish high priest
ἀναντίρρητος, ον undeniable
ἀναντιρρήτως adv. without
objection or hesitation
ἀνάξιος, ον unworthy, in-
competent, incapable
ἀναξίως adv. in an improper
manner
ἀνάπαυσις, εως f relief, rest;
resting-place; ceasing, stop-
ping
ἀναπαύω (fut. pass. ἀναπα-
ήσομαι) give relief, refresh;
midd. rest, relax; rest upon
(of the Spirit)
ἀναπείθω incite, persuade
ἀνάπειρος, ου m see ἀνάπηρος
ἀναπέμπω send; send back;
send up

ἀναπηδάω jump up
ἀνάπηρος, ου m a cripple
ἀναπίπτω (aor. ἀνέπεσον)
sit; sit at table; lean
ἀναπληρόω meet (require-
ments) (pass. come true Mt
13.14); make up for; com-
plete the full measure of
(1 Th 2.16); occupy, fill
(1 Cor 14.16)
ἀναπολόγητος, ον without
excuse
ἀναπτύσσω open, unroll
ἀνάπτω (aor. pass. ἀνήφθην)
kindle, set ablaze
ἀναρίθμητος, ον innumerable
ἀνασείω incite, stir up
ἀνασκευάζω disturb, unsettle,
upset
ἀνασπάω pull out; draw up
ἀνάστα 2 aor. impv. of ἀνίστημι
ἀναστάς 2 aor. ptc. of ἀνίστημι
ἀνάστασις, εως f resurrection;
πτῶσις καὶ ἀ. downfall and
rise (Lk 2.34)
ἀναστατόω agitate, unsettle;
incite a revolt (Ac 21.38)
ἀνασταυρόω crucify; crucify
again
ἀναστενάζω give a deep groan
ἀνάστηθι 2 aor. impv. of
ἀνίστημι
ἀναστῆναι 2 aor. inf. of ἀνίστημι
ἀναστήσας 1 aor. ptc. of
ἀνίστημι
ἀναστήσω fut. of ἀνίστημι

ἀναστρέφω (aor. pass. ἀνεστράφην) return; pass. live, conduct oneself; stay, live (Mt 17.22)

ἀναστροφή, ῆς f manner of life, conduct

ἀναστῶ 2 aor. subj. of ἀνίστημι

ἀνατάσσομαι compile, draw up, write

ἀνατέλλω (aor. ἀνέτειλα; pf. ἀνατέταλκα) intrans. rise (perhaps shine 2 Pe 1.19); dawn (Mt 4.16); be a descendant (He 7.14); trans. cause to rise (Mt 5.45)

ἀνατίθεμαι (aor. ἀνεθέμην) lay before, present

ἀνατολή, ῆς f sg. rising; perhaps day, dawn (of salvation Lk 1.78); pl. (and sg. Re 21.13) east

ἀνατρέπω overturn; bring ruin to

ἀνατρέφω bring up, rear, train

ἀναφαίνω (aor. ptc. ἀναφάνας) come in sight of, sight; pass. appear

ἀναφέρω (aor. ἀνήνεγκον, inf. ἀνενέγκαι and ἀνενεγκεῖν) offer (of sacrifice); lead or take up; bear the burden of; take away

ἀναφωνέω call out, exclaim

ἀναχθῆναι aor. pass. inf. of ἀνάγω

ἀνάχυσις, εως f flood, excess

ἀναχωρέω withdraw; go away; return (Mt 2.12)

ἀνάψυξις, εως f refreshment; spiritual strength

ἀναψύχω refresh, cheer up

ἀνδραποδιστής, οῦ m kidnapper, slavedealer

Ἀνδρέας, ου m Andrew

ἀνδρίζομαι act like a man

Ἀνδρόνικος, ου m Andronicus (Ro 16.7)

ἀνδροφόνος, ου m murderer

ἀνεβαλόμην aor. of ἀναβάλλομαι

ἀνέβην aor. of ἀναβαίνω

ἀνέγκλητος, ον beyond reproach, without fault

ἀνέγνων aor. of ἀναγινώσκω

ἀνέδειξα aor. of ἀναδείκνυμι

ἀνέθαλον aor. of ἀναθάλλω

ἀνεθέμην aor. of ἀνατίθεμαι

ἀνέθην aor. pass. of ἀνίημι

ἀνεῖλον aor. of ἀναιρέω

ἀνείς aor. ptc. of ἀνίημι

ἀνειχόμην impf. of ἀνέχομαι

ἀνεκδιήγητος, ον indescribable (in a good sense)

ἀνεκλάλητος, ον that cannot be expressed in words

ἀνέκλειπτος, ον never decreasing, inexhaustible

ἀνεκρίθην aor. pass. of ἀνακρίνω

ἀνεκτός, όν tolerable

ἀνέλαβον aor. of ἀναλαμβάνω

ἀνελεήμων, ον unmerciful

ἀνελεῖ fut. 3 sg. of ἀναιρέω

ἀνελεῖν aor. inf. of ἀναιρέω

ἀνέλεος, ον merciless

ἀνελήμφθην aor. pass. of
ἀναλαμβάνω
ἀνέλοι aor. opt. 3 sg. of
ἀναιρέω
ἀνέλω aor. subj. of ἀναιρέω
ἀνελῶ fut. of ἀναιρέω
ἀνεμίζομαι be driven by wind
ἀνεμνήσθην aor. pass. of
ἀναμιμνήσκω
ἄνεμος, ου m wind; ἐκ τῶν
τεσσάρων ἄ. from all directions (Mt 24.31)
ἀνένδεκτος, ον impossible
ἀνενέγκαι and ἀνενεγκεῖν
aor. inf. of ἀναφέρω
ἀνεξεραύνητος, ον unfathom-
able, i.e. impossible of explanation by human minds
ἀνεξίκακος, ον tolerant, patient
ἀνεξιχνίαστος, ον untrace-
able, i.e. impossible of understanding by human minds;
fathomless (Eph 3.8)
ἀνεπαίσχυντος, ον with no
need to be ashamed
ἀνέπεσον aor. of ἀναπίπτω
ἀνεπίλημπτος, ον above reproach
ἀνέρχομαι (aor. ἀνῆλθον) go
or come up
ἄνεσις, εως f relief; ἔχω ἄ.
have some liberty (Ac 24.23)
ἀνέστην 2 aor. of ἀνίστημι
ἀνέστησα 1 aor. of ἀνίστημι
ἀνεστράφην aor. pass. of
ἀναστρέφω
ἀνεσχόμην aor. of ἀνέχομαι
ἀνετάζω examine, interrogate

ἀνέτειλα aor. of ἀνατέλλω
ἄνευ prep. with gen. without;
apart from the knowledge and
will of (Mt 10.29)
ἀνεύθετος, ον unsuitable
ἀνευρίσκω (aor. ἀνεῦρον)
find (by searching)
ἀνέχομαι (impf. ἀνειχόμην;
aor. ἀνεσχόμην) endure; be
patient with, give patient
attention to
ἀνεψιός, οῦ m cousin
ἀνέῳγα pf. of ἀνοίγω
ἀνέῳγμαι pf. pass. of ἀνοίγω
ἀνέῳξα aor. of ἀνοίγω
ἀνεῴχθην aor. pass. of ἀνοίγω
ἀνήγαγον aor. of ἀνάγω
ἀνήγγειλα aor. of ἀναγγέλλω
ἀνηγγέλην aor. pass. of ἀναγγέλλω
ἄνηθον, ου n dill (a seasoning
plant)
ἀνήκει impers. it is proper or
right; τὸ ἀνῆκον the appro-
priate thing
ἀνῆλθον aor. of ἀνέρχομαι
ἀνηλώθην aor. pass. of ἀναλίσκω
ἀνήλωσα aor. of ἀναλίσκω
ἀνήμερος, ον fierce, vicious
ἀνήνεγκον aor. of ἀναφέρω
ἀνήρ, ἀνδρός m man; husband
(ἔχω ἀ. or γινώσκω ἀ. be
a married woman); person
ἀνηρέθην aor. pass. of ἀναιρέω
ἀνήφθην aor. pass. of ἀνάπτω
ἀνήχθην aor. pass. of ἀνάγω
ἀνθέξομαι fut. of ἀντέχομαι

ἀνθίστημι (aor. ἀντέστην; pf. ἀνθέστηκα) *resist, oppose, withstand; hold one's ground* (Eph 6.13)

ἀνθομολογέομαι *give thanks*

ἄνθος, ους n *flower; blossom*

ἀνθρακιά, ᾶς f *charcoal fire*

ἄνθραξ, ακος m *charcoal* (ἄ. πυρός *burning coals* Ro 12.20)

ἀνθρωπάρεσκος, ον *one who acts merely to please men*

ἀνθρώπινος, η, ον *human; characteristic of mankind; ἀ. λέγω speak in familiar words* (Ro 6.19)

ἀνθρωποκτόνος, ου m *murderer*

ἄνθρωπος, ου m *man, human being, person, one (friend, sir, man in address); pl. people; mankind, humanity (κατὰ ἄ. according to human standards); husband* (Mt 19.10); *son* (Mt 10.35); *servant* (Lk 12.36)

ἀνθύπατος, ου m *proconsul* (official in charge of a Roman senatorial province)

ἀνίημι (pres. ptc. ἀνιείς; aor. subj. ἀνῶ, ptc. ἀνείς; aor. pass. ἀνέθην) *loosen, unlash; stop, cease; desert, fail*

ἄνιπτος, ον *not washed according to ritual law*

ἀνίστημι (fut. ἀναστήσω; 1 aor. ἀνέστησα, ptc. ἀναστήσας; 2 aor. ἀνέστην, subj. ἀναστῶ, impv. ἀνά- στα and ἀνάστηθι, inf. ἀναστῆναι, ptc. ἀναστάς) trans. (in fut. and 1 aor. act.) *raise (of the dead); appoint (of prophets); help get up* (Ac 9.41); ἀ. σπέρμα τῷ ἀδελφῷ αὐτοῦ *have children in the name of his (deceased) brother* (Mt 22.24); intrans. (in 2 aor. and all midd. forms) *rise, stand up; appear, come; depart; get ready (to go); rebel* (Ac 5.36f); *come back to life* (Lk 9.8, 19)

Ἅννα, ας f *Anna* (Lk 2.36)

Ἅννας, α m *Annas* (Jewish high priest)

ἀνόητος, ον *foolish; ignorant*

ἄνοια, ας f *stupidity, foolishness; rage, fury*

ἀνοίγω (aor. ἀνέῳξα [ἠνέῳξα and ἤνοιξα]; pf. ἀνέῳγα; pf. pass. ἀνέῳγμαι and ἠνέῳγμαι; aor. pass. ἀνεῴχθην [ἠνεῴχθην, ἠνοίχθην and ἠνοίγην]) trans. *open* (ἀ. τὸ στόμα *speak, teach); restore, heal* (of sight or hearing); intrans. (only in pf. ἀνέῳγα) *open* (τὸ στόμα ἡμῶν ἀ. πρὸς ὑμᾶς *we have spoken frankly to you* 2 Cor 6.11)

ἀνοικοδομέω *rebuild*.

ἄνοιξις, εως f *(act of) opening*

ἀνομία, ας f *wickedness, lawlessness, sin* (ὁ ἄνθρωπος τῆς ἀ. *the personification of lawlessness* 2 Th 2.3; τὸ μυστήριον τῆς ἀ. *the secret power of lawlessness* 2 Th 2.7)

ἄνομος, ον *lawless, outside the law, criminal; a person outside the* (Jewish) *law, Gentile*

ἀνόμως adv. *without the* (Jewish) *law*

ἀνορθόω *restore, rebuild; strengthen;* pass. *straighten up*

ἀνόσιος, ον *irreligious, impious*

ἀνοχή, ῆς f *forbearance, tolerance*

ἀνταγωνίζομαι *struggle*

ἀντάλλαγμα, τος n *something offered in exchange*

ἀναναπληρόω *complete*

ἀνταποδίδωμι (fut. **ἀνταποδώσω**, aor. inf. **ἀνταποδοῦναι**; fut. pass. **ἀνταποδοθήσομαι**) *repay; return*

ἀνταπόδομα, τος n *repayment; retribution*

ἀνταπόδοσις, εως f *compensation*

ἀνταποκρίνομαι *reply; answer back*

ἀντεῖπον aor. of **ἀντιλέγω**

ἀντελαβόμην aor. of **ἀντιλαμβάνομαι**

ἀντέχομαι (fut. **ἀνθέξομαι**) *be loyal to; hold firmly to; help*

ἀντί prep. with gen. (original mng. *opposite*) *for, in place of, instead of; in behalf of; because of* (ἀνθ' ὧν *because;*

therefore); *for, as* (1 Cor 11.15)

ἀντιβάλλω *exchange;* ἀ. λόγους *discuss, converse*

ἀντιδιατίθεμαι *oppose* (ὁ ἀ. *opponent*)

ἀντίδικος, ου m *opponent at law; enemy*

ἀντίθεσις, εως f *contradiction*

ἀντικαθίστημι (aor. **ἀντικατέστην**) *resist*

ἀντικαλέω *invite in return*

ἀντίκειμαι *oppose, be against* (ὁ ἀ. *enemy, opponent*)

ἄντικρυς prep. with gen. *opposite, off*

ἀντιλαμβάνομαι (aor. **ἀντελαβόμην**) *help, come to the help of; benefit from* or *devote oneself to* (1 Tm 6.2)

ἀντιλέγω (aor. **ἀντεῖπον**) *object to, oppose* (εἰς σημεῖον ἀντιλεγόμενον *for a controversial sign* Lk 2.34); *contradict, refute; be rebellious* or *obstinate;* οἱ ἀ. ἀνάστασιν μὴ εἶναι *those who say there is no resurrection* (Lk 20.27)

ἀντίλημψις, εως f *ability to help; helper*

ἀντιλογία, ας f *argument, dispute; hostility, hatred, rebellion*

ἀντιλοιδορέω *reply with a curse*

ἀντίλυτρον, ου n *ransom, means to effect freedom*

ἀντιμετρέω *measure out in return*

ἀντιμισθία, ας f *response, return* (τὴν αὐτὴν ἀ. πλατύνθητε *show us the same feelings that we have for you* 2 Cor 6.13); *punishment*

'Αντιόχεια, ας f *Antioch:* (1) in Syria (4 G–3); (2) in Pisidia (4 F–2)

'Αντιοχεύς, έως m *a man of Antioch*

ἀντιπαρέρχομαι (aor. ἀντιπαρῆλθον) *pass by on the other side of the road*

'Αντιπᾶς, ᾶ m *Antipas* (Re 2.13)

'Αντιπατρίς, ίδος f *Antipatris* (2 B–5, 4 G–4)

ἀντιπέρα prep. with gen. *opposite*

ἀντιπίπτω *resist, fight against*

ἀντιστρατεύομαι *war against*

ἀντιτάσσομαι *oppose, resist*

ἀντίτυπος, ον *copy* (He 9.24); *counterpart, figure pointing to* (1 Pe 3.21)

ἀντίχριστος, ου m *Antichrist* (of one who claims to be Christ or is opposed to Christ)

ἀντλέω (pf. ptc. ἠντληκώς) *draw* (water)

ἄντλημα, τος n *bucket*

ἀντοφθαλμέω *head into, face*

ἄνυδρος, ον *waterless; desert*

ἀνυπόκριτος, ον *sincere, genuine*

ἀνυπότακτος, ον *disorderly, disobedient; outside of one's control, not made subject*

ἄνω adv. *above; up, upwards;* ἕως ἄνω *to the brim* (Jn 2.7)

ἀνῶ aor. subj. of ἀνίημι

ἄνωθεν adv. *from above; again; from the beginning* (Lk 1.3); *for a long time* or *from the very first* (Ac 26.5)

ἀνωτερικός, ή, όν *upper; inland*

ἀνώτερον adv. *first, above* (of a previous statement); *to a better seat* (Lk 14.10)

ἀνωφελής, ές *useless(ness); harmful*

ἀξίνη, ης f *axe*

ἄξιος, α, ον *worthy, deserving; in keeping with, as evidence of* (repentance); *proper, fitting* (1 Cor 16.4; 2 Th 1.3); ἄ. πρός *to be compared with* (Ro 8.18)

ἀξιόω *consider worthy, make worthy* (pass. sometimes *deserve*); *think* (something) *best; desire*

ἀξίως adv. *in a manner worthy of* or *suitable to*

ἀόρατος, ον *invisible, unseen*

'Αουλία alt. form of 'Ιουλία

ἀπαγγέλλω (fut. ἀπαγγελῶ; aor. ἀπήγγειλα, opt. 3 sg. ἀπαγγείλοι; aor. pass. ἀπηγγέλην) *tell, inform; proclaim; call upon, command; acknowledge, confess*

ἀπάγχομαι (aor. ἀπηγξάμην) *hang oneself*

ἀπάγω (aor. ἀπήγαγον; aor. pass. inf. ἀπαχθῆναι) *trans.*

lead away by force; lead; bring before; lead astray (1 Cor 12.2); *put to death* (Ac 12.19); intrans. *lead* (of a road)

ἀπαίδευτος, ον *ignorant, stupid*

ἀπαίρω (aor. pass. 3 sg. ἀπήρθη, subj. **ἀπαρθῶ**) *take away*

ἀπαιτέω *demand in return; demand*

ἀπαλγέω *lose all feeling, become insensitive*

ἀπαλλάσσω (pf. pass. inf. ἀπηλλάχθαι) trans. *set free* (ἀπηλλάχθαι ἀπ᾽ αὐτοῦ to *settle the matter with him* Lk 12.58); intrans. *leave, depart* (Ac 19.12)

ἀπαλλοτρίοομαι *be a stranger to, have no connection with*

ἀπαλός, ή, όν *putting out leaves*

ἀπαντάω *meet*

ἀπάντησις, εως f *meeting*

ἅπαξ adv. *once, one time; once for all time;* ἅ. καὶ δίς *more than once, again and again;* εἰδότας ἅ. πάντα *though you are fully aware of all this* (Jd 5)

ἀπαράβατος, ον *permanent, untransferable*

ἀπαρασκεύαστος, ον *unprepared*

ἀπαρθῶ aor. pass. subj. of ἀπαίρω

ἀπαρνέομαι *disown, renounce claim to* ·

ἀπαρτισμός, οῦ m *completion*

ἀπαρχή, ῆς f *first-portion* (Jewish term for anything set apart to God before the remainder could be used); *first;* equivalent to ἀρραβών (Ro 8.23)

ἅπας, ασα, αν (alternative form of πᾶς) *all; whole;* pl. *everyone, everything*

ἀπασπάζομαι *say good-bye to*

ἀπατάω *deceive, lead astray*

ἀπάτη, ης f *deception;* pl. *deceitful ways* (2 Pe 2.13)

ἀπάτωρ, ορος *without* (*record of*) *a father*

ἀπαύγασμα, τος n *brightness, radiance*

ἀπαχθῆναι aor. pass. inf. of ἀπάγω

ἀπέβαλον aor. of ἀποβάλλω

ἀπέβην aor. of ἀποβαίνω

ἀπέδειξα aor. of ἀποδείκνυμι

ἀπεδίδουν impf. of ἀποδίδωμι

ἀπεδόμην aor. midd. of ἀποδίδωμι

ἀπέθανον aor. of ἀποθνήσκω

ἀπεθέμην aor. midd. of ἀποτίθημι

ἀπείθεια, ας f *disobedience* (υἱοὶ τῆς ἀ. *persons disobedient to God*)

ἀπειθέω *disobey; be an unbeliever*

ἀπειθής, ές *disobedient, rebellious*

ἀπειλέω threaten; warn

ἀπειλή, ῆς f threat; threatening

ἄπειμι (from εἰμί; ptc. ἀπών) be away, be absent

ἄπειμι (from εἶμι; impf. 3 pl. ἀπῇεσαν) go, come

ἀπειπάμην (aor. only) renounce, put aside

ἀπείραστος, ον unable to be tempted

ἄπειρος, ον inexperienced in, unacquainted with

ἀπεκαλύφθην aor. pass. of ἀποκαλύπτω

ἀπεκατεστάθην aor. pass. of ἀποκαθίστημι

ἀπεκατέστην aor. of ἀποκαθίστημι

ἀπεκδέχομαι await expectantly; wait

ἀπεκδύομαι disarm; put off, discard

ἀπέκδυσις, εως f putting off, setting (oneself) free from

ἀπεκριθείς alt. form of ἀποκριθείς

ἀπεκρίθην aor. pass. of ἀποκρίνομαι

ἀπεκτάνθην aor. pass. of ἀποκτείνω

ἀπέκτεινα aor. of ἀποκτείνω

ἀπέλαβον aor. of ἀπολαμβάνω

ἀπελαύνω (aor. ἀπήλασα) drive away

ἀπελεγμός, οῦ m discredit, a bad reputation

ἀπελεύθερος, ου m a freedman

ἀπελεύσομαι fut. of ἀπέρχομαι

ἀπελήλυθα pf. of ἀπέρχομαι

ἀπέλιπον aor. of ἀπολείπω

'Απελλῆς, οῦ m Apelles (Ro 16.10)

ἀπελπίζω expect in return

ἀπέναντι prep. with gen. opposite; before, in full view of; contrary to, against

ἀπενεγκεῖν aor. inf. of ἀποφέρω

ἀπενεχθῆναι aor. pass. inf. of ἀποφέρω

ἀπέπεσα aor. of ἀποπίπτω

ἀπέπλευσα aor. of ἀποπλέω

ἀπεπνίγην aor. pass. of ἀποπνίγω

ἀπέραντος, ον endless

ἀπερισπάστως adv. without distraction; perhaps without reservation

ἀπερίτμητος, ον stubborn (lit. uncircumcised)

ἀπέρχομαι (fut. ἀπελεύσομαι; aor. ἀπῆλθον; pf. ἀπελήλυθα) go; go away, leave; be over or past; spread (Mt 4.24); ἀ. ὀπίσω σαρκὸς ἑτέρας commit sexual immorality (Jd 7)

ἀπεστάλην aor. pass. of ἀποστέλλω

ἀπέσταλκα pf. of ἀποστέλλω

ἀπέστειλα aor. of ἀποστέλλω

ἀπέστησα and ἀπέστην aor. of ἀφίσταμαι

ἀπεστράφην aor. pass. of ἀποστρέφω

ἀπέχω trans. *receive in full; have back* (Phm 15); intrans. *be distant;* midd. *abstain from, avoid, keep free* (from something); impers. perhaps = *it is enough* or *the account is settled* (Mk 14.41)

ἀπήγαγον aor. of ἀπάγω

ἀπηγξάμην aor. of ἀπάγχομαι

ἀπῇεσαν impf. 3 pl. of ἄπειμι

ἀπήλασα aor. of ἀπελαύνω

ἀπῆλθον aor. of ἀπέρχομαι

ἀπηλλάχθαι pf. pass. inf. of ἀπαλλάσσω

ἀπήνεγκα aor. of ἀποφέρω

ἀπήρθη aor. pass. 3 sg. of ἀπαίρω

ἀπιστέω *fail* or *refuse to believe; prove* or *be unfaithful*

ἀπιστία, ας f *unbelief; unfaithfulness*

ἄπιστος, ον *unfaithful, unbelieving* (ὁ ἄ. *unbeliever); incredible* (Ac 26.8)

ἁπλότης, ητος f *generosity, liberality; sincerity, single-hearted devotion*

ἁπλοῦς, ῆ, οῦν *sound, healthy; generous*

ἁπλῶς adv. *generously*

ἀπό prep. with gen. *from; away from; by means of; of; because of, as a result of; since, ever since; about, for; with;* ἀπὸ μιᾶς πάντες *one after another, one and all* (Lk 14.18)

ἀποβαίνω (fut. ἀποβήσομαι;

aor. ἀπέβην) *get out* (of boats);* ἀ. εἰς *result in, lead to*

ἀποβάλλω (aor. ἀπέβαλον) *throw off* (clothes); *lose* (courage)

ἀποβλέπω *keep one's eyes on, give one's attention to*

ἀπόβλητος, ον *rejected*

ἀποβολή, ῆς f *loss; rejection*

ἀπογίνομαι (aor. ptc. ἀπογενόμενος) *die,* i.e. *have no part in*

ἀπογραφή, ῆς f *registration, census*

ἀπογράφω *register, enroll*

ἀποδείκνυμι (aor. ἀπέδειξα; pf. midd. ἀποδέδειγμαι) *attest, commend; claim, proclaim; place, set forth; prove* (Ac 25.7)

ἀπόδειξις, εως f *proof, demonstration*

ἀποδεκατόω *give a tenth, tithe; exact tithes from*

ἀπόδεκτος, ον *pleasing*

ἀποδέχομαι *welcome; receive, accept*

ἀποδημέω *leave* (home) *on a journey, go away*

ἀπόδημος, ον *away from home on a journey*

ἀποδίδωμι (ptc. ἀποδιδούς, ptc. neut. ἀποδιδοῦν (Re 22.2); impf. ἀπεδίδουν; aor. subj. 2 sg. ἀποδῷς, 3 sg. ἀποδῷ and ἀποδοῖ, impv. ἀπόδος, inf. ἀποδοῦναι, ptc. ἀποδούς; aor.

midd. **ἀπεδόμην**; aor. pass. inf. **ἀποδοθῆναι**) *give; pay, render; give back, repay, return; reward* (with good or evil); *keep, fulfill* (of vows); *yield* (Re 22.2); ἀ. λόγον *give account*

ἀποδιορίζω *cause divisions;* perhaps *make false distinctions between people*

ἀποδοκιμάζω *reject* (after testing)

ἀποδοχή, ῆς f *acceptance*

ἀποθανοῦμαι fut. of **ἀποθνήσκω**

ἀποθέμενος aor. midd. ptc. of **ἀποτίθημι**

ἀποθέσθαι aor. midd. inf. of **ἀποτίθημι**

ἀπόθεσθε aor. midd. impv. 2 pl. of **ἀποτίθημι**

ἀπόθεσις, εως f *removal* (ἀ. τοῦ σκηνώματος *death* 2 Pe 1.14)

ἀποθήκη, ης f *barn, granary*

ἀποθησαυρίζω *acquire as a treasure*

ἀποθλίβω *crowd in upon*

ἀποθνήσκω (fut. **ἀποθανοῦμαι**; aor. **ἀπέθανον**) *die; face death, be at death's door; be mortal*

ἀποθῶμαι aor. midd. subj. of **ἀποτίθημι**

ἀποίσω fut. of **ἀποφέρω**

ἀποκαθίστημι and **ἀποκαθιστάνω** (fut. **ἀποκαταστήσω**; aor. **ἀπεκατέστην**; aor. pass. **ἀπεκατ**-**εστάθην**) *reestablish, restore; cure, make well; send* or *bring back* (He 13.19)

ἀποκαλύπτω (aor. pass. **ἀπεκαλύφθην**) *reveal, disclose*

ἀποκάλυψις, εως f *revelation*

ἀποκαραδοκία, ας f *eager longing, deep desire*

ἀποκαταλλάσσω (aor. pass. **ἀποκατηλλάγην**) *reconcile*

ἀποκατάστασις, εως f *restoration*

ἀποκαταστήσω fut. of **ἀποκαθίστημι**

ἀπόκειμαι *be stored away;* impers. *be one's lot* (He 9.27)

ἀποκεφαλίζω *behead*

ἀποκλείω *close, lock*

ἀποκόπτω *cut off* or *away;* midd. *mutilate* or *castrate oneself*

ἀπόκριμα, τος n *sentence* (of death)

ἀποκρίνομαι (aor. pass. **ἀπεκρίθην**, ptc. **ἀποκριθείς**) act. in mng. *answer, reply; respond* (e.g. Mk 9.5); *say, declare; continue* (of discourse)

ἀπόκρισις, εως f *answer, reply*

ἀποκρύπτω *hide, keep secret*

ἀπόκρυφος, ον *secret; stored away*

ἀποκτείνω and **ἀποκτέννω, -νύω** (fut. **ἀποκτενῶ**; aor. **ἀπέκτεινα**; aor. pass. **ἀπεκτάνθην**) *kill, put to death; murder*

ἀποκυέω *give birth to, breed*

αποκυλίω - αποστέλλω

ἀποκυλίω *roll away*
ἀπολαμβάνω (fut. ἀπολήμψομαι; aor. ἀπέλαβον) *receive; get back, recover;* midd. *take aside* (Mk 7.33)
ἀπόλαυσις, εως f *enjoyment, pleasure*
ἀπολείπω (aor. ἀπέλιπον, ptc. ἀπολιπών) *leave behind; abandon, desert* (Jd 6); pass. *remain* (impers. *it remains* or *it is certain* He 4.6)
ἀπόλλυμι (fut. ἀπολέσω and ἀπολῶ; aor. ἀπώλεσα, subj. 3 sg. ἀπολέσῃ, inf. ἀπολέσαι; pf. ptc. ἀπολωλώς; fut. midd. ἀπολοῦμαι; aor. midd. ἀπωλόμην) *destroy; kill; lose;* midd. *be lost, perish, be ruined; die; pass away* (He 1.11); pf. ptc. *lost*
Ἀπολλύων, ονος m *Apollyon, Destroyer*
Ἀπολλωνία, ας f *Apollonia* (4 D-2)
Ἀπολλῶς gen. and acc. ῶ m *Apollos*
ἀπολογέομαι *speak in one's own behalf, defend oneself*
ἀπολογία, ας f *verbal defense, defense* (ἀλλὰ ἀ. *what eagerness to prove your innocence* 2 Cor 7.11); *answer, reply*
ἀπολούομαι *cleanse oneself; wash away* (sin)
ἀπολύτρωσις, εως f *setting free, deliverance, release*
ἀπολύω *release, set free; send*

away; send off; divorce; forgive: midd. *leave* (Ac 28.25)
ἀπολωλώς pf. ptc. of ἀπόλλυμι
ἀπομάσσομαι *wipe off* (as a protest)
ἀπονέμω *show* (of respect)
ἀπονίπτω *wash*
ἀποπίπτω (aor. ἀπέπεσα) *fall from*
ἀποπλανάω *mislead, deceive;* pass. *wander away*
ἀποπλέω (aor. ἀπέπλευσα) *set sail, sail away*
ἀποπληρόω *satisfy* or *meet* (requirements)
ἀποπνίγω (aor. pass. ἀπεπνίγην) *choke; drown*
ἀπορέω *be at a loss, be uncertain, be disturbed*
ἀπορία, ας f *despair, perplexity*
ἀπορίπτω *jump overboard*
ἀπορφανίζω *separate from*
ἀποσκίασμα, τος n *shadow, darkness*
ἀποσπάω *draw* or *lead away; draw* (of swords); pass. *leave, go off* (from someone)
ἀποστάς aor. ptc. of ἀφίσταμαι
ἀποστασία, ας f *apostasy, rebellion*
ἀποστάσιον, ου n (with or without βιβλίον) *written notice of divorce*
ἀποστεγάζω *unroof*
ἀποστέλλω (fut. ἀποστελῶ; aor. ἀπέστειλα, subj. ἀποστείλω [in Ac 7.34 this may

be a dialectical peculiarity of the pres. ind.]; pf. ἀπέσταλκα; aor. pass. ἀπεστάλην) send; send out or away

ἀποστερέω defraud, rob, steal; deny, refuse (μὴ ἀ. ἀλλήλους do not deny marital relations to one another 1 Cor 7.5); pf. pass. ptc. no longer have (1 Tm 6.5)

ἀποστῆναι aor. inf. of ἀφίσταμαι

ἀποστήσομαι fut. of ἀφίσταμαι

ἀπόστητε aor. impv. 2 pl. of ἀφίσταμαι

ἀποστολή, ῆς f apostleship; mission

ἀπόστολος, ου m apostle; messenger

ἀποστοματίζω attack with questions

ἀποστρέφω (aor. pass. ἀπεστράφην) turn away; remove, banish; put back; mislead (perhaps incite to revolt Lk 23.14); midd. (and aor. pass.) turn away from, refuse, reject, desert

ἀποστυγέω hate

ἀποσυνάγωγος, ον excommunicated or banished from the synagogue

ἀποτάσσομαι say good-bye; leave; give up, part with

ἀποτελέω accomplish, perform; pass. be full grown

ἀποτίθημι (aor. midd. ἀπεθέμην, subj. ἀποθῶμαι,

impv. 2 pl. ἀπόθεσθε, inf. ἀποθέσθαι, ptc. ἀποθέμενος) throw off, be done with; take off (clothes); put (in prison)

ἀποτινάσσω shake off

ἀποτίνω (fut. ἀποτίσω) pay (someone) back

ἀποτολμάω be or become bold

ἀποτομία, ας f severity

ἀποτόμως adv. severely, sharply

ἀποτρέπομαι avoid, keep away from

ἀπουσία, ας f absence

ἀποφέρω (fut. ἀποίσω; aor. ἀπήνεγκα, inf. ἀπενεγκεῖν; aor. pass. inf. ἀπενεχθῆναι) take, carry; carry away; lead away by force (Mk 15.1; Jn 21.18)

ἀποφεύγω (aor. ptc. ἀποφυγών) escape

ἀποφθέγγομαι speak, declare; address (generally used in connection with an inspired utterance)

ἀποφορτίζομαι unload

ἀπόχρησις, εως f process of being used

ἀποχωρέω go away, leave

ἀποχωρίζομαι separate; perhaps vanish or split open (Re 6.14)

ἀποψύχω faint, lose heart

'Αππίου Φόρον Forum of Appius (market town south of Rome) (4 A-1)

ἀπρόσιτος, ον unapproachable

ἀπρόσκοπος, ον *blameless, faultless; inoffensive; clear* (of conscience)

ἀπροσωπολήμπτως adv. *impartially*

ἄπταιστος, ον *free from stumbling*

ἅπτω (aor. ptc. ἅψας; aor. midd. ἡψάμην) *light, ignite;* midd. *take hold of, touch* (γυναικὸς μὴ ἅ. *not to marry* 1 Cor 7.1); *harm, injure*

Ἀπφία, ας f *Apphia* (Phm 2)

ἀπωθέομαι (aor. ἀπωσάμην) *push aside; reject; fail to listen to* (one's conscience)

ἀπώλεια, ας f *destruction, utter ruin; hell* (ὁ υἱὸς τῆς ἀ. *one bound to be lost* or *one destined for hell* Jn 17.12; 2 Th 2.3)

ἀπώλεσα aor. of ἀπόλλυμι

ἀπωλόμην aor. midd. of ἀπόλλυμι

ἀπωσάμην aor. of ἀπωθέομαι

ἀρά, ᾶς f *cursing, curse(s)*

ἄρα *inferential particle consequently, therefore, then, thus, so;* sometimes with εἰ or ἐπεί for emphasis

ἆρα *interrogative particle expecting a negative response*

Ἀραβία, ας f *Arabia* (2 E–4, 3 E–4, 4 H–4)

ἆραι aor. inf. of αἴρω

Ἀράμ m *Aram* (Mt 1.3, 4; Lk 3.33)

ἄραφος, ον *seamless*

Ἄραψ, βος m *Arab*

ἀργέω *be idle* or *inoperative*

ἀργός, ή, όν *idle, unemployed; lazy* (γαστέρες ἀ. *lazy gluttons* Tt 1.12); *careless; ineffective, useless*

ἀργύριον, ου n *silver coin, money; silver*

ἀργυροκόπος, ου m *silversmith*

ἄργυρος, ου m *silver; silver coin, money; silver image* (Ac 17.29)

ἀργυροῦς, ᾶ, οῦν *made of silver*

ἀρεῖ fut. 3 sg. of αἴρω

Ἄρειος πάγος m *Areopagus, Hill of Mars* (where the Athenian court convened)

Ἀρεοπαγίτης, ου m *Areopagite* (member of the court of Areopagus)

ἀρεσκεία, ας f *desire to please*

ἀρέσκω (aor. ἤρεσα, inf. ἀρέσαι) *try to please; please, be acceptable to*

ἀρεστός, ή, όν *pleasing;* οὐκ ἀρεστόν ἐστιν *it is not right* (Ac 6.2)

Ἀρέτας, α m *Aretas* (in 2 Cor 11.32 Aretas IV, king of Nabatean Arabia)

ἀρετή, ῆς f *moral excellence, goodness; redemptive acts, power* (of God)

Ἀρηί alt. form of Ἀρνί

ἀρήν, ἀρνός m *lamb*

ἀρθήσομαι fut. pass. of αἴρω

ἀριθμέω *count, number*

ἀριθμός, οῦ m *number, total*

'Αριμαθαία, ας f *Arimathea* (2 B–5)

'Αρίσταρχος, ου m *Aristarchus*

ἀριστάω *eat breakfast; eat a meal*

ἀριστερός, ά, όν *left* (opposite right); *left hand* (Mt 6.3); ὅπλον ἀ. *weapon to defend oneself* (2 Cor 6.7)

'Αριστόβουλος, ου m *Aristobulus* (Ro 16.10)

ἄριστον, ου n *meal, noon meal; feast*

ἀρκετός, ή, όν *enough; it is enough*

ἀρκέω *be enough* or *sufficient;* pass. *be content* or *satisfied*

ἄρκος, ου m and f *bear*

ἅρμα, τος n *chariot, carriage*

'Αρμαγεδών *Armageddon* (cryptic name)

'Αρμίν alt. form of 'Αδμίν

ἁρμόζομαι *promise* or *give in marriage*

ἁρμός, οῦ m *joint* (of the body)

ἄρνας acc. pl. of ἀρήν

ἀρνέομαι *deny; disown, renounce; refuse* (He 11.24)

'Αρνί m *Arni* (Lk 3.33)

ἀρνίον, ου n *lamb, sheep*

ἀροτριάω *plow*

ἄροτρον, ου n *plow*

ἁρπαγείς aor. pass. ptc. of ἁρπάζω

ἁρπαγή, ῆς f *taking* (something) *by violence* or *greed; violence, greed; seizure* (He 10.34)

ἁρπαγμός, οῦ m *something to grasp after; something to hold on to*

ἁρπάζω (aor. pass. ἡρπάγην, ptc. ἁρπαγείς) *take by force; take away, carry off; catch up* (into heaven); perhaps *attack* (Jn 10.12)

ἅρπαξ, αγος adj. *grasping, greedy* (ὁ ἅ. *swindler); savage* (of wolves)

ἀρραβών, ῶνος m *pledge, guarantee* (of what is to come)

ἄρρητος, ον *too sacred to put in words*

ἄρρωστος, ον *sick, ill*

ἀρσενοκοίτης, ου m *male sexual pervert*

ἄρσην, εν gen. ενος *male; man*

'Αρτεμᾶς, ᾶ m *Artemas* (Tt 3.12)

"Αρτεμις, ιδος f *Artemis* (Roman n me *Diana*)

ἀρτέμων, ωνος m *foresail*

ἄρτι adv. *now, at the present time* (ἀπ' ἄρτι *hereafter, from now on, again); just now; at once*

ἀρτιγέννητος, ον *newborn*

ἄρτιος, α, ον *fully qualified*

ἄρτος, ου m *bread, a loaf; food;* ἄ. τῆς προθέσεως or πρόθεσις τῶν ἄ. cf. πρόθεσις ἀρτύω *season; restore flavor* (to salt)

'Αρφαξάδ m *Arphaxad* (Lk 3.36)

ἀρχάγγελος, ου m *archangel*

ἀρχαῖος, α, ον *old, ancient, former; early; original*

'Αρχέλαος, ου m *Archelaus* (Mt 2.22)

ἀρχή, ῆς f *beginning, first* (τὴν ἀ. ὅ τι καὶ λαλῶ ὑμῖν *what I have told you from the very beginning* or *why do I talk to you at all?* Jn 8.25); *origin, first cause; ruling power, authority, ruler* (whether earthly or spiritual); *what is elementary, elementary principle* (He 5.12; 6.1); *corner* (of a cloth)

ἀρχηγός, οῦ m *leader, pioneer, founder, originator*

ἀρχιερατικός, όν *highpriestly*

ἀρχιερεύς, έως m *high priest; member of high priestly family*

ἀρχιποίμην, ενος m *chief shepherd*

"Αρχιππος, ου m *Archippus* (Col 4.17; Phm 2)

ἀρχισυνάγωγος, ου m *president of a synagogue*

ἀρχιτέκτων, ονος m *expert builder*

ἀρχιτελώνης, ου m *tax superintendent*

ἀρχιτρίκλινος, ου m *head steward*

ἀρχοστασία gender and mng. not certain, but may be: (1) neut. pl. of ἀρχοστάσιον, mng. in the pl. *elections* or (2) a misreading of the papyrus hand for διχοστασία, mng. *divisions, dissensions*

ἄρχω *rule, govern;* midd. *begin;* often redundant adding little meaning, if any, to the verb with which it is associated

ἄρχων, οντος m *ruler; official, authority; judge* (Lk 12.58); ἄ. τῶν Ἰουδαίων *member of the Sanhedrin* (Jn 3.1)

ἄρωμα, τος n *aromatic spice* or *oil*

'Ασά alt. form of **'Ασάφ**

ἀσάλευτος, ον *immovable; unshakable*

'Ασάφ m *Asaph* (Mt 1.7, 8)

ἄσβεστος, ον *unquenchable*

ἀσέβεια, ας f *godlessness, wickedness*

ἀσεβέω *live* or *act in an ungodly way*

ἀσεβής, ές *godless, impious*

ἀσέλγεια, ας f *sensuality, indecency, vice*

ἄσημος, ον *insignificant*

'Ασήρ m *Asher* (Lk 2.36; Re 7.6)

ἀσθένεια, ας f *weakness* (of any sort); *illness* (πνεῦμα ἀσθενείας *a spirit causing illness* Lk 13.11)

ἀσθενέω *be sick* or *ill; be weak*

ἀσθένημα, τος n *weakness*
ἀσθενής, ές *sick; weak; delicate* (of parts of the body); *helpless* (Ro 5.6)
'Ασία, ας f *Asia* (4 E–2)
'Ασιανός, οῦ m *one from the Roman province of Asia*
'Ασιάρχης, ου m *Asiarch* (high ranking official of the province of Asia)
ἀσιτία, ας f *lack of appetite* (πολλῆς τε ἀσιτίας ὑπαρχούσης *after they had gone for a long time without food* Ac 27.21)
ἄσιτος, ον *without food*
ἀσκέω *endeavor, do one's best*
ἀσκός, οῦ m *wine-skin*
ἀσμένως adv. *gladly, warmly*
ἄσοφος, ον *senseless, foolish*
ἀσπάζομαι *greet* (perhaps *greet with politeness* or *respect* Mt 5.47); *welcome; visit briefly, pay one's respects; take leave of, say goodbye;* impv. *remember me to* (someone)
ἀσπασμός, οῦ m *greeting*
ἄσπιλος, ον *pure, spotless; without defect*
ἀσπίς, ίδος f *snake*
ἄσπονδος, ον *irreconcilable; merciless*
'Ασσά alt. form of 'Ασάφ
ἀσσάριον, ου n *assarion* (Roman copper coin worth 1/16 denarius)
ἆσσον adv. *as close as possible*
'Ασσος, ου f *Assos* (4 E–2)

ἀστατέω *be homeless, wander from place to place*
ἀστεῖος, α, ον *pleasing; beautiful*
ἀστήρ, έρος m *star*
ἀστήρικτος, ον *unsteady, weak; insincere*
ἄστοργος, ον *lacking normal human affection, inhuman*
ἀστοχέω (lit. *miss the mark*) *lose one's way, leave the way*
ἀστραπή, ῆς f *lightning; ray* (Lk 11.36)
ἀστράπτω *flash; dazzle*
ἄστρον, ου n *star, constellation*
'Ασύγκριτος, ου m *Asyncritus* (Ro 16.14)
ἀσύμφωνος, ον *in disagreement*
ἀσύνετος, ον *without understanding, dull; senseless, foolish*
ἀσύνθετος, ον *faithless, disloyal*
ἀσφάλεια, ας f *security, safety* (ἐν πάσῃ ἀ. *most securely* Ac 5.23); *accurate information, full truth* (Lk 1.4)
ἀσφαλής, ές *safe, sure; safeguard* (Php 3.1); *definite* (Ac 25.26); *the facts* or *reason* (Ac 21.34; 22.30)
ἀσφαλίζω *secure, fasten*
ἀσφαλῶς adv. *safely, under close guard; for certain, beyond a doubt*
ἀσχημονέω *behave improperly*
ἀσχημοσύνη, ης f *shameless act(s); shame of nakedness*

ἀσχήμων, ον *unpresentable* (τὰ ἀ. *private bodily parts* 1 Cor 12.23)

ἀσωτία, ας f *dissipation, reckless living*

ἀσώτως adv. *recklessly, immorally*

ἀτακτέω *be lazy or idle*

ἄτακτος, ον *lazy, idle*

ἀτάκτως adv. *in idleness or laziness*

ἄτεκνος, ον *childless*

ἀτενίζω *fix one's eyes on, look straight at, stare*

ἄτερ prep. with gen. *without, apart from*

ἀτιμάζω *treat shamefully, dishonor* (pass. *suffer disgrace* Ac 5.41); *degrade* (Ro 1.24)

ἀτιμία, ας f *disgrace, dishonor, shame; humiliation;* εἰς ἀ. *for common use* (Ro 9.21; 2 Tm 2.20)

ἄτιμος, ον *unhonored, dishonored, despised; insignificant or unattractive in appearance* (of bodily parts)

ἀτμίς, ίδος f *vapor, mist*

ἄτομος, ον *indivisible;* ἐν ἀ. *in a moment, in a flash* (1 Cor 15.52)

ἄτοπος, ον *improper, wrong, evil; harmful, unusual* (Ac 28.6)

Ἀττάλεια, ας f *Attalia* (4 F-3)

αὐγάζω *see;* perhaps *bring light;* εἰς τὸ . . . εὐαγγελίου *so as not to see the light*

of the gospel shining on them or so that the gospel cannot dawn upon them and bring them light (2 Cor 4.4)

αὐγή, ῆς f *daybreak, dawn*

Αὔγουστος, ου m *Augustus* (= Σεβαστός, title given emperor Octavian)

αὐθάδης, ες *arrogant, self-willed*

αὐθαίρετος, ον *of one's own accord*

αὐθεντέω *domineer, have authority over*

αὐλέω *play a flute* (τὸ αὐλούμενον *what is played on a flute* 1 Cor 14.7)

αὐλή, ῆς f *(an enclosed) courtyard, court* (of a temple); *palace; house; fold* (for sheep)

αὐλητής, οῦ m *flute player*

αὐλίζομαι *spend the night*

αὐλός, οῦ m *flute*

αὐξάνω and αὔξω (fut. αὐξήσω; aor. ηὔξησα; aor. pass. ηὐξήθην) intrans. *grow, spread, increase; become more important* (Jn 3.30); *reach full growth* (Mt 13.32); trans. *make grow, increase*

αὔξησις, εως f *growth*

αὔριον adv. *tomorrow, the next day; in a short while, soon*

αὐστηρός, ά, όν *hard, severe, strict*

αὐτάρκεια, ας f *what is necessary; self-sufficiency; satisfaction* αὐτάρκης, ες resourceful, self-sufficient; satisfied

αὐτόθι adv. there, in that place

αὐτοκατάκριτος, ον self-condemned

αὐτόματος, η, ον by itself, on its own

αὐτόπτης, ου m eyewitness

αὐτός, ή, ό self, of oneself, even, very; preceded by the article the same; as a third person pro. he, she, it; ἐπὶ τὸ αὐτό together; κατὰ τὸ αὐτό so, the same way; at the same time

αὐτοῦ adv. here; there

αὐτόφωρος, ον in the act

αὐτόχειρ, ος with one's own hand(s)

αὐχέω boast, make wild claims

αὐχμηρός, ά, όν dark

ἀφαιρέω (fut. ἀφελῶ; aor. ἀφεῖλον [same mng. in act. and midd.], inf. ἀφελεῖν; aor. midd. subj. ἀφέλωμαι) take away, remove; cut off

ἀφανής, ές hidden, able to be hidden

ἀφανίζω ruin, destroy; make unsightly, disfigure; pass. perish; vanish, disappear

ἀφανισμός, οῦ m disappearing, destruction

ἄφαντος, ον invisible (ἄ. ἐγένετο he disappeared Lk 24.31)

ἀφεδρών, ῶνος m latrine

ἀφέθην aor. pass. of ἀφίημι

ἀφεθήσομαι fut. pass. of ἀφίημι

ἀφειδία, ας f severe discipline

ἀφεῖλον aor. of ἀφαιρέω

ἀφείς aor. ptc. of ἀφίημι

ἀφεῖς probably pres. 2 sg. of ἀφίημι (Re 2.20)

ἀφελεῖν aor. inf. of ἀφαιρέω

ἀφελότης, ητος f simplicity, humility

ἀφελῶ fut. of ἀφαιρέω

ἀφέλωμαι aor. midd. subj. of ἀφαιρέω

ἄφες (2 pl. ἄφετε) aor. impv. of ἀφίημι

ἄφεσις, εως f forgiveness, cancellation (of sins); release (of prisoners)

ἀφέωνται pf. pass. 3 pl. of ἀφίημι

ἀφή, ῆς f ligament

ἀφῆκα aor. of ἀφίημι

ἀφήσω fut. of ἀφίημι

ἀφθαρσία, ας f imperishability, immortality; ἐν ἀ. with undying (love) (Eph 6.24)

ἄφθαρτος, ον imperishable; immortal

ἀφθορία, ας f integrity, honesty

ἀφίδω aor. subj. of ἀφοράω

ἀφίημι (pres. 2 sg. ἀφεῖς, 1 pl. ἀφίομεν, 3 pl. ἀφίουσιν, inf. ἀφιέναι; impf. 3 sg. ἤφιεν; fut. ἀφήσω; aor. ἀφῆκα, impv. ἄφες, 2 pl. ἄφετε, subj. ἀφῶ, ptc. ἀφείς; aor. pass. ἀφέθην; fut. pass. ἀφεθήσομαι; pf. pass. 3 pl. ἀφέωνται) cancel;

forgive, remit (of sin or debts); allow, let be, tolerate (ἄφες ἴδωμεν Wait! Let us see! or simply Let us see! Mt 27.49; Mk 15.36); leave; leave behind, forsake, neglect; let go, dismiss, divorce; ἀφῆκεν τὸ πνεῦμα he died (Mt 27.50); ἀ. φωνὴν μεγάλην give a loud cry (Mk 15.37)

ἀφικνέομαι (aor. ἀφικόμην) reach, be known to

ἀφιλάγαθος, ον enemy to goodness

ἀφιλάργυρος, ον not greedy for money

ἀφίλετο alt. aor. midd. 3 sg. of ἀφαιρέω

ἄφιξις, εως f departure

ἀφίουσιν pres. 3 pl. of ἀφίημι

ἀφίσταμαι (deponent in all forms except aorist; impf. 3 sg. ἀφίστασο; fut. ἀποστήσομαι; aor. ἀπέστησα and ἀπέστην, impv. 2 pl. ἀπόστητε, inf. ἀποστῆναι, ptc. ἀποστάς) intrans. leave, go away; desert, commit apostasy; keep away; trans. incite to revolt (Ac 5.37)

ἄφνω adv. suddenly

ἀφόβως adv. without fear; without reverence; ἀ. γίνομαι be at ease, feel welcome (1 Cor 16.10)

ἀφομοιόω be like, resemble

ἀφοράω (aor. subj. ἀφίδω) fix one's eyes on; ὡς ἂν ἀφίδω τὰ περὶ ἐμέ as soon

as I know my situation (Php 2.23)

ἀφορίζω (fut. ἀφοριῶ and ἀφορίσω) separate, take away; exclude (from one's company); set apart, appoint

ἀφορμή, ῆς f opportunity, occasion

ἀφρίζω foam at the mouth

ἀφρός, οῦ m foam

ἀφροσύνη, ης f folly, foolishness (ἐν ἀ. foolishly 2 Cor 11.17, 21)

ἄφρων, ον gen. ονος fool; foolish, senseless; ignorant, unlearned

ἀφυπνόω fall asleep

ἀφυστερέω withhold

ἀφῶ aor. subj. of ἀφίημι

ἄφωνος, ον dumb, silent; without meaning (1 Cor 14.10)

Ἀχάζ m Ahaz (Mt 1.9)

Ἀχαΐα, ας f Achaia (4 C–2)

Ἀχαϊκός, οῦ m Achaicus (1 Cor 16.17)

ἀχάριστος, ον ungrateful

ἀχειροποίητος, ον not made by human hand(s); περιτομῇ ἀ. not in a physical sense (Col 2.11)

ἀχθήσομαι fut. pass. of ἄγω

Ἀχίμ m Achim (Mt 1.14)

ἀχλύς, ύος f mistiness

ἀχρειόομαι be worthless or debased

ἀχρεῖος, ον worthless; mere

ἄχρηστος, ον of little use, useless

ἄχρι (and ἄχρις): (1) prep. with gen. *until; to, as far as;* (2) conj. *until;* ἄχρι οὗ *until; as; when; while, as long as*

ἄχυρον, ου n *chaff* (of grain)

ἄψας aor. ptc. of ἅπτω

ἀψευδής, ές *who never lies, trustworthy*

ἄψινθος, ου m and f *wormwood* (as a proper name Re 8.11)

ἄψυχος, ον *inanimate*

B

β *beta* (second letter of the Greek alphabet); *second* (in titles of NT writings)

Βάαλ m (appears with feminine article ἡ) *Baal* (Semitic deity)

Βαβυλών, ῶνος f *Babylon* (3 F–3)

βαθμός, οῦ m *standing, position, status*

βάθος, ους n *depth; greatness* (ἡ κατὰ β. πτωχεία *extreme poverty* 2 Cor 8.2); *deep water* (Lk 5.4)

βαθύνω *go deep*

βαθύς, εῖα, ύ *deep* (τὰ β. *the deep secrets* Re 2.24); ὄρθρου βαθέως *at early dawn* (Lk 24.1)

βάϊον, ου n *palm branch*

Βαλαάμ m *Balaam* (2 Pe 2.15; Jd 11; Re 2.14)

Βαλάκ m *Balak* (Re 2.14)

βαλλάντιον, ου n *purse*

βάλλω (fut. βαλῶ; aor. ἔβα-λον; pf. βέβληκα; pass. aor. ἐβλήθην; fut. βληθή-σομαι; pf. βέβλημαι; plpf. ἐβεβλήμην) trans. *throw, throw down; put, place* (pf. pass. ptc. often *lying*); *offer, give; pour; sow* (seed); *bring* (peace); *invest, deposit* (money); *banish* (fear); *shed* (figs); *swing* (a sickle); τὰ βαλλόμενα *money put into a purse* (Jn 12.6); intrans. *sweep down* (of a storm)

βαπτίζω *baptize; wash*

βάπτισμα, τος n *baptism*

βαπτισμός, οῦ m *ritual washing, ablution, baptism; washing* (of hands)

βαπτιστής, οῦ m *Baptist* (of John)

βάπτω (pf. pass. βέβαμμαι) *dip* (βεβα. αἵματι *covered with blood* Re 19.13)

Βαραββᾶς, ᾶ m *Barabbas*

Βαράκ m *Barak* (He 11.32)

Βαραχίας, ου m *Barachiah* (Mt 23.35)

βάρβαρος, ον *non-Greek; uncivilized; foreigner; native* (Ac 28.2, 4)

βαρέω *burden, weigh down; overcome*

βαρέως adv. *with difficulty*

Βαρθολομαῖος, ου m *Bartholomew*

Βαριησοῦς, οῦ m *Bar-Jesus* (Ac 13.6)

Βαριωνᾶ and **Βαριωνᾶς, ᾶ** m *Bar-Jona* (Mt 16.17)

Βαρναβᾶς, ᾶ m *Barnabas*

βάρος, ους n *burden; weight, fulness* (of glory); *importance* (ἐν β. εἶναι *make demands, make one's weight felt* 1 Th 2.7)

Βαρσαββᾶς, ᾶ m *Barsabbas:* (1) Joseph (Ac 1.23); (2) Judas (Ac 15.22)

Βαρτιμαῖος, ου m *Bartimaeus* (Mk 10.46)

βαρύς, εῖα, ύ *heavy; hard, difficult; important, weighty; serious; fierce* (Ac 20.29)

βαρύτιμος, ον *very expensive*

βασανίζω *torment, disturb; toss about* (of waves); β. ἐν τῷ ἐλαύνειν *strain at the oars* (Mk 6.48)

βασανισμός, οῦ m *torture; torment*

βασανιστής, οῦ m *jailer, torturer*

βάσανος, ου f *torment; pain*

βασιλεία, ας f *reign, rule;*

kingdom, domain (λαβεῖν β. *to be made king* Lk 19.12, 15)

βασίλειος, ον *royal; palace* (Lk 7.25)

βασιλεύς, έως m *king*

βασιλεύω *rule, reign; become like a king* (1 Cor 4.8)

βασιλικός, ή, όν *royal, belonging to the king; royal official* or *relative of the royal family*

βασίλισσα, ης f *queen*

βάσις, εως f *foot* (of the body)

βασκαίνω *bewitch, place under a spell*

βαστάζω *carry* (*carry a child in the womb* Lk 11.27); *endure, bear, tolerate; take away, remove; support, sustain* (Ro 11.18); *pick up* (Jn 10.31)

βάτος, ου m and f *bush; thornbush* (Lk 6.44)

βάτος, ου m *bath* (a liquid measure of 65 pints or 8.1 gallons)

βάτραχος, ου m *frog*

βατταλογέω *babble, use many words* (perhaps onomatopoeic usage)

βδέλυγμα, τος n *something detestable;* τὸ β. τῆς ἐρημώσεως *sacrilegious object causing the desecration* (of a sacred place)

βδελυκτός, ή, όν *detestable, vile*

βδελύσσομαι *detest;* pf. pass. ptc. *vile, corrupt* (Re 21.8) βέβαιος, α, ον *reliable; firm, well-founded; confirmed, verified; effective* (of wills)

βεβαιόω *confirm, verify, prove to be true; strengthen, sustain*

βεβαίωσις, εως f *confirmation, establishing firmly*

βέβαμμαι pf. pass. of βάπτω

βέβηλος, ον *vile, godless, irreligious*

βεβηλόω *desecrate*

βέβληκα pf. of βάλλω

βεβρωκώς pf. ptc. of βιβρώσκω

Βεελζεβούλ m *Beelzebul* (= the Devil)

Βελιάρ m *Belial* (= the Devil)

βελόνη, ης f *sewing needle*

βέλος, ους n *arrow*

βέλτιον adv. *well, very well*

Βενιαμείν m *Benjamin*

Βερνίκη, ης f *Bernice* (Ac 25.13, 23; 26.30)

Βέροια, ας f *Beroea* (4 C–2)

Βεροιαῖος, α, ον *Beroean*

Βέρος, ου m *Berus* (Ac 20.4)

Βεωορσόρ alt. form of Βεώρ

Βεώρ m *Beor* (2 Pe 2.15)

Βηθαβαρά f *Bethabara* (a place of uncertain location, Jn 1.28)

Βηθανία, ας f *Bethany* (2 C–6)

Βηθεσδά f *Bethesda* (appears in some mss. as an alternative reading for Bethzatha, Jn 5.2)

Βηθζαθά f *Bethzatha* (pool in northeast Jerusalem)

Βηθλέεμ f *Bethlehem* (1 C–6, 1i A–2, 2 C–6)

Βηθσαϊδά f *Bethsaida* (2 D–3)

Βηθφαγή f *Bethphage* (village near Jerusalem, perhaps east of Bethany)

βῆμα, τος n *judicial bench, place of judgment, court;* β. ποδός *space enough for a foot* (Ac 7.5)

Βηρεύς, εως m *Bereus* (Ro 16.15)

βήρυλλος, ου m and f *beryl* (a semiprecious stone, usually green or bluish-green in color)

βία, ας f *force, violence; use of force*

βιάζω *exercise force* (if midd.) or *suffer violence* (if pass.) (Mt 11.12); *enter by force* (Lk 16.16)

βίαιος, α, ον *violent, strong*

βιαστής, οῦ m *violent or eager person*

βιβλαρίδιον, ου n *little book or scroll*

βιβλίον, ου n *book, scroll; written statement* (of divorce)

βίβλος, ου f *book; record* (Mt 1.1)

βιβρώσκω (pf. ptc. βεβρωκώς) *eat*

Βιθυνία, ας f *Bithynia* (4 F–2)

βίος, ου m *life; livelihood, living; property, possessions*

βιόω *live*

βίωσις, εως f *way of life*

βιωτικός, ή, όν *pertaining to everyday life*

βλαβερός, ά, όν *harmful*

βλάπτω *harm, injure*

βλαστάνω and βλαστάω (aor.
ἐβλάστησα) intrans. *sprout;*
trans. *yield, produce*
Βλάστος, ου m *Blastus* (Ac
12.20)
βλασφημέω *speak against
God, blaspheme; speak
against, slander, insult*
βλασφημία, ας f *speaking
against God, blasphemy;
speaking against, slander, insulting talk*
βλάσφημος, ον *speaking
against God, blasphemous;
insulting, slanderous*
βλέμμα, τος n *what is seen*
βλέπω *see; look* (on or *at);
be able to see, gain one's
sight; beware of; consider,
regard; see to* (something);
perceive, discover, find
βληθήσομαι fut. pass. of
βάλλω
βλητέος, α, ον (verbal adj.
from βάλλω) *must be put
or poured*
Βοανηργές *Boanerges* (Mk
3.17)
βοάω *call, cry out, shout*
Βόες m *Boaz* (Mt 1.5)
βοή, ῆς f *shout, outcry, cry*
βοήθεια, ας f *help, support;*
perhaps *rope, cable* (Ac 27.17)
βοηθέω *help*
βοηθός, οῦ m *helper*
βόθυνος, ου m *ditch, pit*
βολή, ῆς f *a throw* (of a stone)
βολίζω *take a sounding* (for
depth of water)

Βόος m *Boaz* (Lk 3.32)
βόρβορος, ου m *mud, mire*
βορρᾶς, ᾶ m *the north*
βόσκω *tend, feed* (ὁ βόσκων
herdsman); midd. graze, feed
Βοσόρ m *Bosor* (2 Pe 2.15)
βοτάνη, ης f *vegetation, crop*
βότρυς, υος m *bunch* (of
grapes)
βουλεύομαι *plan, decide; deliberate, consider*
βουλευτής, οῦ m *council
member* (of the Sanhedrin)
βουλή, ῆς f *purpose, intention; plan, decision* (τίθημι
β. *advise, be in favor of*
Ac 27.12)
βούλημα, τος n *will, desire;
purpose, intention*
βούλομαι (aor. ἐβουλήθην)
*want, desire, wish; be willing;
intend, plan*
βουνός, οῦ m *hill*
βοῦς, βοός m *ox*
βραβεῖον, ου n *prize*
βραβεύω *act as judge or
umpire, rule*
βραδύνω *be delayed; be negli-
gent about*
βραδυπλοέω *sail slowly*
βραδύς, εῖα, ύ *slow*
βραδύτης, ητος f *slowness,
negligence*
βραχίων, ονος m *arm*
βραχύς, εῖα, ύ *little, short,
small;* βραχύ τι *for a little
while* (He 2.7,9), *a small
amount* (Jn 6.7); διὰ βρα-
χέων *briefly* (He 13.22)

βρέφος, ους n *baby, infant;
childhood*

βρέχω *rain; send rain; wet*

βροντή, ῆς f *thunder*

βροχή, ῆς f *rain*

βρόχος, ου m *restriction* (lit.
noose)

βρυγμός, οῦ m *grinding,
gnashing*

βρύχω *grind, gnash*

βρύω *pour out, gush*

βρῶμα, τος n *food; solid food*

βρώσιμος, ον *eatable* (ἔχετέ

τι β. *do you have anything
to eat?* Lk 24.41)

βρῶσις, εως f *food; eating; a
meal* (He 12.16); *rust* (Mt
6.19, 20)

βυθίζω *sink; drag down, plunge*

βυθός, οῦ m *open sea*

βυρσεύς, έως m *tanner,
leather worker*

βύσσινος, η, ον *made of fine
linen*

βύσσος, ου f *fine linen*

βωμός, οῦ m *altar*

Γ

γ *gamma* (third letter of the
Greek alphabet); *third* (in
titles of NT writings)

Γαββαθα *Gabbatha* (Jn 19.13)
(Aramaic word)

Γαβριήλ m *Gabriel* (Lk 1.19,
26)

γάγγραινα, ης f *gangrene,
cancer*

Γάδ m *Gad* (Re 7.5)

Γαδαρηνός, ή, όν *of Gadara*
(*Gadara* 2 D–4)

Γάζα, ης f *Gaza* (1 A–7,
2 A–7, 3 C–4)

γάζα, ης f *treasury*

γαζοφυλάκιον, ου n *Temple
treasury; offering box*

Γάϊος, ου m *Gaius:* (1) of
Derbe (Ac 20.4); (2) of
Macedonia (Ac 19.29); (3)

of Corinth (Ro 16.23; 1 Cor
1.14); (4) recipient of 3 Jn
(3 Jn 1)

γάλα, γάλακτος n *milk*

Γαλάτης, ου m *a Galatian*

Γαλατία, ας f *Galatia* (4 F–2,
4 G–2)

Γαλατικός, ή, όν *Galatian*

γαλήνη, ης f *calm* (of the
sea)

Γαλιλαία, ας f *Galilee* (2 C–3)

Γαλιλαῖος, α, ον *Galilean*

Γαλλία, ας f *Gaul*

Γαλλίων, ωνος m *Gallio* (Ac
18.12ff)

Γαμαλιήλ m *Gamaliel* (Ac
5.34; 22.3)

γαμέω *marry* (aor. sometimes
ἔγημα, subj. γήμω, ptc.
γήμας) (of men or women)

γαμίζω give (a bride) in marriage; perhaps marry (1 Cor 7.38)

γαμίσκω give (a bride) in marriage

γάμος, ου m wedding, wedding feast or celebration; banquet hall, wedding hall (Mt 22.10); marriage (He 13.4)

γάρ conj. for, since, then; indeed, certainly; τί γάρ what! why!

γαστήρ, τρός f womb (ἐν γ. ἔχω conceive or be pregnant); glutton (Tt 1.12)

Γαύδη alt. form of **Καῦδα**

γέ enclitic particle adding emphasis to the word with which it is associated

γέγονα and **γεγένημαι** pf. of **γίνομαι**

γέγονει plpf. 3 sg. of **γίνομαι**

γέγραπται pf. pass. 3 sg. of **γράφω**

γέγραφα pf. of **γράφω**

Γεδεών m Gideon (He 11.32)

γέεννα, ης f hell; υἱὸς γεέννης one destined for hell

Γεθσημανί Gethsemane (garden at the foot of the Mt. of Olives)

γείτων, ονος m and f neighbor

γελάω laugh

γέλως, ωτος m laughter

γεμίζω fill

γέμω be full; be covered with (Re 4.6, 8)

γενεά, ᾶς f generation, contemporaries; period, age (of time); family, posterity (posterity or perhaps origin Ac 8.33)

γενεαλογέομαι descend from

γενεαλογία, ας f genealogy

γενέσθαι aor. inf. of **γίνομαι**

γενέσια, ων n pl. birthday celebration

γένεσις, εως f birth; lineage; τὸ πρόσωπον τῆς γ. one's natural face (Jas 1.23); τροχὸς τῆς γ. course of existence (Jas 3.6)

γενετή, ῆς f birth

γενηθήτω aor. impv. 3 sg. of **γίνομαι**

γένημα, τος n product, harvest (γ. τῆς ἀμπέλου wine)

γενήσομαι fut. of **γίνομαι**

γεννάω be father of; bear, give birth to (perhaps conceive); pass. be born; lead to, cause (2 Tm 2.23)

γέννημα, τος n offspring; γ. ἐχιδνῶν you snakes!

Γεννησαρέτ f Gennesaret (2 D-3)

γέννησις, εως f birth

γεννητός, ή, όν born; ἐν γ. γυναικῶν among all mankind (Mt 11.11; Lk 7.28)

γένοιτο aor. opt. 3 sg. of **γίνομαι**

γένος, ους n family, race, nation, people; offspring, descendants; sort, kind

Γερασηνός, ή, όν of Gerasa (Gerasa 2 D-5)

Γεργεσηνός, ή, όν of Gergesa (Gergesa 2 D-3)

γερουσία, ας f *Council* (i.e.
the Sanhedrin)
γέρων, οντος m *old man,
grown man*
γεύομαι *taste; eat; experience*
γεωργέω *cultivate* (of land)
γεώργιον, ου n a *(cultivated)
field*
γεωργός, οῦ m *farmer; tenant
farmer; vinedresser*
γῆ, γῆς f *the earth; land,
country, region; soil, ground;
mankind*
γῆρας, ως or ους dat. γήρει
n *old age*
γηράσκω *become old, age*
γίνομαι (fut. γενήσομαι; aor.
ἐγενόμην, opt. 3 sg. γέ-
νοιτο, inf. γενέσθαι, ptc.
γενόμενος; pf. γέγονα and
γεγένημαι; aor. pass. ἐγενήθην, impv. 3 sg. γενη-
θήτω; plpf. 3 sg. ἐγεγόνει
and γεγόνει) *become, be;
happen, take place, arise*
(aor. often impers. *it hap-
pened* or *came about); come
into being, be born* or *created;
be done* (of things), *become
something* (of persons); *come,
go* (γ. κατά *arrive off* Ac
27.7); *appear* (Mk 1.4; Jn
1.6); *marry* (Ro 7.3, 4); μὴ
γένοιτο *no indeed!;* sometimes with dat. of person
have, possess, receive (e.g.
Mt 18.12)
γινώσκω (fut. γνώσομαι;
aor. ἔγνων, impv. γνῶθι,
γνώτω, subj. 3 sg. γνῷ

and γνοῖ, inf. γνῶναι, ptc.
γνούς; pf. ἔγνωκα; plpf.
ἐγνώκειν; aor. pass. ἐγ-
νώσθην; fut. pass. γνωσ-
θήσομαι) *know, have knowledge of* (of sexual relations
Mt 1.25: Lk 1.34); *find out,
learn, understand; perceive,
discern; to have knowledge;
acknowledge, recognize;* impv.
be very certain, remember
γλεῦκος, ους n *new wine*
(γ. μεμεστωμένος *be drunk*
Ac 2.13)
γλυκύς, εῖα, ύ *sweet*
γλῶσσα, ης f *tongue; language; utterance*
γλωσσόκομον, ου n *money
box, money bag*
γναφεύς, έως m *one who
bleaches* (cloth)
γνήσιος, α, ον *genuine; true,
loyal; genuineness* (2 Cor
8.8)
γνησίως adv. *genuinely*
γνοῖ and γνῷ aor. subj. 3
sg. of γινώσκω
γνούς, γνόντος aor. ptc. of
γινώσκω
γνόφος, ου m *darkness*
γνῶθι, γνώτω aor. impv. of
γινώσκω
γνώμη, ης f *purpose, intent,
will; opinion; decision; consent* (Phm 14)
γνῶναι aor. inf. of γινώσκω
γνωρίζω *make known, dis-
close; know*
γνωσθήσομαι fut. pass. of
γινώσκω

γνῶσις, εως f knowledge; esoteric knowledge; κατὰ γ. with understanding or consideration (1 Pe 3.7)

γνώσομαι fut. of γινώσκω

γνώστης, ου m one familiar with

γνωστός, ή, όν known; acquaintance, friend; what can be known (Ro 1.19); notable, extraordinary (Ac 4.16)

γογγύζω grumble, complain; mutter, whisper

γογγυσμός, οῦ m complaining; whispering; quarreling

γογγυστής, οῦ m habitual grumbler

γόης, ητος m imposter, charlatan

Γολγοθᾶ acc. ᾶν f Golgotha (Aramaic name of a hill near Jerusalem where executions took place)

Γόμορρα, ας f and ων n Gomorrah (city located at the southern part of the Dead Sea which God destroyed because of its evil)

γόμος, ου m cargo

γονεύς, έως m parent

γόνυ, γόνατος n knee

γονυπετέω kneel

γράμμα, τος n letter of the alphabet (οὐ γράμματι not literal Ro 2.?9); Scripture; letter, communication (Ac 28.21); bill, account (Lk 16.6, 7); learning (πῶς οὗτος γ. οἶδεν how does he know so much? Jn 7.15)

γραμματεύς, έως m scribe, expert in the Jewish law (possibly with reference to Christians Mt 13.52; 23.34); town clerk (Ac 19.35); man of letters, scholar (1 Cor 1.20)

γραπτός, ή, όν written, inscribed

γραφή, ῆς f Scripture; sacred writing; passage of Scripture (sg.), OT Scriptures (pl.)

γράφω (pf. γέγραφα; pf. pass. 3 sg. γέγραπται; aor. pass. ἐγράφην) write; record, compose; sign one's name (2 Th 3.17); cover with writing (Re 5.1)

γραώδης, ες silly, foolish (lit. such as old women tell)

γρηγορέω be or keep awake; watch, be alert; be alive (1 Th 5.6)

γυμνάζω train, exercise; discipline

γυμνασία, ας f training, discipline

γυμνιτεύω be dressed in rags

γυμνός, ή, όν naked (ἐπὶ γ. on his body Mk 14.51); uncovered, bare, exposed; poorly dressed, in need of clothes; perhaps wearing only an undergarment (Jn 21.7)

γυμνότης, ητος f nakedness; without sufficient clothing, poverty

γυναικάριον, ου n morally weak woman

γυναικεῖος, α, ον *female*
(γ. σκεῦος *wife* 1 Pe 3.7)
γυνή, αικός f *woman,
wife*

Γώγ m *Gog* (cryptic name)
γωνία, ας f *corner;* κεφαλὴ
γωνίας *main corner-stone,
keystone*

Δ

δαιμονίζομαι *be demon pos-
sessed*
δαιμόνιον, ου n *demon, evil
spirit; a god* (Ac 17.18)
δαιμονιώδης, ες *demonic, dev-
ilish*
δαίμων, ονος m *demon, evil
spirit*
δάκνω *bite*
δάκρυον, ου n *tear* (as in
weeping)
δακρύω *weep*
δακτύλιος, ου m *ring* (for a
finger)
δάκτυλος, ου m *finger*
Δαλμανουθά f *Dalmanutha* (a
place of uncertain location
near the western shore of
the Sea of Galilee)
Δαλματία, ας f *Dalmatia* (4
B–1)
δαμάζω *subdue, tame; control*
δάμαλις, εως f *heifer*
Δάμαρις, ιδος f *Damaris* (Ac
17.34)
Δαμασκηνός, ή, όν *of Da-
mascus*
Δαμασκός, οῦ f *Damascus*

(1 E–1, 2 E–1, 3 D–3,
4 H–4)
δανείζω (aor. subj. δανίσω)
lend; midd. *borrow*
δάνειον, ου n *debt*
δανειστής, οῦ m *moneylender*
Δανιήλ m *Daniel*
δαπανάω *spend* (δ. ἐπ᾽ αὐτοῖς *pay their expenses* Ac
21.24)
δαπάνη, ης f *cost, expense*
δαρήσομαι fut. pass. of δέρω
Δαυίδ m *David*
δέ *but, to the contrary, rather;
and; now, then, so;* δὲ καί
but also, but even; μὲν . . .
δέ *on the one hand . . . on
the other hand*
δέδεκται pf. 3 sg. of δέχομαι
δεδεκώς pf. ptc. of δέω
δέδεμαι pf. pass. of δέω
δέδομαι pf. pass. of δίδωμι
δέδωκα pf. of δίδωμι
δεδώκειν plpf. of δίδωμι
δέῃ subj. of δεῖ
δεήθητι aor. pass. impv. of
δέομαι
δέησις, εως f *prayer, petition*
δεθῆναι aor. pass. inf. of δέω

δεῖ (subj. δέῃ, inf. δεῖν, ptc. δέον; impf. ἔδει) impers. be necessary, must; should, ought; be proper; impf. had to, should have

δεῖγμα, τος n example, warning

δειγματίζω disgrace (δ. ἐν παρρησίᾳ make a public spectacle of Col 2.15); expose

δείκνυμι (fut. δείξω; aor. ἔδειξα, impv. δεῖξον; aor. pass. ptc. δειχθείς) show, point out; reveal, explain; prove

δειλία, ας f cowardice; timidity

δειλιάω be afraid

δειλός, ή, όν cowardly, afraid

δεῖνα m and f such a one, a certain one

δεινός ή, όν terrible (ἄλλα δεινά, other terrible sufferings)

δεινῶς adv. terribly; with hostility

δειπνέω eat, dine

δεῖπνον, ου n feast, banquet; supper, main meal

δείρας aor. ptc. of δέρω

δεισιδαιμονία, ας f religion

δεισιδαίμων, ον gen. ονος religious; comp. δεισιδαιμονέστερος very religious

δειχθείς aor. pass. ptc. of δείκνυμι

δέκα ten

δέκα ὀκτώ eighteen

δεκαπέντε fifteen

Δεκάπολις, εως f Decapolis (originally a league of ten Hellenistic cities) (2 D–5)

δεκατέσσαρες fourteen

δεκάτη, ης f a tenth part, tithe

δέκατος, η, ον tenth

δεκατόω collect tithes; pass. pay tithes

δεκτός, ή, όν acceptable, welcome; favorable (of time)

δελεάζω lure, entice; catch, trap

δένδρον, ου n tree

δεξιολάβος, ου m (uncertain mng.) perhaps soldier, infantryman

δεξιός, ά, όν right (opposite left); ἐν δ., ἐκ δ., ἐπὶ δ. at the right hand; δεξιὰς ἔδωκαν they shook hands (Ga 2.9); ὅπλον δ. weapon used to attack (2 Cor 6.7)

δέομαι (impf. 3 sg. ἐδεῖτο; aor. ἐδεήθην, impv. δεήθητι) ask, beg (often= interj. please!); pray; implore

δέον ptc. of δεῖ

δέος, ους n awe, godly fear

Δερβαῖος, α, ον of Derbe

Δέρβη, ης f Derbe (4 F–3)

δέρμα, τος n skin

δερμάτινος, η, ον of leather

δέρω (aor. ἔδειρα, ptc. δείρας; fut. pass. δαρήσομαι) beat, strike, hit

δεσμεύω tie (up), bind

δέσμη, ης f bundle

δέσμιος, ου m prisoner

δεσμός, οῦ m bond, chain; imprisonment, prison

δεσμοφύλαξ, ακος m jailer, prison guard

δεσμωτήριον, ου n *jail, prison*

δεσμώτης, ου m *prisoner*

δεσπότης, ου m *Lord, Master* (of God and Christ); *slave owner, master* (of a household)

δεῦρο adv. *come, come here;* ἄχρι τοῦ δεῦρο *thus far* (Ro 1.13)

δεῦτε adv. *come* (of command or exhortation)

δευτεραῖος, α, ον *in two days* or *on the second day*

δευτερόπρωτος, ον (of doubtful mng.) *the next or the one after the next*

δεύτερος, α, ον *second;* (τό) δ., πάλιν δ., ἐν τῷ δ. or ἐκ δ. *a second time; in the second place, secondly* (1 Cor 12.28); *afterward, the next time* (Jd 5)

δέχομαι (pf. 3 sg. δέδεκται) *receive, accept; take; welcome; bear with* (2 Cor 11.16)

δέω (aor. ἔδησα, subj. δήσω; pf. ptc. δεδεκώς; pf. pass. δέδεμαι; aor. pass. inf. δεθῆναι) *bind, tie* (δέδεμαι γυναικί *be married* 1 Cor 7.27); *imprison; compel* (Ac 20.22); *forbid, prohibit* (Mt 16.19; 18.18)

δή *indeed; then, therefore, now*

δῆλος, η, ον *evident* (ἡ λαλιά σου δ. σε ποιεῖ *your speech gives you away* Mt 26.73); δῆλον (ὅτι) *it is evident (that)*

δηλόω *make clear, show; indicate; inform*

Δημᾶς, ᾶ m *Demas* (Col 4.14; 2 Tm 4.10; Phm 24)

δημηγορέω *make a speech*

Δημήτριος, ου m *Demetrius:* (1) a silversmith in Ephesus (Ac 19.24, 38); (2) a church leader (3 Jn 12)

δημιουργός, οῦ m *builder, creator*

δῆμος, ου m *people, crowd; public assembly*

δημόσιος, α, ον *public* (δημοσίᾳ *publicly, in public*)

δηνάριον, ου n *denarius* (Roman silver coin equivalent to the day's wage of a common laborer)

δήποτε adv. with οἵῳ *whatever*

δηποτοῦν cf. οἱοσδηποτοῦν

δήπου adv. *it is clear, of course*

δήσω aor. subj. of δέω

διά prep. with: (1) gen. *through, by means of, with; during, throughout* (διὰ παντός *continually*); *through, among, throughout;* (2) acc. *because of, on account of, for the sake of; through, by* (rarely); διὰ τοῦτο *therefore, for this reason;* διὰ (τό) with inf. *because;* διὰ τί *why?*

Δία acc. of Ζεύς

διαβαίνω (aor. διέβην, ptc. διαβάς) *cross, cross over, come over*

διαβάλλω (aor. pass. **διε-βλήθην**) *bring charges*

διαβεβαιόομαι *speak confidently, insist on, give special emphasis*

διαβλέπω *see clearly;* perhaps *look hard* or *have one's eyes come into focus* (Mk 8.25)

διάβολος, ου m *the Devil;* as adj. **ος, ον** *given to malicious gossip*

διαγγέλλω (aor. pass. subj. **διαγγελῶ**) *proclaim, preach; give notice of*

διαγίνομαι *pass* (of time)

διαγινώσκω *investigate, examine; decide, determine*

διάγνωσις, εως f *decision*

διαγογγύζω *complain, grumble*

διαγρηγορέω *become fully awake* or *stay awake*

διάγω *lead, spend* (of a life)

διαδέχομαι *receive possession of*

διάδημα, τος n *diadem, crown*

διαδίδωμι (aor. **διέδωκα**, impv. 2 sg. **διάδος**; impf. pass. 3 sg. **διεδίδετο**) *distribute, divide, give*

διάδοχος, ου m *successor*

διαζώννυμι (aor. **διέζωσα**; aor. midd. **διεζωσάμην**; pf. pass. ptc. **διεζωσμένος**) *wrap around, put on* (clothes)

διαθήκη, ης f *covenant;* pl. *ordinances* (of a covenant) or simply *covenant; will, testament* (Ga 3.15); both

covenant and *will* (He 9.16, 17; Ga 3.17)

διαθήσομαι fut. of **διατίθεμαι**

διαίρεσις, εως f *variety, difference*

διαιρέω (aor. **διεῖλον**) *divide, distribute, apportion*

διακαθαίρω (aor. inf. **διακαθᾶραι**) *clean out, thresh out*

διακαθαρίζω (fut. **διακαθαριῶ**) *clean out, thresh out*

διακατελέγχομαι *defeat* (by debate), *refute*

διακονέω *serve, wait on; care for, see after, provide for; serve as a deacon* (1 Tm 3.10, 13)

διακονία, ας f *ministry, service; contribution, help, support; mission;* perhaps *office of deacon* or *authority* (Ro 12.7)

διάκονος, ου m and f *servant; helper, minister; deacon; deaconess* (Ro 16.1); ἆρα Χριστὸς ἁμαρτίας δ. *Does Christ serve the interests of sin?* (Ga 2.17)

διακόσιοι, αι, α *two hundred*

διακούω *hear* (a legal case)

διακρίνω (aor. pass. **διεκρίθην**) *evaluate, judge; recognize, discern; make a distinction* (between persons); *consider* or *make superior* (1 Cor 4.7); midd. (and aor. pass.) *doubt, hesitate; dispute, debate, take issue* διάκρισις, εως f ability to discriminate; arguing, dispute (Ro 14.1)

διακωλύω prevent (impf. tried to prevent Mt 3.14)

διαλαλέω discuss, talk about

διαλέγομαι (aor. pass. διελέχθην) discuss, debate; address, speak

διαλείπω (aor. διέλιπον) cease, stop

διάλεκτος, ου f language

διαλιμπάνω stop, quit

διαλλάσσομαι (aor. impv. διαλλάγηθι) be reconciled to, make peace with

διαλογίζομαι discuss, argue; consider, reason; wonder, question

διαλογισμός, οῦ m thought, opinion, motive (κριταὶ δ. πονηρῶν perhaps persons who make judgments based on evil motives Jas 2.4); reasoning; doubt, question; argument, dispute

διαλύω scatter, disperse

διαμαρτύρομαι declare solemnly and emphatically; charge under solemn oath; warn (Lk 16.28)

διαμάχομαι protest violently

διαμένω stay, remain, continue

διαμερίζω divide; distribute, divide among; δ. γλῶσσαι ὡσεὶ πυρός like tongues of fire spreading out (Ac 2.3)

διαμερισμός, οῦ m division, disunity

διανέμω (aor. pass. διενεμήθην) spread

διανεύω make signs

διανόημα, τος n thought

διάνοια, ας f mind, understanding; intention, purpose; thought, attitude

διανοίγω (aor. pass. διηνοίχθην) open (cf. μήτρα Lk 2.23); explain (Ac 17.3)

διανυκτερεύω spend the night

διανύω complete, continue

διαπαρατριβή, ῆς f constant arguing or irritation

διαπεράω cross over

διαπλέω (aor. διέπλευσα) sail across

διαπονέομαι be greatly annoyed

διαπορεύομαι go or travel through; go by (Lk 18.36)

διαπορέω be very confused; wonder

διαπραγματεύομαι make a profit, earn

διαπρίομαι be furious or enraged

διαρπάζω plunder, steal, take away

διαρρήγνυμι and διαρήσσω (aor. διέρρηξα) tear, rip; break (Lk 8.29)

διασαφέω explain; tell, report

διασείω take money by violence or force

διασκορπίζω scatter; squander, waste

διασπάω pull or tear apart

διασπείρω (aor. pass. **διεσπάρην**) scatter

διασπορά, ᾶς f dispersion (of the Jews or Christians scattered throughout the Graeco-Roman world)

διαστάς aor. ptc. of **διΐστημι**

διαστέλλομαι (aor. **διεστειλάμην**) order, command (δ. πολλά give strict orders Mk 5.43)

διάστημα, τος n interval

διαστήσας aor. ptc. of **διΐστημι**

διαστολή, ῆς f distinction, difference

διαστρέφω (pf. pass. **διέστραμμαι**) pervert, distort (pf. pass. ptc. depraved, crooked, wrong); divert, turn away; mislead, lead astray

διασώζω (aor. pass. **διεσώθην**) bring safely through, rescue; cure; pass. escape (Ac 28.1, 4)

διαταγή, ῆς f decree, ordinance (εἰς δ. ἀγγέλων handed down by angels Ac 7.53)

διάταγμα, τος n order, decree

διαταράσσομαι (aor. **διεταράχθην**) be deeply confused or troubled

διατάσσω (aor. pass. ptc. **διαταγείς** and **διαταχθείς**; pf. pass. **διατέταγμαι**) command, order; give instructions; arrange (Ac 20.13)

διατελέω continue, go, be

διατηρέω keep; treasure up

διατίθεμαι (fut. **διαθήσομαι**; aor. **διεθέμην**) make (of covenants or wills); ὁ δ. one who makes a will (He 9.16f); δ. βασιλείαν give (someone) the right to rule (Lk 22.29)

διατρίβω remain, stay

διατροφή, ῆς f food

διαυγάζω dawn

διαυγής, ές transparent, translucent

διαφέρω (aor. subj. **διενέγκω**) intrans. be worth more than, be superior to (τὰ δ. what is best or right Ro 2.18; Php 1.10); differ, differ from; trans. carry through (Mk 11.16); spread (Ac 13.49); drive about (pass. drift Ac 27.27); impers. οὐδέν μοι διαφέρει it does not matter to me (Ga 2.6)

διαφεύγω (aor. subj. **διαφύγω**) escape

διαφημίζω spread around

διαφθείρω (aor. pass. **διεφθάρην**; pf. pass. **διέφθαρμαι**) destroy, ruin; pass. wear away, decay (2 Cor 4.16); be depraved (1 Tm 6.5)

διαφθορά, ᾶς f decay, rotting (of a dead body)

διάφορος, ον different; comp. διαφορώτερος superior, far superior

διαφυλάσσω protect, take care of

διαχειρίζομαι *kill, murder*

διαχλευάζω *make fun, sneer*

διαχωρίζομαι *leave, go away*

διδακτικός, ή, όν *able to teach*

διδακτός, ή, όν *taught; imparted*

διδασκαλία, ας f *what is taught, teaching, doctrine; act of teaching, instruction*

διδάσκαλος, ου m *teacher, rabbi*

διδάσκω (aor. pass. ἐδιδά-χθην) *teach*

διδαχή, ῆς f *what is taught, teaching; act of teaching, instruction*

δίδραχμον, ου n *didrachma, two-drachma* (Greek coin with the approximate value of two denarii; annual Temple-tax required of each Jew)

Δίδυμος, ου m *Didymus* (mng. *twin*)

δίδωμι (διδῶ Re 3.9) (3 pl. διδόασιν, impv. 2 sg. δίδου, inf. διδόναι, ptc. διδούς; impf. 3 sg. ἐδίδου, 3 pl. ἐδίδουν and ἐδίδο-σαν; fut. δώσω; aor. ἔδω-κα, subj. 3 sg. δῷ, δοῖ and δώη, opt. 3 sg. δώη, impv. δός; inf. δοῦναι, ptc. δούς; pf. δέδωκα; pf. pass. δέδομαι; plpf. (ἐ)δεδώκειν; aor. pass. ἐδόθην, ptc. δοθείς; fut. pass. δοθήσομαι) *give;*

grant, allow, permit; place, put; appoint; establish; give out, pay; produce, yield, cause; entrust; bring (offerings); *inflict* (punishment); δ. ἑαυτόν *venture to go* (Ac 19.31); cf. ἐργασία (Lk 12.58)

διέβην aor. of διαβαίνω

διεγείρω (aor. διήγειρα; aor. pass. ptc. διεγερθείς) *awake, wake up; rise, grow rough* (of the sea)

διέζωσα aor. of διαζώννυμι

διεθέμην aor. of διατίθεμαι

διεῖλον aor. of διαιρέω

διελεύσομαι fut. of διέρχο-μαι

διελέχθην aor. pass. of δια-λέγομαι

διεληλυθώς pf. ptc. of διέρ-χομαι

διελθεῖν aor. inf. of διέρχο-μαι

διέλιπον aor. of διαλείπω

διενέγκω aor. subj. of δια-φέρω

διενθυμέομαι *think over, try to understand*

διέξοδος, ου f (doubtful mng.) δ. τῶν ὁδῶν perhaps *where the roads leave the city* or *along the main streets*

διερμηνευτής, οῦ m *interpreter*

διερμηνεύω *interpret, explain; translate* (Ac 9.36)

διέρχομαι (fut. διελεύσομαι:

aor. **διῆλθον**, inf. **διελ- θεῖν**; pf. **διελήλυθα**, ptc. **διεληλυθώς**) go or pass through; cross over; go or pass by; go about; come, go; spread (Lk 5.15)

διερωτάω learn by inquiry

διεσπάρην aor. pass. of **δια- σπείρω**

διεστειλάμην aor. of **δια- στέλλομαι**

διέστην aor. of **διΐστημι**

διέστραμμαι pf. pass. of **δια- στρέφω**

διεταράχθην aor. of **διατα- ράσσομαι**

διετής, ές two years old

διετία, ας f two-year period

διεφθάρην aor. pass. of **δια- φθείρω**

διέφθαρμαι pf. pass. of **δια- φθείρω**

διήγειρα aor. of **διεγείρω**

διηγέομαι tell, relate

διήγησις, εως f account, narrative

διῆλθον aor. of **διέρχομαι**

διηνεκής, ές continuous; εἰς τὸ δ. for all time; con- tinually, perpetually

διηνοίχθην aor. pass. of **δια- νοίγω**

διθάλασσος, ον between the seas; τόπος δ. sandbank, reef or cross-currents (Ac 27.41)

διϊκνέομαι go all the way through, penetrate

διΐστημι (aor. **διέστην**, ptc. **διαστάς** and **διαστήσας**)

part; pass (of time); sail farther on (Ac 27.28)

διϊσχυρίζομαι insist

δικαιοκρισία, ας f righteous judgment

δίκαιος, α, ον conforming to the standard, will, or char- acter of God; upright, right- eous, good; just, right; proper; in a right relationship with God; fair, honest; innocent

δικαιοσύνη, ης f what God requires; what is right, right- eousness, uprightness, justice; righting wrong; (God's) put- ting (man) in a right rela- tionship (with Himself); re- ligious duties or acts of charity (Mt 6.1)

δικαιόω put into a right rela- tionship (with God); acquit, declare and treat as righteous; show or prove to be right; set free (Ac 13.38; Ro 6.7); δ. τὸν θεόν acknowledge God's justice or obey God's righteous demands (Lk 7.29)

δικαίωμα, τος n regulation, requirement; righteous deed, judgment; acquittal (Ro 5.16)

δικαίως adv. justly, uprightly (γίνομαι δ. live uprightly 1 Th 2.10); ἐκνήφω δ. come to one's senses (1 Cor 15.34)

δικαίωσις, εως f putting into a right relationship (with God); setting free, acquittal

δικαστής, οῦ m judge

δίκη, ης f punishment; divine

justice, Justice (as a goddess Ac 28.4)

δίκτυον, ου n *fishing-net*

δίλογος, ον *two-faced, insincere*

διό conj. *therefore, for this reason*

διοδεύω *go about; travel through*

Διονύσιος, ου m *Dionysius* (Ac 17.34)

διόπερ (emphatic of **διό**) *therefore indeed, for this very reason*

διοπετής, ές *fallen from heaven*

διόρθωμα, τος n *improvement, reform*

διόρθωσις, εως f *new order, reformation*

διορύσσω (aor. pass. inf. **διορυχθῆναι**) *dig through, break in*

Διός gen. of **Ζεύς**

Διόσκουροι, ων m *Dioscuri* (mng. *heavenly twins*)

διότι conj. *because, for; therefore;* perhaps *that*

Διοτρέφης, ους m *Diotrephes* (3 Jn 9)

διπλοῦς, ῆ, οῦν *double* (δι- πλόω τὰ δ. *repay double* Re 18.6); comp. *twice as much, much more* (Mt 23.15)

διπλόω *double*

δίς adv. *twice;* ἅπαξ καὶ δίς *more than once* (Php 4.16; 1 Th 2.18)

δισμυριάς, άδος f *twenty thousand*

διστάζω *doubt, be doubtful*

δίστομος, ον *double-edged*

δισχίλιοι, αι, α *two thousand*

διϋλίζω *strain out, filter out*

διχάζω *turn against*

διχοστασία, ας f *division, dissension*

διχοτομέω *cut in pieces; punish severely*

διψάω *be thirsty; long for* (Mt 5.6)

δίψος, ους n *thirst*

δίψυχος, ον *of divided loyalty, undecided;* perhaps *hypocrite*

διωγμός, οῦ m *persecution*

διώκτης, ου m *persecutor*

διώκω *persecute* (*pursue, chase* Re 12.13); *seek after, strive for; drive out* or *away; practice* (hospitality); *follow, run after* (Lk 17.23)

δόγμα, τος n *rule, regulation, law; order, decree*

δογματίζομαι *obey rules and regulations*

δοθείς aor. pass. ptc. of **δίδωμι**

δοθήσομαι fut. pass. of **δίδωμι**

δοῖ aor. subj. 3 sg. of **δίδωμι**

δοκέω (aor. ἔδοξα) *trans. think, suppose, consider, imagine;* intrans. *seem; be recognized, have a reputation* (Mk 10.42; Ga 2.2, 6, 9); *be disposed* (1 Cor 11.16);

impers. *it seems, it seems
good, proper* or *best*
δοκιμάζω *test, examine; interpret, discern, discover; approve; prove, demonstrate*
δοκιμασία, ας f *test, testing*
δοκιμή, ῆς f *character, worth;
proof, evidence* (2 Cor 13.3);
πολλὴ δ. *severe ordeal* (2 Cor
8.2)
δοκίμιον, ου n *testing, act of
testing; genuineness*
δόκιμος, ον *approved, genuine*
(δ. γίνομαι *stand the test*
Jas 1.12); *respected, valued*
δοκός, οῦ f *log, beam of wood*
δόλιος, α, ον *deceitful, dishonest*
δολιόω (impf. 3 pl. **ἐδολιοῦσαν**) *deceive, be treacherous*
δόλος, ου m *deceit, treach-
ery*
δολόω *distort, falsify*
δόμα, τος n *gift*
Δονεῖ m *Doni* (Lk 3.33)
δόξα, ης f *glory, splendor,
grandeur* (in gen. often *glorious*); *power, kingdom; praise;
honor; pride* (δόξα καὶ χαρά
pride and joy 1 Th 2.20);
*brightness, brilliance; revealed
presence of God, God himself;
heaven* (1 Tm 3.16); *glorious
heavenly being* (2 Pe 2.10;
Jd 8); δὸς δόξαν τῷ θεῷ
*promise before God to tell the
truth* (Jn 9.24)
δοξάζω *praise, honor; glorify,*

exalt; pf. pass. ptc. *glorious*
(1 Pe 1.8)
Δορκάς, άδος f *Dorcas* (mng.
gazelle, deer Ac 9.36, 39)
δός aor. impv. of **δίδωμι**
δόσις, εως f *giving; gift*
δότης, ου m *giver*
Δουβέριος, α, ον *of Doberus*
(a city in Macedonia)
δουλαγωγέω *bring under control*
δουλεία, ας f *slavery;* δουλείας ἔνοχος *enslaved* (He
2.15)
δουλεύω *serve* (as a slave);
be a slave, be enslaved
δούλη, ης f *female servant* or
slave
δοῦλος, η, ον *as a slave*
δοῦλος, ου m *slave, servant*
δουλόω *enslave, make* (someone) *a slave* (pass. *be a slave);*
pass. *be bound* (of marriage
vows)
δοῦναι aor. inf. of **δίδωμι**
δούς aor. ptc. of **δίδωμι**
δοχή, ῆς f *banquet; reception*
δράκων, οντος m *dragon*
(figurative term for the
Devil)
δραμών aor. ptc. of **τρέχω**
δράσσομαι *catch, trap*
δραχμή, ῆς f *drachma* (Greek
silver coin with approximate
value of a denarius)
δρέπανον, ου n *sickle*
δρόμος, ου m *course* (of life)
Δρούσιλλα, ης f *Drusilla*
(Ac 24.24)

δύναμαι (2 sg. δύνῃ, δύνασε and δύνασαι; opt. δυναίμην; impf. ἐδυν- and ἠδυν-; aor. ἠδυνάσθην and ἠδυνήθην) can, be able to, be capable of; can do, able to do

δύναμις, εως f power, strength; act of power, miracle (miracle worker 1 Cor 12.28f); supernatural power(s), the Power, God (Mt 26.64; Mk 14.62; cf. Ac 8.10); ability, capacity, means (Mt 25.15; 2 Cor 1.8; 8.3); meaning, significance (1 Cor 14.11)

δυναμόω strengthen, make strong

δύνασε pres. 2 sg. of δύναμαι

δυνάστης, ου m ruler, king; Sovereign, Lord (of God); official (Ac 8.27)

δυνατέω be able; be powerful, be strong

δυνατός, ή, όν possible; strong; powerful; able, capable of; influential, leading (Ac 25.5; 1 Cor 1.26); person of strong faith or conscience (Ro 15.1); well versed (Ac 18.24); ὁ δ. the Mighty God (Lk 1.49)

δύνω (aor. ἔδυν) set (of the sun)

δύο gen. and acc. δύο dat. δυσίν two; δύο δύο or ἀνὰ δύο two by two, in twos; two each (Jn 2.6; Lk 9.3);

κατὰ δύο two at a time; εἰς δύο in two

δυσβάστακτος, ον hard to carry

δυσεντέριον, ου n dysentery

δυσερμήνευτος, ον hard to explain

δύσις, εως f west

δύσκολος, ον hard, difficult

δυσκόλως adv. with difficulty (πῶς δ. how hard it is)

δυσμή, ῆς f west (always pl.)

δυσνόητος, ον difficult to understand

δυσφημέω slander, speak ill of, insult

δυσφημία, ας f slander, insult

δῷ and δώῃ aor. subj. 3 sg. of δίδωμι

δώδεκα twelve

δωδέκατος, η, ον twelfth

δωδεκάφυλον, ου n the twelve tribes

δώῃ aor. opt. 3 sg. of δίδωμι

δῶμα, τος n roof, housetop

δωρεά, ᾶς f gift

δωρεάν adv. without cost, as a free gift; for nothing, needlessly (Ga 2.21); without cause or for no reason (Jn 15.25)

δωρέομαι give; bestow upon

δώρημα, τος n gift

δῶρον, ου n gift; offering; τὰ δ. offering box (Lk 21.4)

δωροφορία, ας f bringing of a gift or collection

E

ἔα *ah!* (exclamation expressing deep emotion; in some contexts it is best left untranslated)

ἐάν conj. *if; even if, though; when;* sometimes equivalent to ἄν (e.g. Mt 5.19); *ἐὰν μή unless; ἐάνπερ if only*

ἑαυτοῦ, ῆς, οῦ (not used in nominative) reflexive pro. *himself, herself, itself, themselves;* possessive pro. *his, hers,* etc.; reciprocal pro. *one another, each other;* τὸ ἑαυτοῦ *one's own interest or advantage*

ἐάω (ptc. ἐῶν, impv. 2 pl. ἐᾶτε; impf. 3 sg. εἴα, 3 pl. εἴων; fut. ἐάσω; aor. εἴασα) *allow, permit; leave, let go* (Ac 23.32; 27.40); ἐᾶτε ἕως τούτου perhaps *enough, no more of this* (Lk 22.51)

ἔβαλον aor. of βάλλω

ἑβδομήκοντα *seventy*

ἑβδομηκοντάκις *seventy times* (ἑ. ἑπτά *seventy-seven times* Mt 18.22)

ἕβδομος, η, ον *seventh*

ἐβεβλήμην plpf. pass. of βάλλω

Ἔβερ m *Eber* (Lk 3.35)

ἐβλήθην aor. pass. of βάλλω

ἑβραϊκός, ή, όν *Hebrew* (i.e. *Aramaic*)

Ἑβραῖος, ου m *Hebrew person*

Ἑβραΐς, ΐδος f *Hebrew language* (i.e. *Aramaic*)

Ἑβραϊστί adv. *in Hebrew or Aramaic*

ἐγγίζω *approach, come or draw near*

ἐγγράφω (pf. pass. ἐγγέγραμμαι) *write; record*

ἔγγυος, ου m *guarantor, guarantee*

ἐγγύς adv. *near, close to; on the verge of*

ἐγγύτερον (comp. of the adv. ἐγγύς) *nearer*

ἐγεγόνει plpf. 3 sg. of γίνομαι

ἐγείρω (fut. ἐγερῶ; aor. ἤγειρα; pf. pass. ἐγήγερμαι; aor. pass. ἠγέρθην; fut. pass. ἐγερθήσομαι) trans. *raise* (the dead); *raise up, bring into being; wake, rouse* (Mt 8.25; Ac 12.7); *cause, stir up* (Php 1.17); *lift out* (Mt 12.11); *make* (Mt 3.9; Lk 3.8); intrans. act. (impv. only) *Get up! Come!* intrans. pass. *get up, rise* (impv. *Get up! Come!*); *appear* (of prophets); *rise up in arms*

ἐγενήθην aor. pass. of γίνομαι

ἐγενόμην aor. of γίνομαι

ἔγερσις, εως f resurrection

ἔγημα aor. of γαμέω

ἐγκάθετος, ου m spy

ἐγκαίνια, ων n Jewish Feast of Dedication, Hanukkah

ἐγκαινίζω put into force, inaugurate; open (He 10.20)

ἐγκακέω become discouraged; tire of

ἐγκαλέω bring charges against, accuse

ἐγκαταλείπω (aor. ἐγκατέλιπον) forsake, abandon, desert; leave, leave behind; neglect

ἐγκατέλειπας and ἐγκατέλιπας alt. aor. 2 sg. of ἐγκαταλείπω

ἐγκατοικέω live (ἐν) among

ἐγκαυχάομαι boast

ἐγκεντρίζω graft (of branches)

ἔγκλημα, τος n charge, accusation (ἔχω ἔ. be charged with a crime Ac 23.29)

ἐγκομβόομαι put on

ἐγκοπή, ῆς f obstacle, hindrance

ἐγκόπτω (aor. ἐνέκοψα) prevent, hinder; detain (Ac 24.4)

ἐγκράτεια, ας f self-control

ἐγκρατεύομαι exercise self-control

ἐγκρατής, ές self-controlled

ἐγκρίνω class or classify with

ἐγκρύπτω (aor. ἐνέκρυψα) place or mix in

ἔγκυος, ον pregnant

ἐγνώκειν plpf. of γινώσκω

ἔγνων aor. and ἔγνωκα pf. of γινώσκω

ἐγνώσθην aor. pass. of γινώσκω

Ἔγυπτος alt. form of Αἴγυπτος

ἐγχρίω rub on (of ointment)

ἐγώ 1 pers. pro. ἐμοῦ (μου), ἐμοί (μοι), ἐμέ (με) I, me; pl. ἡμεῖς, ἡμῶν, ἡμῖν, ἡμᾶς we, us

ἐδαφίζω (fut. ἐδαφιῶ) raze to the ground, completely destroy

ἔδαφος, ους n ground

ἐδεδώκειν plpf. of δίδωμι

ἐδεήθην aor. of δέομαι

ἔδειξα aor. of δείκνυμι

ἔδειρα aor. of δέρω

ἐδιδάχθην aor. pass. of διδάσκω

ἐδίδοσαν impf. 3 pl. of δίδωμι

ἐδίδου impf. 3 sg. of δίδωμι

ἐδίδουν impf. 3 pl. of δίδωμι

ἐδόθην aor. pass. of δίδωμι

ἐδολιοῦσαν impf. 3 pl. of δολιόω

ἔδοξα aor. of δοκέω

ἑδραῖος, α, ον firm, steadfast

ἑδραίωμα, τος n support, foundation

ἔδραμον aor. of τρέχω

ἔδυν aor. of δύνα

ἔδωκα aor. of δίδωμι

Ἑζεκίας, ου m Hezekiah (Mt 1.9, 10)

ἔζην impf. of ζάω

ἐθελοθρησκία, ας f *self-im-posed piety* or *religion*

ἔθεντο aor. midd. 3 pl. of τίθημι

ἔθηκα aor. of τίθημι

ἐθίζω (pf. pass. εἴθισμαι) *accustom*

ἐθνάρχης, ου m *governor, official*

ἐθνικός, ή, όν *pagan, heathen, Gentile*

ἐθνικῶς adv. *like a Gentile*

ἔθνος, ους n *nation, people;* τὰ ἔ. *non-Jews, Gentiles; pagans, heathen, unbelievers*

ἔθος, ους n *custom, practice*

ἔθου aor. midd. 2 sg. of τίθημι

ἔθρεψα aor. of τρέφω

εἰ *if; whether; that; if only, surely; since;* εἴ τις, εἴ τι *who(ever), what(ever);* εἴπερ *since, if it is true that* εἴγε *if indeed*

εἴα impf. 3 sg. and εἴων impf. 3 pl. of ἐάω

εἴασα aor. of ἐάω

εἶδα and εἶδον aor. of ὁράω

εἰδέα, ας f *appearance*

εἰδέναι inf. of οἶδα

εἰδήσω fut. of οἶδα

εἰδός alt. form of εἰδώς

εἶδος, ους n *visible form, outward appearance; sight, seeing* (2 Cor 5.7); *kind, sort* (1 Th 5.22)

εἰδῶ subj. of οἶδα

εἰδωλεῖον, ου n *idol's temple*

εἰδωλόθυτον, ου n *meat offered to idols*

εἰδωλολάτρης, ου m *idolater*

εἰδωλολατρία, ας f *idolatry*

εἴδωλον, ου n *idol, image; false god*

εἰδώς, εἰδυῖα masc. and fem. ptc. of οἶδα

εἴθισμαι pf. pass. of ἐθίζω

εἰκῆ adv. *in vain, for nothing; without reason; thoughtlessly, without proper consideration*

εἴκοσι *twenty*

εἴκω (aor. εἶξα) *yield, give in to*

εἰκών, όνος f *likeness, image; form, appearance; statue*

εἰλάμην aor. of αἱρέομαι

εἰλευθέρωσεν alt. aor. 3 sg. of ἐλευθερόω

εἴληπται pf. pass. 3 sg. of λαμβάνω

εἴληφα pf. of λαμβάνω

εἰλικρίνεια, ας f *sincerity*

εἰλικρινής, ές *pure; sincere; honest*

εἶλκον impf. of ἕλκω

εἵλκυσα aor. of ἕλκω

εἵλκωμαι pf. of ἑλκόομαι

εἰμί (impv. ἴσθι, ἔστω and ἤτω, 3 pl. ἔστωσαν; inf. εἶναι; impf. ἦν and ἤμην; fut. ἔσομαι) *be, exist; happen, take place; live; be located in; remain, stay; come* (Jn 7.28, 29; 19.9); *go* (Jn 7.34, 36);* οὐκ ἔστιν *it is not possible* (1 Cor 11.20; He 9.5); ὅ ἐστιν, τοῦτ' ἔστιν *that means, that is to say;* εἰμὶ ἐκ *belong to, be one of*

εἵνεκεν = ἕνεκα
εἶξα aor. of εἴκω
εἴπερ *since, if it is true that*
εἶπον aor. of λέγω
εἰργασάμην aor. of ἐργάζομαι
εἴργασμαι pf. of ἐργάζομαι
εἴρηκα pf. of λέγω
εἰρήκει plpf. 3 sg. of λέγω
εἰρηνεύω *live* or *be at peace*
εἰρήνη, ης f *peace, harmony;* often used in invocations and greetings; *order* (opposite *disorder*)
εἰρηνικός, ή, όν *peaceful; peace-loving*
εἰρηνοποιέω *make peace*
εἰρηνοποιός, οῦ m *peacemaker*
εἰς prep. with acc. *into, to; in, at, on, upon, by, near; among; against; concerning; as;* εἰς τό with inf. denotes purpose and sometimes result
εἷς, μία, ἕν gen. ἑνός, μιᾶς, ἑνός *one; a, an, single; only one;* εἷς τις = τις *a certain one, someone, one;* εἷς τὸν ἕνα *one another* (1 Th 5.11); καθ' ἕνα *one by one* (1 Cor 14.31)
εἰσάγω (aor. εἰσήγαγον) *lead* or *bring in* or *into*
εἰσακούω *hear* (of prayer); *obey*
εἰσδέχομαι *welcome, receive, accept*

εἰσδραμοῦσα aor. ptc. fem. of εἰστρέχω
εἴσειμι ([εἶμι] inf. εἰσιέναι; pres. 3 pl. εἰσίασιν; impf. 3 sg. εἰσῄει) *enter, go in*
εἰσενεγκεῖν aor. inf. of εἰσφέρω
εἰσέρχομαι (fut. εἰσελεύσομαι; aor. εἰσῆλθον; pf. εἰσελήλυθα) *come* or *go* (*in* or *into*), *enter; have part in, share in; fall into* (temptation); *arise* (of arguments); εἰσ. καὶ ἐξέρχομαι *live among*
εἰσήγαγον aor. of εἰσάγω
εἰσήνεγκον aor. of εἰσφέρω
εἰσκαλέομαι *invite in*
εἴσοδος, ου f *coming, visit; entrance, access; reception, welcome*
εἰσπηδάω *rush in*
εἰσπορεύομαι *go* or *come in, enter;* εἰσ. καὶ ἐκπορεύομαι εἰς *live in* or *among*
εἱστήκειν plpf. of ἵστημι
εἰστρέχω (aor. ptc. fem. εἰσδραμοῦσα) *run in*
εἰσφέρω (aor. εἰσήνεγκον, inf. εἰσενεγκεῖν) *bring in, carry in, lead in*
εἶτα adv. *then, and then; moreover, after all* or *in the case of* (He 12.9)
εἴτε conj. *if, whether;* εἴτε ... εἴτε *whether ... or, if ... if*
εἶτεν = εἶτα
εἶχον impf. of ἔχω

εἴωθα (pf. with pres. mng.)
be accustomed (τὸ εἰωθός
custom)

εἴων impf. 3 pl. of ἐάω

ἐκ (ἐξ before vowels) prep.
with gen. *from, out from,
away from; by, by means of,
by reason of, because; for;
on, at; of*

ἕκαστος, η, ον *each, every*

ἑκάστοτε adv. *at all times,
always*

ἐκατέστησας alt. aor. 2 sg. of
καθίστημι

ἑκατόν *one hundred;* κατὰ
ἑκατόν *in hundreds*

ἑκατονταετής, ές *a hundred
years old*

ἑκατονταπλασίων, ον *a hun-
dred-fold*

ἑκατοντάρχης, ου and ἑκα-
τόνταρχος, ου m *centurion,
officer* (of the Roman army)

ἐκβαίνω (aor. ἐξέβην) *leave,
go out*

ἐκβάλλω (fut. ἐκβαλῶ; aor.
ἐξέβαλον; plpf. ἐκβεβλή-
κειν; aor. pass. ἐξεβλή-
θην; fut. pass. ἐκβλη-
θήσομαι) *force* or *drive out,
expel, exclude, reject;* without exercise of force: *send
away* or *out; lead out; take
out; bring out;* ἐ. ἔξωθεν
leave out, omit (Re 11.2);
ἐ. εἰς νῖκος τὴν κρίσιν
cause justice to triumph (Mt
12.20)

ἔκβασις, εως f *way out* (of

temptation); *outcome* (of
life)

ἐκβολή, ῆς f *throwing overboard*

ἔκγονον, ου n *grandchild*

ἐκδαπανάομαι *spend oneself
fully*

ἐκδέχομαι *wait for; wait;
expect, look forward to*

ἔκδηλος, ον *clearly evident*

ἐκδημέω *be away from home;
leave home*

ἐκδίδομαι (fut. ἐκδώσομαι;
aor. ἐξεδόμην) *let out, lease,
rent*

ἐκδιηγέομαι *tell* or *relate*
(*fully*)

ἐκδικέω *help* (someone) *get
justice; avenge, punish* (ἐ.
ἐμαυτόν *take revenge* Ro
12.19)

ἐκδίκησις, εως f *rendering of
justice; retribution, punishment, revenge*

ἔκδικος, ου m *one who pun-
ishes*

ἐκδιώκω *persecute harshly;
drive out*

ἔκδοτος, ον *given over, handed
over*

ἐκδοχή, ῆς f *expectation, pros-
pect*

ἐκδύω *strip, take off;* midd.
strip oneself, be naked

ἐκδώσομαι fut. of ἐκδίδομαι

ἐκεῖ adv. *there, in that place;
there, to that place*

ἐκεῖθεν adv. *from there*

ἐκείνης adv. *there* (Lk 19.4)

ἐκεῖνος, η, ο demon. adj. *that; he, she, it*

ἐκεῖσε adv. *there, at that place*

ἐκέκραξα aor. of κράζω

ἐκέρασα aor. of κεράννυμι

ἐκέρδησα aor. of κερδαίνω

ἐκζητέω *seek or search diligently; charge with, require from* (Lk 11.50f)

ἐκζήτησις, εως f *senseless speculation;* perhaps *argument, controversy*

ἐκθαμβέομαι *be greatly surprised or alarmed; be greatly distressed* (Mk 14.33)

ἔκθαμβος, ον *greatly surprised or alarmed*

ἐκθαυμάζω *be completely amazed*

ἔκθετος, ον *abandoned out of doors*

ἐκκαθαίρω (aor. impv. ἐκκαθάρατε) *clean out, make clean*

ἐκκαίομαι (aor. ἐξεκαύθην) *be inflamed* (of lust)

ἐκκεντέω *pierce*

ἐκκέχυμαι pf. pass. of ἐκχέω

ἐκκλάω *break off*

ἐκκλείω *exclude, shut out*

ἐκκλησία, ας f *church, congregation; assembly, gathering* (of religious, political, or unofficial groups)

ἐκκλίνω *turn away; turn aside*

ἐκκολυμβάω *swim away*

ἐκκομίζω *carry out for burial*

ἐκκόπτω (aor. pass. ἐξεκόπην; fut. pass. ἐκκοπήσομαι) *cut off or down; remove*

ἐκκρέμαμαι (impf. ἐξεκρεμάμην) *hang upon*

ἐκλαλέω *tell*

ἐκλάμπω *shine*

ἐκλανθάνομαι (pf. ἐκλέλησμαι) *forget completely*

ἔκλαυσα aor. of κλαίω

ἐκλέγομαι (aor. 2 sg. ἐξελέξω) *choose, select*

ἐκλείπω (aor. subj. ἐκλίπω) *fail, give out; cease, end; leave, leave behind* (Ac 18.19)

ἐκλεκτός, ή, όν *chosen, elect;* perhaps *choice, select* (1 Pe 2.6)

ἐκλήθην aor. pass. of καλέω

ἐκλογή, ῆς f *election, choosing; what is selected or chosen*

ἐκλύομαι *give up; faint, give out*

ἐκμάσσω (aor. ἐξέμαξα) *wipe; dry*

ἐκμυκτηρίζω *make fun of, ridicule*

ἐκνεύω *leave without being noticed*

ἐκνήφω *come to one's senses*

ἑκούσιος, α, ον *willing*

ἑκουσίως adv. *willingly; deliberately*

ἔκπαλαι adv. *for a long time, long ago*

ἐκπειράζω *put to the test, tempt*

ἐκπέμπω *send out; send off or away*

ἐκπερισσῶς adv. *emphatically, again and again*

ἐκπετάννυμι (aor. ἐξεπέτασα) *hold out*

ἐκπηδάω *rush out*

ἐκπίπτω (aor. ἐξέπεσον, inf. ἐκπεσεῖν; pf. ἐκπέπτωκα) *fall off* or *away; lose, forfeit; run aground* (of ships); *fail, become ineffective* (Ro 9.6)

ἐκπλέω (aor. ἐξέπλευσα, inf. ἐκπλεῦσαι) *sail, set sail*

ἐκπληρόω *fulfill, make come true*

ἐκπλήρωσις, εως f *completion, end*

ἐκπλήσσομαι (aor. ἐξεπλάγην) *be amazed*

ἐκπνέω (aor. ἐξέπνευσα) *die*

ἐκπορεύομαι *go* or *come out* (ἐ. εἰς ὁδόν *set out on a journey* Mk 10.17); *come from; rise* (of the dead); *spread* (Lk 4.37)

ἐκπορνεύω *live immorally*

ἐκπτύω *despise, reject*

ἐκριζόω *uproot*

ἐκρίθην aor. pass. of κρίνω

ἐκρύβην aor. pass. of κρύπτω

ἔκστασις, εως f *amazement; trance, vision* (ἐγένετο ἐπ᾽ αὐτὸν ἔ. *he had a vision* Ac 10.10; cf. Ac 11.5; 22.17)

ἐκστρέφομαι (pf. ἐξέστραμμαι) *be perverted* or *corrupt*

ἐκσῴζω (aor. inf. ἐκσῶσαι) *save, keep safe*

ἐκταράσσω *stir up trouble, agitate*

ἐκτεθείς aor. ptc. of ἐκτίθεμαι

ἐκτείνω (fut. ἐκτενῶ; aor. ἐξέτεινα) *stretch out, extend* (οὐκ ἐ. τὰς χεῖρας ἐπ᾽ ἐμέ *you did not arrest me* Lk 22.53); *lay out* (anchors)

ἐκτελέω *finish, complete*

ἐκτένεια, ας f *earnestness*

ἐκτενέστερον adv. *more earnestly*

ἐκτενής, ές *constant, unfailing*

ἐκτενῶς adv. *earnestly; constantly*

ἐκτίθεμαι (aor. ἐξετέθην, ptc. ἐκτεθείς) *explain, expound; be abandoned* or *left out of doors* (Ac 7.21)

ἐκτινάσσω *shake off; shake out*

ἕκτος, η, ον *sixth*

ἐκτός: (1) prep. with gen. *outside; out of; except;* (2) conj. ἐκτὸς εἰ μή *except, unless;* (3) τὸ ἐ. *the outside*

ἐκτρέπομαι (fut. ἐκτραπήσομαι; aor. ἐξετράπην) *wander, go astray, stray after; avoid* (1 Tm 6.20); perhaps *be disabled* (He 12.13)

ἐκτρέφω *feed; raise* (children)

ἔκτρομος, ον *trembling*

ἔκτρωμα, τος n *abnormal birth, miscarriage*

ἐκφέρω (fut. ἐξοίσω; aor. ἐξήνεγκα, inf. ἐξενεγκεῖν) *carry* or *bring out; yield, produce* (He 6.8); ἐ. ἔξω *lead out* (Mk 8.23)

ἐκφεύγω (aor. ἐξέφυγον, inf. ἐκφυγεῖν) escape; flee, run away

ἐκφοβέω frighten, terrify

ἔκφοβος, ον frightened, terrified

ἐκφύω put out (leaves)

ἐκχέω and ἐκχύννω (fut. ἐκχεῶ; aor. ἐξέχεα, inf. ἐκχέαι; pf. pass. ἐκκέχυμαι; aor. pass. ἐξεχύθην; fut. pass. ἐκχυθήσομαι) pour out; shed (blood); pass. plunge into, abandon oneself to (Jd 11)

ἐκχωρέω leave, go away

ἐκψύχω die

ἑκών, οῦσα, όν of one's own free will

ἔλαθον aor. of λανθάνω

ἐλαία, ας f olive tree; olive

ἔλαιον, ου n olive oil; oil

ἐλαιών, ῶνος m olive orchard

Ἐλαμίτης, ου m an Elamite (Elam 3 G–3)

ἐλάσσων, ον (comp. of μικρός) lesser, inferior; younger; less (than)

ἐλαττονέω be in need, have too little

ἐλαττόω make lower; pass. become less important

ἐλαύνω (pf. ἐλήλακα) drive (of wind or demons); row

ἐλαφρία, ας f vacillation (τῇ ἑ. χρῶμαι be fickle 2 Cor 1.17)

ἐλαφρός, ά, όν light, easy to bear; slight, insignificant

ἐλάχιστος, η, ον (superl. of μικρός) least, smallest; very little, insignificant; ἐλαχιστότερος less than the least (Eph 3.8)

ἔλαχον aor. of λαγχάνω

Ἐλεάζαρ m Eleazar (Mt 1.15)

ἐλεάω and ἐλεέω be merciful (pass. be shown mercy, receive mercy); show kindness (Ro 12.8)

ἐλεγμός, οῦ m refutation of error

ἔλεγξις, εως f rebuke; ἔχω ἔ. be rebuked (2 Pe 2.16)

ἔλεγχος, ου m verification, certainty

ἐλέγχω (aor. pass. ἠλέγχθην) show (someone his) fault or error, convince (someone) of (his) fault or error; show (something) up for what it is; prove guilty, condemn; rebuke, reprove

ἐλεεινός, ή, όν pitiable

ἐλεέω cf. ἐλεάω

ἐλεημοσύνη, ης f giving money to a needy person; money given to a needy person, gift

ἐλεήμων, ον gen. ονος merciful

ἔλεος, ους n mercy, compassion

ἐλευθερία, ας f freedom, liberty

ἐλεύθερος, α, ον free; free person (opposite slave); independent; exempt (from taxes) ἐλευθερόω *free, set free*

ἐλεύκανα aor. of λευκαίνω

ἔλευσις, εως f *coming*

ἐλεύσομαι fut. of ἔρχομαι

ἐλεφάντινος, η, ον *of ivory*

ἐλήλακα pf. of ἐλαύνω

ἐλήλυθα pf. of ἔρχομαι

ἐλθεῖν aor. inf. of ἔρχομαι

'Ελιακίμ m *Eliakim* (Mt 1.13; Lk 3.30)

ἔλιγμα, τος n *package, roll*

'Ελιέζερ m *Eliezer* (Lk 3.29)

'Ελιούδ m *Eliud* (Mt 1.14, 15)

'Ελισάβετ f *Elizabeth*

'Ελισαῖος, ου m *Elisha* (Lk 4.27)

ἑλίσσω *roll up*

ἑλκόομαι (pf. εἵλκωμαι) *be covered with sores*

ἕλκος, ους n *sore, boil*

ἕλκω (impf. εἷλκον; fut. ἑλκύσω; aor. εἵλκυσα, subj. 3 sg. ἑλκύσῃ) *draw, attract; drag* (of coercion); *haul in; draw* (of swords)

'Ελλάς, άδος f *Greece* (4 C–3)

"Ελλην, ηνος m *a Greek; non-Jew, Gentile, pagan*

'Ελληνικός, ή, όν *Greek* (ἐν τῇ 'Ε. *in Greek* Re 9.11)

'Ελληνίς, ίδος f *Greek* or *Gentile woman*

'Ελληνιστής, οῦ m *a Hellenist* (one who uses the Greek language and customs)

'Ελληνιστί adv. *in the Greek language*

ἐλλογέω and ἐλλογάω *charge to one's account, keep record of*

'Ελμαδάμ m *Elmadam* (Lk 3.28)

ἐλόμενος aor. ptc. of αἱρέομαι

ἐλπίζω (fut. ἐλπιῶ; aor. ἤλπισα; pf. ἤλπικα) *hope, hope for; hope in; expect*

ἐλπίς, ίδος f *hope* (παρ' ἐ. ἐπ' ἐ. *hoping against hope* Ro 4.18); *ground* or *basis of hope; what is hoped for*

'Ελύμας, α m *Elymas* (Ac 13.8)

ελωι (Aramaic word) *my God*

ἔμαθον aor. of μανθάνω

ἐμαυτοῦ, ῆς reflexive pro. *myself;* possessive pro. *my own* (1 Cor 10.33)

ἐμβαίνω (aor. ἐνέβην, ptc. ἐμβάς, inf. ἐμβῆναι) *get into, embark; go* or *step in*

ἐμβάλλω (aor. inf. ἐμβαλεῖν) *throw* (*in*)

ἐμβάπτω (aor. ptc. ἐμβάψας) *dip*

ἐμβατεύω (doubtful mng.) perhaps *take one's stand on* (what one has seen in a vision) or *claim special powers because of* (what one has seen in a vision)

ἐμβιβάζω *put aboard*

ἐμβλέπω *look straight at; consider; see*

ἐμβριμάομαι *speak harshly to; criticize harshly;* ἐ. ἐν ἐμαυτῷ or ἐ. ἐν πνεύματι *be deeply moved* (Jn 11.33, 38) ἔμεινα aor. of μένω

ἐμέω spit out; vomit

ἐμμαίνομαι be enraged or infuriated

Ἐμμανουήλ m Emmanuel (Mt 1.23)

Ἐμμαοῦς f Emmaus (2 B–6)

ἐμμένω (aor. ἐνέμεινα) remain faithful to, obey; live, stay

Ἑμμώρ m Hamor (Ac 7.16)

ἐμνήσθην aor. of μιμνήσκομαι

ἐμός, ή, όν possessive adj. my, mine

ἐμπαιγμονή, ῆς f mocking, ridicule

ἐμπαιγμός, οῦ m public ridicule; perhaps public torture

ἐμπαίζω (aor. ἐνέπαιξα; aor. pass. ἐνεπαίχθην) ridicule, make fun of; trick, deceive

ἐμπαίκτης, ου m one who makes fun (of another), mocker

ἐμπεριπατέω live (ἐν) among

ἐμπί(μ)πλημι and ἐμπιπλάω (aor. ἐνέπλησα; pf. pass. ἐμπέπλησμαι; aor. pass. ἐνεπλήσθην) fill, satisfy; enjoy

ἐμπί(μ)πρημι (aor. ἐνέπρησα) set on fire, burn down

ἐμπίπτω (fut. ἐμπεσοῦμαι; aor. ἐνέπεσον) fall into or among

ἐμπλέκομαι (aor. pass. ptc. ἐμπλακείς) be mixed up in or involved in

ἐμπλοκή, ῆς f elaborate braiding (of hair)

ἐμπνέω breathe (threats)

ἐμπορεύομαι be in business; exploit, make profit of

ἐμπορία, ας f business

ἐμπόριον, ου n market

ἔμπορος, ου m merchant

ἔμπροσθεν: (1) prep. with gen. before, in front of; (2) adv. ahead, forward, in front

ἐμπτύω spit on

ἐμφανής, ές visible; revealed

ἐμφανίζω i n f o r m , m a k e known, report; reveal (pass. appear He 9.24); ἐ. κατά bring charges against (Ac 24.1; 25.2)

ἔμφοβος, ον full of fear, terrified, afraid

ἐμφυσάω breathe on

ἔμφυτος, ον i m p l a n t e d , planted

ἐν prep. with dat. in, on, at; near, by, before; among, within; by, with; into (= εἰς); to, for (rarely); ἐν τῷ with inf. during, while, as; ἐν ὀνόματι ὅτι because (Mk 9.41)

ἐναγκαλίζομαι take into one's arms; put one's arms round

ἐνάλιον, ου n sea creature, fish

ἔναντι prep. with gen. before, in the presence of; in the judgment of

ἐναντίον prep. with gen. in the judgment of; before; ἐ.

τοῦ λαοῦ *in public* (Lk
20.26)

ἐναντιόομαι *oppose, contradict, deny*

ἐναντίος, α, ον *against, contrary, opposed; hostile* (1 Th
2.15); **ἐξ ἐ.** *opposite* (Mk
15.39); **ὁ ἐξ ἐ.** *enemy* (Tt
2.8)

ἐνάρχομαι *begin, make a beginning*

ἔνατος, η, ον *ninth*

ἐνγ- see **ἐγγ-**

ἐνδεής, ές *needy, poor*

ἔνδειγμα, τος n *evidence,
proof*

ἐνδείκνυμαι (aor. **ἐνεδειξάμην**) *show, give indication
of; do* (2 Tm 4.14)

ἔνδειξις, εως f *evidence; indication*

ἔνδεκα *eleven*

ἐνδέκατος, η, ον *eleventh*

ἐνδέχεται impers. *it is possible, it is imaginable; perhaps
it is right*

ἐνδημέω *be at home, be present*

ἐνδιδύσκω *dress or clothe in;*
midd. *dress oneself in*

ἔνδικος, ον *just, deserved*

ἐνδοξάζομαι *receive glory, be
honored*

ἔνδοξος, ον *glorious, splendid;
fine, expensive* (of clothes);
honored, respected (of men)

ἔνδυμα, τος n *clothing, garment*

ἐνδυναμόω *strengthen, make
strong;* pass. *become strong*

(**ἐ.** *μᾶλλον grow stronger
and stronger* Ac 9.22)

ἐνδύνω *enter on the sly, worm
in*

ἔνδυσις, εως f *wearing, putting on*

ἐνδύω *dress, clothe;* midd.
put on, wear

ἐνδώμησις, εως f *foundation; material* (for building)

ἐνέβην aor. of **ἐμβαίνω**

ἐνέγκας aor. ptc. of **φέρω**

ἐνεγκεῖν and **ἐνέγκαι** aor.
inf. of **φέρω**

ἐνεδειξάμην aor. of **ἐνδείκνυμαι**

ἐνέδρα, ας f *ambush, plot*

ἐνεδρεύω *lie in ambush, lie in
wait; plot*

ἐνειλέω *wrap in*

ἔνειμι (ptc. **ἐνών**) *be in* or
inside (**τὰ ἐ.** *what is inside*
Lk 11.41)

ἕνεκα (**ἕνεκεν** and **εἵνεκεν**)
prep. with gen. *because of,
for the sake of;* **ἕ.** *τούτου*
or **ἕ.** *τούτων for this reason;*
οὗ ἕ. *because* (Lk 4.18);
τίνος **ἕ.** *why?* (Ac 19.32);
ἕ. with *τοῦ* and inf. *in order
that* (2 Cor 7.12)

ἐνέκρυψα aor. of **ἐγκρύπτω**

ἐνέμεινα aor. of **ἐμμένω**

ἐνενήκοντα *ninety*

ἐνεός, ά, όν *speechless*

ἐνεπαίχθην aor. pass. of
ἐμπαίζω

ἐνέπεσον aor. of **ἐμπίπτω**

ἐνέπλησα aor. of **ἐμπίμπλημι**

ἐνεπλήσθην aor. pass. of ἐμπίμπλημι

ἐνέπρησα aor. of ἐμπίμπρημι

ἐνέργεια, ας f (*supernatural*) *working, power* or *activity*

ἐνεργέω (generally of supernatural activity) intrans. *work, be at work, be operative; be effective* (πολὺ ἰσχύει ἐ. *has powerful effects* Jas 5.16); trans. *effect, accomplish*

ἐνέργημα, τος n *working, activity*

ἐνεργής, ές *active, effective*

ἐνέστηκα pf. of ἐνίστημι

ἐνεστώς and ἐνεστηκώς pf. ptc. of ἐνίστημι

ἐνετειλάμην aor. of ἐντέλλομαι

ἐνετράπην aor. pass. of ἐντρέπω

ἐνέτυχον aor. of ἐντυγχάνω

ἐνευλογέω *bless*

ἐνεχθείς aor. pass. ptc. of φέρω

ἐνέχω *have a grudge against, be hostile towards;* pass. *be subject to*

ἐνθάδε adv. *here, to this place; here, in this place*

ἔνθεν adv. *from here, from this place*

ἐνθυμέομαι *think about; think*

ἐνθύμησις, εως f (*inmost*) *thought, idea; imagination*

ἔνι (= ἔνεστιν) *there is*

ἐνιαυτός, οῦ m *year* (κατ' ἐ. *yearly*)

ἐνίστημι (pf. ἐνέστηκα, ptc. ἐνεστηκώς and ἐνεστώς; fut. midd. ἐνστήσομαι) *be impending, be present,* pf. *have come, arrived* (pf. ptc. *present, imminent*)

ἐνισχύω intrans. *regain strength;* trans. *strengthen*

ἐνκ- see ἐγκ-

ἐννέα *nine*

ἐννεύω *inquire by making signs*

ἔννοια, ας f *attitude, thought; intention, purpose*

ἔννομος, ον *subject to law; regular, legal* (Ac 19.39)

ἔννυχα adv. *in the night;* ἔ. λιάν *long before daylight* (Mk 1.35)

ἐνοικέω *live in*

ἐνορκίζω *place* (someone) *under a solemn charge* (ἐ. ὑμᾶς τὸν κύριον *I solemnly charge you in the name of the Lord* 1 Th 5.27)

ἐνότης, ητος f *unity*

ἐνοχλέω *trouble; cause trouble*

ἔνοχος, ον *liable, answerable, guilty; deserving* (of death); *guilty of sin against* (1 Cor 11.27); ἔ. δουλείας *enslaved* (He 2.15); ἔ. εἰς τὴν γέενναν *in danger of going to hell* (Mt 5.22)

ἐνπ- see ἐμπ-

ἐνστήσομαι fut. midd. of ἐνίστημι

ἔνταλμα, τος n *commandment, rule*

ἐνταφιάζω *prepare for burial*
ἐνταφιασμός, οῦ m *preparation for burial, burial*
ἐντέλλομαι (fut. ἐντελοῦμαι; aor. ἐνετειλάμην, ptc. ἐντειλάμενος; pf. ἐντέταλμαι) *command, order, give orders*
ἐντεῦθεν adv. *from here; on this side* (ἐ. καὶ ἐ. *on each side* Jn 19.18); *from this very source* (Jas 4.1)
ἔντευξις, εως f *prayer, petition*
ἔντιμος, ον *valuable, precious; honored, esteemed, distinguished*
ἐντολή, ῆς f *commandment; command, order; instruction* (Ac 17.15)
ἐντόπιος, α, ον *local;* pl. *residents*
ἐντός prep. with gen. *within, in the midst of, among;* τὸ ἐ. *what is inside, contents* (of a cup)
ἐντρέπω (aor. pass. ἐνετράπην; fut. pass. ἐντραπήσομαι) *make ashamed;* pass. *respect, regard; be ashamed, be made ashamed*
ἐντρέφομαι *live on, feed oneself on*
ἔντρομος, ον *trembling, full of fear*
ἐντροπή, ῆς f *shame*
ἐντρυφάω *revel, carouse*
ἐντυγχάνω (aor. ἐνέτυχον) *turn to* (God on behalf of),

plead; appeal (perhaps *bring complaints* Ac 25.24)
ἐντυλίσσω *wrap in; fold* or *roll up*
ἐντυπόω *engrave, carve*
ἐνυβρίζω *insult, outrage*
ἔνυξα aor. of νύσσω
ἐνυπνιάζομαι *dream, have visions*
ἐνύπνιον, ου n *dream*
ἐνφ- see ἐμφ-
ἐνών ptc. of ἔνειμι
ἐνώπιον prep. with gen. *before, in the presence of, in front of; in the judgment of; among;* ἁμαρτάνω ἐ. *sin against* (Lk 15.18, 21)
Ἐνώς m *Enos* (Lk 3.38)
ἐνωτίζομαι *pay close attention to*
Ἐνώχ m *Enoch*
ἐξ = ἐκ before vowels
ἕξ *six*
ἐξαγγέλλω (aor. ἐξήγγειλα) *proclaim, declare, tell*
ἐξαγοράζω *set free;* midd. *make the most of, make good use of*
ἐξάγω (aor. ἐξήγαγον) *lead* or *bring out*
ἐξαιρέω (aor. ἐξεῖλον, impv. ἔξελε; aor. midd. ἐξειλάμην, inf. ἐξελέσθαι) *pull out;* midd. *rescue, deliver, save;* perhaps *rescue* or *select, choose* (Ac 26.17)
ἐξαίρω (aor. impv. 2 pl. ἐξάρατε) *remove, drive out*
ἐξαιτέομαι (aor. ἐξητησά-

μην) ask permission; demand

ἐξαίφνης adv. suddenly, unexpectedly

ἐξακολουθέω follow, obey; depend on (2 Pe 1.16)

ἐξακόσιοι, αι, α six hundred

ἐξαλείφω wipe away or out, remove; cancel, destroy

ἐξάλλομαι jump up

ἐξανάστασις, εως f resurrection

ἐξανατέλλω (aor. ἐξανέτειλα) sprout, spring up

ἐξανίστημι (aor. ἐξανέστησα, subj. 3 sg. ἐξαναστήσῃ) trans. have (σπέρμα) children; intrans. stand up

ἐξαπατάω deceive, lead astray

ἐξάπινα adv. suddenly

ἐξαπορέομαι despair

ἐξαποστέλλω (fut. ἐξαποστελῶ; aor. ἐξαπέστειλα; aor. pass. ἐξαπεστάλην) send off or away; send out or forth

ἐξάρατε aor. impv. 2 pl. of ἐξαίρω

ἐξαρτίζω be completed (of time); equip

ἐξαστράπτω flash like lightning

ἐξαυτῆς adv. at once, immediately; at that moment

ἐξέβαλον aor. of ἐκβάλλω

ἐξέβην aor. of ἐκβαίνω

ἐξεβλήθην aor. pass. of ἐκβάλλω

ἐξεγείρω (fut. ἐξεγερῶ; aor.

ἐξήγειρα) raise; bring into power (Ro 9.17)

ἐξεδόμην aor. of ἐκδίδομαι

ἐξεῖλον aor. of ἐξαιρέω

ἔξειμι ([εἶμι] inf. ἐξιέναι, ptc. ἐξιών; impf. 3 pl. ἐξῄεσαν) go away, depart, leave; head for, get to (Ac 27.43)

ἐξεκαύθην aor. of ἐκκαίομαι

ἐξεκόπην aor. pass. of ἐκκόπτω

ἐξεκρεμάμην impf. of ἐκκρέμαμαι

ἔξελε aor. impv. of ἐξαιρέω

ἐξελέξω aor. 2 sg. of ἐκλέγομαι

ἐξελέσθαι aor. midd. inf. of ἐξαιρέω

ἐξελεύσομαι fut. of ἐξέρχομαι

ἐξελήλυθα pf. of ἐξέρχομαι

ἐξέλκω lure away, draw away

ἐξέμαξα aor. of ἐκμάσσω

ἐξενεγκεῖν aor. inf. of ἐκφέρω

ἐξέπεσον aor. of ἐκπίπτω

ἐξεπέτασα aor. of ἐκπετάννυμι

ἐξεπλάγην aor. of ἐκπλήσσομαι

ἐξέπλευσα aor. of ἐκπλέω

ἐξέπνευσα aor. of ἐκπνέω

ἐξέραμα, τος n vomit

ἐξεραυνάω make a careful search

ἐξέρχομαι (fut. ἐξελεύσομαι; aor. ἐξῆλθον; pf. ἐξελήλυθα) come or go out or *forth; get out, escape, get away; originate* (ἐ. ἐκ τῆς ὀσφύος *descend from* He 7.5); *be gone, disappear* (Ac 16.19)

ἐξεστακέναι pf. inf. of ἐξί-στημι

ἐξέστην and ἐξέστησα aor. of ἐξίστημι

ἔξεστι (ptc. ἐξόν) impers. *it is proper, permitted* or *lawful; it is possible*

ἐξέστραμμαι pf. of ἐκστρέφομαι

ἐξετάζω *look for; make a careful search; ask*

ἐξετέθην aor. of ἐκτίθεμαι

ἐξετράπην aor. of ἐκτρέπομαι

ἐξέφυγον aor. of ἐκφεύγω

ἐξέχεα aor. of ἐκχέω

ἐξεχύθην aor. pass. of ἐκχέω

ἐξέωσαι aor. inf. of ἐξωθέω

ἐξήγαγον aor. of ἐξάγω

ἐξήγγειλα aor. of ἐξαγγέλλω

ἐξήγειρα aor. of ἐξεγείρω

ἐξηγέομαι *tell, relate, explain, report; make known, reveal* (Jn 1.18)

ἐξῄεσαν impf. 3 pl. of ἔξειμι

ἐξήκοντα *sixty*

ἐξῆλθον aor. of ἐξέρχομαι

ἐξήνεγκα aor. of ἐκφέρω

ἐξήραμμαι pf. pass. of ξηραίνω

ἐξήρανα aor. of ξηραίνω

ἐξηράνθην aor. pass. of ξηραίνω

ἑξῆς adv. *on the next day;* ἐν τῷ ἑ. *soon afterwards* (Lk 7.11)

ἐξητησάμην aor. of ἐξαιτέομαι

ἐξηχέομαι *ring out, sound forth*

ἐξιέναι inf. of ἔξειμι

ἕξις, εως f *use, practice*

ἐξίστημι and ἐξιστάνω (aor. ἐξέστην and ἐξέστησα; pf. inf. ἐξεστακέναι; impf. midd. ἐξιστάμην) intrans. *be amazed* or *surprised; be out of one's mind;* trans. *amaze, surprise*

ἐξισχύω *be fully able*

ἐξιών ptc. of ἔξειμι

ἔξοδος, ου f *departure, death; the Exodus* (from Egypt)

ἐξοίσω fut. of ἐκφέρω

ἐξολεθρεύω *destroy, put to death*

ἐξομολογέω *agree, consent;* midd. *confess, admit; acknowledge; praise; thank*

ἐξόν ptc. of ἔξεστι

ἐξορκίζω *put* (someone) *under oath* (κατὰ τοῦ θεοῦ *in the name of God*)

ἐξορκιστής, οῦ m *exorcist* (one who drives out evil spirits with magic formulas)

ἐξορύσσω *dig out, open; gouge out*

ἐξουδενέω *treat with contempt, despise; reject*

ἐξουθενέω *despise, treat with*

contempt; look down on, count as nothing; reject

ἐξουσία, ας f *authority, right, liberty; ability, capability; supernatural power; ruling power, government, official; jurisdiction* (Lk 23.7); *disposal* (Ac 5.4); ἐ. ἔχειν ἐπὶ τῆς κεφαλῆς *have a covering on her head* (perhaps as a symbol of subjection to her husband's authority 1 Cor 11.10)

ἐξουσιάζω *have power over, be master of;* pass. *be made a slave* (1 Cor 6.12)

ἐξουσιαστικός, ή, όν *authoritative*

ἐξοχή, ῆς f *prominence;* κατ' ἐ. *prominent* (Ac 25.23)

ἐξυπνίζω *awake, wake up*

ἔξυπνος, ον *awake*

ἔξω: (1) adv. *out, outside; away;* (2) prep. with gen. *out of, outside;* (3) ὁ ἔξω *outsider, unbeliever; outer, physical* (2 Cor 4.16); *foreign* (Ac 26.11)

ἔξω fut. of **ἔχω**

ἔξωθεν: (1) adv. *from outside, outside;* (2) prep. with gen. *from outside, outside;* (3) τὸ ἔ. *the outside;* ὁ ἔ. *outsider, unbeliever* (1 Tm 3.7); *outward, external* (1 Pe 3.3)

ἐξωθέω (aor. ἐξῶσα, inf. ἐξῶσαι and ἐξέωσαι) *drive out; run aground, beach* (of ships)

ἐξώτερος, α, ον *outer, outmost*

ἔοικα *be like*

ἑόρακα pf. of **ὁράω**

ἑορτάζω *observe a festival*

ἑορτή, ῆς f *festival, feast* (καθ' ἑ. *at each festival*)

ἐπαγγελία, ας f *promise, what is promised; consent* or *decision* (Ac 23.21)

ἐπαγγέλλομαι (aor. ἐπηγγειλάμην; pf. ἐπήγγελμαι) *promise; profess, claim*

ἐπάγγελμα, τος n *promise; what is promised*

ἐπάγω (aor. inf. ἐπαγαγεῖν, ptc. ἐπάξας) *bring upon*

ἐπαγωνίζομαι *struggle in behalf of*

ἔπαθον aor. of **πάσχω**

ἐπαθροίζομαι *increase, crowd around*

Ἐπαίνετος, ου m *Epaenetus* (Ro 16.5)

ἐπαινέω (aor. ἐπῄνεσα) *commend, praise*

ἔπαινος, ου m *praise, commendation, approval; a praiseworthy thing* (Php 4.8)

ἐπαίρω (aor. ἐπῆρα, inf. ἐπᾶραι, ptc. ἐπάρας; aor. pass. ἐπήρθην) *raise, lift up; hoist* (sails); midd. *rise up in opposition* (2 Cor 10.5); *put on airs, act haughtily* (2 Cor 11.20)

ἐπαισχύνομαι *be ashamed*

ἐπαιτέω *beg*

ἐπακολουθέω *follow* (τὰ ἐ. σημεῖα *accompanying* or *authenticating signs* Mk 16.20);

appear or *come later; devote oneself to*

ἐπακούω *listen to, give attention to*

ἐπακροάομαι *listen to*

ἐπάν conj. *when, as soon as*

ἐπάναγκες adv. *necessarily;* τὰ ἐ. *the necessary things*

ἐπανάγω (aor. inf. ἐπαναγαγεῖν) *return; put out* (to sea)

ἐπαναμιμνήσκω *remind, remind again*

ἐπαναπαύομαι (fut. pass. ἐπαναπαήσομαι) *rest upon; rely upon*

ἐπανέρχομαι (aor. inf. ἐπανελθεῖν) *return*

ἐπανίσταμαι *turn against, rebel against*

ἐπανόρθωσις, εως f *correcting faults*

ἐπάνω: (1) prep. with gen. *on, upon; over, above; more than;* (2) adv. *over* (Lk 11.44); *more than* (1 Cor 15.6)

ἐπάξας aor. ptc. of ἐπάγω

ἐπᾶραι aor. inf. of ἐπαίρω

ἐπάρας aor. ptc. of ἐπαίρω

ἐπάρατος, ον *under God's curse*

ἐπαρκέω *assist, help; support*

ἐπαρχεία, ας f *province*

ἔπαυλις, εως f *house, home*

ἐπαύριον adv. *the next day*

Ἐπαφρᾶς, ᾶ m *Epaphras* (Col 1.7; 4.12; Phm 23)

ἐπαφρίζω *foam up, cast up like foam*

Ἐπαφρόδιτος, ου m *Epaphroditus* (Php 2.25; 4.18)

ἐπέβαλον aor. of ἐπιβάλλω

ἐπέβην aor. of ἐπιβαίνω

ἐπεγείρω (aor. ἐπήγειρα) *stir up*

ἐπέγνωκα pf. of ἐπιγινώσκω

ἐπέγνων aor. of ἐπιγινώσκω

ἐπεγνώσθην aor. pass. of ἐπιγινώσκω

ἐπεδίδου impf. 3 sg. of ἐπιδίδωμι

ἐπεδόθην aor. pass. of ἐπιδίδωμι

ἐπέδωκα aor. of ἐπιδίδωμι

ἐπεθέμην aor. midd. of ἐπιτίθημι

ἐπέθηκα aor. of ἐπιτίθημι

ἐπεί conj. *since, because, as; otherwise, for otherwise; when*

ἐπειδή conj. *since, because, for; when, after*

ἐπειδήπερ conj. *inasmuch as, since*

ἐπεῖδον aor. of ἐφοράω

ἔπειμι (fem. ptc. ἐπιοῦσα) *come after, be next* (ἡ ἐπιοῦσα *the next day*)

ἔπεισα aor. of πείθω

ἐπεισαγωγή, ῆς f *bringing in*

ἐπεισέρχομαι (fut. ἐπεισελεύσομαι) *come upon*

ἔπειτα adv. *then, afterwards; next*

ἐπέκειλα aor. of ἐπικέλλω

ἐπέκεινα prep. with gen. *beyond*

ἐπεκεκλήμην plpf. pass. of
  ἐπικαλέω

ἐπεκλήθην aor. pass. of ἐπικαλέω

ἐπεκτείνομαι *stretch toward,*
  reach for

ἐπελαβόμην aor. of ἐπι-
  λαμβάνομαι

ἐπελαθόμην aor. of ἐπιλανθάνομαι

ἐπέλθοι aor. opt. 3 sg. of
  ἐπέρχομαι

ἐπενδύομαι *put on; be fully*
  clothed

ἐπενδύτης, ου m *outer gar-*
  ment

ἐπενεγκεῖν aor. inf. of ἐπιφέρω

ἐπεποίθειν plpf. of πείθω

ἐπέρχομαι (fut. ἐπελεύσο-
  μαι; aor. ἐπῆλθον, ptc.
  ἐπελθών, opt. 3 sg. ἐπέλθοι) *come; come upon; come*
  about (Ac 13.40); *attack* (Lk
  11.22)

ἐπερωτάω *ask; ask for* (Mt
  16.1)

ἐπερώτημα, τος n *promise,*
  answer; appeal; συνειδή-
  σεως ἀγαθῆς ἐ. εἰς θεόν
  perhaps *promise* or *answer*
  made to God from a good
  conscience (1 Pe 3.21)

ἔπεσα aor. of πίπτω

ἐπέστειλα aor. of ἐπι-
  στέλλω

ἐπέστην aor. of ἐφίστημι

ἐπεστράπην aor. pass. of
  ἐπιστρέφω

ἐπετίθεσαν impf. 3 pl. of
  ἐπιτίθημι

ἐπετράπην aor. pass. of ἐπιτρέπω

ἐπέτυχον aor. of ἐπιτυγ-
  χάνω

ἐπεφάνην aor. pass. of ἐπιφαίνω

ἐπέχω (aor. ἐπέσχον) in-
  trans. *notice, give close atten-*
  tion to, keep close watch on;
  stay (ἐ. χρόνον *stay a while*
  Ac 19.22); trans. *hold firmly*
  to or *offer* (Php 2.16)

ἐπηγγειλάμην aor. of ἐπαγγέλλομαι

ἐπήγγελμαι pf. of ἐπαγγέλλομαι

ἐπήγειρα aor. of ἐπεγείρω

ἐπῆλθον aor. of ἐπέρχομαι

ἐπήνεσα aor. of ἐπαινέω

ἔπηξα aor. of πήγνυμι

ἐπῆρα aor. of ἐπαίρω

ἐπηρεάζω *mistreat, insult*

ἐπήρθην aor. pass. of ἐπαίρω

ἐπί prep. with: (1) gen. *on,*
  upon; over; at, by; before, in
  the presence of; when, under,
  at the time of; in the passage
  about (Mk 12.26; Lk 20.37);
  ἐπί or ἐπὶ στόματος *on*
  the evidence of (Mt 18.16;
  2 Cor 13.1; 1 Tm 5.19);
  (2) dat. *on, at, in; with, by,*
  near; over; because of, on the
  basis of; to, for; against; in
  addition to; about, concern-
  ing; of, from (rarely); *after*
  (Lk 1.59); (3) acc. *on, upon;*

*in; against; over; to, for;
around, about, concerning;
towards; among* (rarely); ἐπὶ
τὸ αὐτό *together;* ἐφ' ὅσον
χρόνον *while, as long as;*
ἐπὶ τοῦτο *for this purpose*
(Lk 4.43)

ἐπιβαίνω (aor. **ἐπέβην**, ptc.
ἐπιβάς; pf. **ἐπιβέβηκα**) *go
on board, embark; arrive,
come to; mount* (a donkey)

ἐπιβάλλω (fut. **ἐπιβαλῶ**;
aor. **ἐπέβαλον**) trans. *lay*
(hands) *on; throw* or *place
on* or *upon; sew on* (cloth);
intrans. *beat against* (of
waves); *fall to* (by inheri-
tance); ἐπιβαλὼν ἔκλαιεν
perhaps *he broke down and
cried* (Mk 14.72)

ἐπιβαρέω *be a financial burden;* ἵνα μὴ ἐπιβαρῶ *in order
not to be too hard on you* or
in order not to exaggerate
(2 Cor 2.5)

ἐπιβάς aor. ptc. of **ἐπιβαίνω**

ἐπιβέβηκα pf. of **ἐπιβαίνω**

ἐπιβιβάζω *set* or *place upon*

ἐπιβλέπω *look upon with
care; show more respect to*
(Jas 2.3)

ἐπίβλημα, τος n *piece, patch*

ἐπιβουλή, ῆς f *plot*

ἐπιγαμβρεύω *marry* (according to levirate law)

ἐπίγειος, ον *earthly, of the
earth*

ἐπιγίνομαι (aor. ptc. **ἐπιγε-
νόμενος**) *spring up, come on*

ἐπιγινώσκω (fut. **ἐπιγνώ-
σομαι**; aor. **ἐπέγνων**, subj.
ἐπιγνῶ, ptc. **ἐπιγνούς**; pf.
ἐπέγνωκα; aor. pass. **ἐπεγνώσθην**) *know, perceive,
understand; recognize, acknowledge; find out, learn;
know well*

ἐπίγνωσις, εως f *knowledge, recognition, consciousness* (ἔχω ἐν ἐ. *acknowledge*
Ro 1.28)

ἐπιγραφή, ῆς f *inscription*
(on a coin); *superscription*
(on the cross)

ἐπιγράφω *write on* or *in*

ἔπιδε aor. impv. of **ἐφοράω**

ἐπιδείκνυμι (aor. impv. 2 pl.
ἐπιδείξατε) *show, point out*

ἐπιδέχομαι *receive, welcome;
pay attention to, recognize*
(3 Jn 9)

ἐπιδημέω *visit; live in a place*

ἐπιδιατάσσομαι *add to* (a will)

ἐπιδίδωμι (impf. 3 sg. **ἐπεδίδου**; fut. **ἐπιδώσω**; aor.
ἐπέδωκα, ptc. **ἐπιδούς**,
subj. 3 sg. **ἐπιδῷ**; aor. pass.
ἐπεδόθην) *give, hand; deliver* (letters); *give way* (to
wind) or *give up* (Ac 27.15)

ἐπιδιορθόω *finish setting in
order* or *set in order*

ἐπιδύω *set* (of the sun)

ἐπιείκεια, ας f *kindness, forbearance, graciousness*

ἐπιεικής, ές *gentle, forbearing,
considerate;* τὸ ἐπιεικές =
ἡ ἐπιείκεια (Php 4.5)

ἐπιζητέω seek, desire, want; search for, look for

ἐπιθανάτιος, ον sentenced to death

ἐπιθεῖναι aor. inf. of ἐπιτίθημι

ἐπιθείς aor. ptc. of ἐπιτίθημι

ἐπίθες aor. impv. of ἐπιτίθημι

ἐπίθεσις, εως f laying on (of hands)

ἐπιθήσω fut. of ἐπιτίθημι

ἐπιθυμέω long for, desire; covet; lust for (Mt 5.28)

ἐπιθυμητής, οῦ m one who desires

ἐπιθυμία, ας f desire, longing; lust, passion; covetousness

ἐπιθῶ aor. subj. of ἐπιτίθημι

ἐπικαθίζω sit, sit on

ἐπικαλέω (pf. pass. ἐπικέκλημαι; plpf. pass. ἐπεκεκλήμην; aor. pass. ἐπεκλήθην) call, name, surname; midd. call upon; appeal to (Caesar)

ἐπικάλυμμα, τος n covering, pretext

ἐπικαλύπτω cover (sin)

ἐπικατάρατος, ον under a curse

ἐπίκειμαι lie on or upon; crowd, press hard; be urgent, insist; be in force, be imposed (of regulations)

ἐπικέλλω (aor. ἐπέκειλα) run aground

Ἐπικούρειος, ου m Epicurean (Ac 17.18)

ἐπικουρία, ας f help

ἐπικράνθην aor. pass. of πικραίνω

ἐπικρίνω decide, pass sentence

ἐπιλαμβάνομαι (aor. ἐπελαβόμην) take, take hold of; seize, catch; arrest (Ac 21.33); help, be concerned about or assume the nature of (He 2.16)

ἐπιλανθάνομαι (aor. ἐπελαθόμην, inf. ἐπιλαθέσθαι; pf. ἐπιλέλησμαι) forget, neglect, overlook

ἐπιλέγω call, name; midd. choose

ἐπιλείπω run short (ἐ. με ὁ χρόνος time is running short for me He 11.32)

ἐπιλείχω lick

ἐπιλησμονή, ῆς f forgetfulness

ἐπίλοιπος, ον remaining

ἐπίλυσις, εως f interpretation, explanation

ἐπιλύω explain; settle (a dispute)

ἐπιμαρτυρέω testify, declare

ἐπιμέλεια, ας f care, attention

ἐπιμελέομαι take care of, look after

ἐπιμελῶς adv. carefully, thoroughly

ἐπιμένω (aor. ἐπέμεινα, inf. ἐπιμεῖναι) remain, stay; continue, keep on, persist in

ἐπινεύω consent

ἐπίνοια, ας f intent, purpose

ἔπιον aor. of πίνω

ἐπιορκέω *break an oath, swear falsely*

ἐπίορκος, ου m *perjurer*

ἐπιοῦσα, ης f *the next day*

ἐπιούσιος, ον (of doubtful mng.) *for today; for the coming day; necessary for existence*

ἐπιπίπτω (aor. ἐπέπεσον; pf. ἐπιπέπτωκα) *fall or come upon; press close on;* ἐ. ἐπὶ τὸν τράχηλον *embrace* (Lk 15.20; Ac 20.37)

ἐπιπλήσσω *reprimand, rebuke*

ἐπιποθέω *long for, desire;* perhaps *yearn over* (Jas 4.5)

ἐπιπόθησις, εως f *longing*

ἐπιπόθητος, ον *longed for*

ἐπιποθία, ας f *longing, desire*

ἐπιπορεύομαι *come to*

ἐπιράπτω *sew on*

ἐπιρίπτω *throw on*

ἐπισείω (aor. ptc. nom. masc. pl. ἐπεισείσαντες) *urge on, stir up, incite*

ἐπίσημος, ον *well known, outstanding; notorious* (prisoner Mt 27.16)

ἐπισιτισμός, οῦ m *food, something to eat*

ἐπισκέπτομαι *visit, care for, be concerned about; pick out, look for* (Ac 6.3); perhaps *rise upon* (Lk 1.78)

ἐπισκευάζομαι *make ready, pack up*

ἐπισκηνόω *rest upon, live in*

ἐπισκιάζω *overshadow; fall upon* (of a shadow)

ἐπισκοπεύω alt. form of ἐπισκοπέω

ἐπισκοπέω *see to it, take care; oversee, see after*

ἐπισκοπή, ῆς f *visitation* (of God's presence among men); *office, place of service; office of bishop* (1 Tm 3.1)

ἐπίσκοπος, ου m *overseer, guardian; bishop*

ἐπισπάομαι *remove the marks of circumcision*

ἐπισπείρω *sow in addition*

ἐπίσταμαι *know, understand*

ἐπιστάς aor. ptc. of ἐφίστημι

ἐπίστασις, εως f *pressure, burden; stirring up* (of a crowd)

ἐπιστάτης, ου m *Master* (of Christ)

ἐπιστέλλω (aor. ἐπέστειλα, inf. ἐπιστεῖλαι) *write, instruct by letter*

ἐπιστῆ aor. subj. 3 sg. of ἐφίστημι

ἐπίστηθι aor. impv. of ἐφίστημι

ἐπιστήμων, ον gen. ονος *understanding*

ἐπιστηρίζω *strengthen*

ἐπιστολή, ῆς f *letter*

ἐπιστομίζω *silence*

ἐπιστρέφω (aor. pass. ἐπεστράφην, ptc. ἐπιστραφείς) intrans. (including midd. and aor. pass.) *turn back, return; turn to; turn around;* trans. *turn, turn back*

ἐπιστροφή, ῆς f *conversion*

ἐπισυνάγω (aor. inf. ἐπισυναγαγεῖν and ἐπισυνάξαι) *gather, gather together*

ἐπισυναγωγή, ῆς f *assembling, gathering; meeting* (of worship)

ἐπισυντρέχω *gather rapidly, close in*

ἐπισφαλής, ές *dangerous, risky*

ἐπισχύω *insist, be urgent*

ἐπισωρεύω *accumulate, collect*

ἐπιταγή, ῆς f *command, order; authority* (Tt 2.15)

ἐπιτάσσω *command, order*

ἐπιτελέω *complete, accomplish; finish, end; perform* (of duty); *place upon* (of suffering); *erect* (a tent)

ἐπιτήδειος, α, ον *necessary, suitable*

ἐπιτίθημι (3 pl. ἐπιτιθέασιν, impv. ἐπιτίθει; impf. 3 pl. ἐπετίθεσαν; fut. ἐπιθήσω; aor. ἐπέθηκα, impv. ἐπίθες, subj. ἐπιθῶ, inf. ἐπιθεῖναι, ptc. ἐπιθείς; fut. midd. ἐπιθήσομαι; aor. midd. ἐπεθέμην) *lay* or *put on; place, put; add* (Re 22.18a); ἐ. ὄνομα *surname* (Mk 3.16, 17); ἐ. πληγάς *beat* (Lk 10.30; Ac 16.23); midd. *give, put on board* (Ac 28.10); *attack* (Ac 18.10)

ἐπιτιμάω *command, order, give*

a command; rebuke; scold; ἐ. αὐτῷ perhaps *show him his fault* (Lk 17.3)

ἐπιτιμία, ας f *punishment*

ἐπιτρέπω (aor. pass. ἐπετράπην) *let, allow, permit*

ἐπιτροπή, ῆς f *commission*

ἐπίτροπος, ου m *steward, foreman; guardian*

ἐπιτυγχάνω (aor. ἐπέτυχον, inf. ἐπιτυχεῖν) *obtain, receive, attain*

ἐπιφαίνω (aor. inf. ἐπιφᾶναι; aor. pass. ἐπεφάνην) *appear, give light;* pass. *appear, be revealed*

ἐπιφάνεια, ας f *appearing, appearance, coming*

ἐπιφανής, ές *glorious*

ἐπιφαύσκω (fut. ἐπιφαύσω) *shine* (on), *give light* (to)

ἐπιφέρω (aor. inf. ἐπενεγκεῖν) *bring upon, inflict; pronounce; bring* (a charge against someone)

ἐπιφωνέω *shout, cry out*

ἐπιφώσκω *dawn, draw near, begin* (τῇ ἐ. εἰς μίαν σαββάτων as the first day of the week was dawning Mt 28.1)

ἐπιχειρέω *undertake, attempt, try*

ἐπιχέω *pour on*

ἐπιχορηγέω *supply, give, provide; support;* ἐ. ἐν *add to* (2 Pe 1.5)

ἐπιχορηγία, ας f *supply, support, help*

ἐπιχρίω *smear* or *spread on*

ἐπλάσθην aor. pass. of
πλάσσω

ἐπλήγην aor. pass. of
πλήσσω

ἔπλησα aor. of πίμπλημι

ἐπλήσθην aor. pass. of πίμπλημι

ἔπνευσα aor. of πνέω

ἐποικοδομέω build on or
upon; build up

ἐπονομάζομαι call oneself

ἐποπτεύω see, observe

ἐπόπτης, ου m eyewitness

ἔπος, ους n word; ὡς ἔπος
εἰπεῖν so to speak (He 7.9)

ἐπουράνιος, ον heavenly; ce-
lestial (1 Cor 15.40); ἐν
τοῖς ἐ. in the heavenly
world, in the supernatural
sphere (Eph 1.3, etc.)

ἐπράθην aor. pass. of πι-
πράσκω

ἐπρήσθησαν alt. form of
ἐπρίσθησαν

ἐπρίσθησαν aor. pass. 3 pl.
of πρίζω

ἑπτά seven

ἑπτάκις adv. seven times

ἑπτακισχίλιοι, αι, α seven
thousand

ἑπταπλασίων, ον gen. ονος
seven times as much

ἐπυθόμην aor. of πυνθάνο-
μαι

Ἔραστος, ου m Erastus (Ac
19.22; Ro 16.23; 2 Tm 4.20)

ἐραυνάω search, examine; inquire, try to find out

ἐργάζομαι (aor. εἰρ- and

ἠρ-; pf. εἴργασμαι) in-
trans. work; trade, invest (Mt
25.16); trans. do, bring
about; perform (temple duties); work for (Jn 6.27);
ἐ. τὴν θάλασσαν trade by
sea (Re 18.17)

ἐργασία, ας f gain, profit;
business; practice, doing; δὸς
ἐ. make an effort (Lk 12.58)

ἐργάτης, ου m laborer, worker,
workman; ἐ. ἀδικίας evil-
doer (Lk 13.27)

ἔργον, ου n work, deed, action; task, occupation, undertaking; practical expression;
handiwork, workmanship (1
Cor 9.1); perhaps effect,
result or product (Jas 1.4)

ἐρεθίζω stir up, rouse; make
resentful, embitter

ἐρείδω stick fast

ἐρεύγομαι declare, tell

ἐρημία, ας f deserted place,
uninhabited region, desert

ἐρημόομαι be made waste or
desolate

ἔρημος, ου f deserted place,
uninhabited region, desert

ἔρημος, ον lonely, deserted,
uninhabited; desolate

ἐρήμωσις, εως f desolation,
destruction

ἐρίζω argue, quarrel, protest

ἐριθεία, ας f selfishness, selfish
rivalry, selfish ambition

ἔριον, ου n wool

ἔρις, ιδος f strife, selfish

rivalry, fighting; pl. *quarrels, quarreling*

ἐρίφιον, ου n *goat, kid*

ἔριφος, ου m *goat, kid*

ἔριψα aor. of **ῥίπτω**

Ἑρμᾶς, ᾶ m *Hermas* (Ro 16.14)

ἑρμηνεία, ας f *interpretation, translation*

ἑρμηνεύω *interpret, explain;* pass. *mean, be translated*

Ἑρμῆς, οῦ m *Hermes:* (1) Greek god (Ac 14.12); (2) Roman Christian (Ro 16.14)

Ἑρμογένης, ους m *Hermogenes* (2 Tm 1.15)

ἑρπετόν, οῦ n *reptile*

ἔρραμαι pf. pass. of **ῥαίνω**

ἐρραντισμένος pf. pass. ptc. of **ῥαντίζω**

ἐρρέθην aor. pass. of **λέγω**

ἔρρηξα aor. of **ῥήγνυμι**

ἐρρίζωμαι pf. of **ῥιζόομαι**

ἔρριμμαι pf. pass. of **ῥίπτω**

ἐρρυσάμην aor. of **ῥύομαι**

ἐρρύσθην aor. pass. of **ῥύομαι**

ἔρρωσο (2 pl. **ἔρρωσθε**) pf. impv. of **ῥώννυμαι**

ἐρυθρός, ά, όν *red*

ἔρχομαι (imperf. **ἠρχόμην**, fut. **ἐλεύσομαι**; aor. **ἦλθον** and **ἦλθα**, inf. **ἐλθεῖν**; pf. **ἐλήλυθα**) *come* (**εἰς τὸ χεῖρον ἔ.** *grow worse* Mk 5.26); *appear, make an appearance; go; return* (Jn 4.27, 30; Ro 9.9); *be brought* (Mk 4.21); **ἐ. εἰς προκοπήν** *help the progress* (Php 1.12)

ἐρῶ fut. of **λέγω**

ἐρωτάω *ask* (a question); *ask, request; beg, request urgently, urge*

ἔσβεσα aor. of **σβέννυμι**

ἐσήμανα aor. of **σημαίνω**

ἐσθής, ῆτος f *clothing, apparel*

ἐσθήσεσι dat. pl. of **ἐσθής**

ἐσθίω and **ἔσθω** (fut. **φάγομαι**; aor. **ἔφαγον**, inf. **φαγεῖν**) *eat; consume*

ἔσκυλμαι pf. pass. of **σκύλλω**

Ἐσλί m *Esli* (Lk 3.25)

ἔσοπτρον, ου n *mirror*

ἔσπαρμαι pf. pass. of **σπείρω**

ἑσπέρα, ας f *evening*

Ἑσρώμ m *Hezron* (Mt 1.3; Lk 3.33)

ἐσσόομαι *be worse off, be treated worse*

ἐστάθην aor. pass. of **ἵστημι**

ἐστάναι pf. inf. of **ἵστημι**

ἕστηκα pf. of **ἵστημι**

ἑστηκώς and **ἑστώς** pf. ptc. of **ἵστημι**

ἔστην 2 aor. of **ἵστημι**

ἔστησα 1 aor. of **ἵστημι**

ἐστράφην aor. pass. of **στρέφω**

ἐστρωμένος pf. pass. ptc. of **στρώννυμι**

ἔστρωσα aor. of **στρώννυμι**

ἔστω impv. 3 sg. of **εἰμί**

ἔσχατος, η, ον: (1) adj. *last, final; lowest, most insignificant;* **ἕως ἐ. τῆς γῆς** *to the very ends of the earth,* i.e. *for the whole world* (Ac 1.8; 13.47);* (2) adv. **ἔσχατον**

πάντων last of all (Mk
12.22; 1 Cor 15.8)

ἐσχάτως adv. finally; ἐ. ἔχω
be dying, be very sick (Mk
5.23)

ἔσχηκα pf. of ἔχω

ἔσχον aor. of ἔχω

ἔσω: (1) adv. inside, within;
(2) prep. with gen. inside
(Mk 15.16); (3) ὁ ἔσω one
inside the church, believer (1
Cor 5.12); inner being, inmost being (of man)

ἔσωθεν adv. within, inside,
inwardly; from within; τὸ
ἔ. the inside (Lk 11.39, 40)

ἐσώτερος, α, ον: (1) adj.
inner; (2) prep. with gen.
behind, inside (He 6.19)

ἑταῖρος, ου m friend, companion

ἐταράχθην aor. pass. of ταράσσω

ἐτάφην aor. pass. of θάπτω

ἐτέθην aor. pass. of τίθημι

ἔτεκον aor. of τίκτω

ἑτερόγλωσσος, ον speaking
a foreign (strange?) language

ἑτεροδιδασκαλέω teach a different doctrine; teach a false
doctrine

ἑτεροζυγέω be mismated

ἕτερος, α, ον other, another
(ἐν ἑτέρῳ in another pas-
sage Ac 13.35; He 5.6; γίνομαι ἔ. be altered or changed
Lk 9.29; οὐδὲν ἔ. nothing
else Ac 17.21); different,
strange (σὰρξ ἔ. unnatural

lust Jd 7); next (τῇ ἐ. the
next day Ac 20.15; 27.3)

ἑτέρως adv. otherwise, dif-
ferently

ἐτέχθην aor. pass. of τίκτω

ἔτι adv. still, yet (οὐκ ἔτι
no longer; οὐδὲ ἔτι νῦν
not even yet 1 Cor 3.2);
even; further, in addition,
moreover (τίς ἔτι χρεία
what further need? He 7.11)

ἐτίθει impf. 3 sg. of τίθημι

ἐτίθεσαν and ἐτίθουν impf.
3 pl. of τίθημι

ἑτοιμάζω prepare, make
ready; get everything ready
(Lk 9.52)

ἑτοιμασία, ας f readiness;
equipment

ἕτοιμος, η, ον ready, prepared (ἐν ἑ. ἔχω be ready
2 Cor 10.6); present, at hand
(Jn 7.6); τὰ ἑ. work already
done (2 Cor 10.16)

ἑτοίμως adv. readily; ἑ. ἔχω
be ready or prepared

ἔτος, ους n year (πεντή-
κοντα ἔτη ἔχω be fifty
years old Jn 8.57; κατ' ἔτος
every year Lk 2.41)

ἐτύθην aor. pass. of θύω

εὖ adv. well (εὖ ποιῶ do good,
help); well done! splendid!

Εὔα, ας f Eve (2 Cor 11.3;
1 Tm 2.13)

εὐαγγελίζω act. and midd.
bring the good news, preach
the good news (sometimes
preach the good news to, e.g.

Ac 8.25); *preach, proclaim;* pass. *hear the good news* (of persons); *be preached* (of things)

εὐαγγέλιον, ου n *good news, gospel*

εὐαγγελιστής, οῦ m *one who preaches the good news, evangelist*

εὐαρεστέω *please, be pleasing to*

εὐάρεστος, ον *acceptable, pleasing*

εὐαρέστως adv. *in an acceptable way*

Εὔβουλος, ου m *Eubulus* (2 Tm 4.21)

εὖγε adv. *well done! splendid!*

εὐγενής, ές *of high* or *noble birth; of high social status; open-minded* (Ac 17.11)

εὐδία, ας f *fair weather*

εὐδοκέω *be pleased; take delight* or *pleasure in; choose, will, resolve; be content* (2 Cor 12.10)

εὐδοκία, ας f *good will, pleasure, favor; desire, purpose, choice*

εὐεργεσία, ας f *service; act of kindness*

εὐεργετέω *do good*

εὐεργέτης, ου m *benefactor* (honorary title of men in high positions)

εὔθετος, ον *fit, suitable, useful*

εὐθέως adv. *immediately, at once; soon*

εὐθυδρομέω *sail a straight (direct?) course*

εὐθυμέω *take courage; be happy*

εὔθυμος, ον *encouraged*

εὐθύμως adv. *cheerfully, confidently*

εὐθύνω *make straight;* ὁ εὐθύνων *helmsman* or *pilot* (of a ship)

εὐθύς, εῖα, ύ gen. **έως** *straight; right, upright*

εὐθύς adv. *immediately, at once; then*

εὐθύτης, ητος f *uprightness, justice*

εὐκαιρέω *have time* or *opportunity; spend time*

εὐκαιρία, ας f *opportune moment, good chance*

εὔκαιρος, ον *suitable, timely*

εὐκαίρως adv. *when the time is right; when convenient*

εὐκοπώτερος, α, ον (comp. of **εὔκοπος** *easy*) *easier;* εὐκοπώτερόν ἐστιν *it is easier*

εὐλάβεια, ας f *godly fear, reverence*

εὐλαβέομαι *act in reverence, be moved with fear; take heed, take care*

εὐλαβής, ές *devout, reverent*

εὐλογέω *bestow a blessing upon, act graciously toward* (with God or Christ as subj.); *praise* (with God or Christ as obj.); *ask God's blessing upon* (food) εὐλογητός, ή, όν blessed; praised; the Blessed One (of God Mk 14.61)

εὐλογία, ας f blessing; praise; consecration; gift, contribution (2 Cor 9.5); flattery (Ro 16.18); ἐπ᾽ εὐλογίαις bountifully (2 Cor 9.6)

εὐμετάδοτος, ον liberal, generous

Εὐνίκη, ης f Eunice (2 Tm 1.5)

εὐνοέω make friends, come to terms

εὔνοια, ας f good will; eagerness, zeal

εὐνουχίζω castrate, make a eunuch of

εὐνοῦχος, ου m eunuch

εὐξαίμην aor. opt. of εὔχομαι

Εὐοδία, ας f Euodia (Php 4.2)

εὐοδόομαι have things go well (for oneself); earn, gain (money); be possible (for one to do something)

εὐπάρεδρον, ου n devotion

εὐπειθής, ές open to reason, willing to give in (to someone else)

εὐπερίσπαστος, ον easily distracting

εὐπερίστατος, ον holding on tightly and causing entanglement

εὐποιΐα, ας f doing of good

εὐπορέομαι have financial means

εὐπορία, ας f wealth, prosperity

εὐπρέπεια, ας f beauty, loveliness

εὐπρόσδεκτος, ον acceptable

εὐπροσωπέω make a good showing

Εὐρακύλων, ωνος m northeast wind, Euraquilo

εὑρίσκω (impf. εὑ- and ηὑ-; fut. εὑρήσω; aor. εὗρον, opt. 3 pl. εὕροιεν; pf. εὕρηκα; aor. pass. εὑρέθην; fut. pass. εὑρεθήσομαι) find, discover, come upon; obtain, secure, receive; pass. be found, be, appear; εὑ. εἰς θάνατον proved to mean death (Ro 7.10)

Εὐροκλύδων, ωνος m southeast wind, Euroclydon

εὐρύχωρος, ον wide, roomy

εὐσέβεια, ας f godliness, godly life; religion; pl. good deeds or godly living (2 Pe 3.11)

εὐσεβέω worship; τὸν ἴδιον οἶκον εὐ. carry out one's religious duties towards one's family (1 Tm 5.4)

εὐσεβής, ές godly, religious

εὐσεβῶς adv. in a godly manner

εὔσημος, ον intelligible, easily understood

εὔσπλαγχνος, ον tenderhearted, kind

εὐσχημόνως adv. properly; respectably

εὐσχημοσύνη, ης f modesty, propriety

εὐσχήμων, ον gen. ονος

respected, of high standing; presentable or *more presentable* (parts of the body); τὸ εὖ. *good order* (1 Cor 7.35)

εὐτόνως adv. *vehemently, vigorously*

εὐτραπελία, ας f *vulgar* or *dirty talk*

Εὔτυχος, ου m *Eutychus* (Ac 20.9)

εὐφημία, ας f *good reputation* or *report*

εὔφημος, ον *worthy of praise*

εὐφορέω *produce good crops*

εὐφραίνω (aor. pass. **ηὐφράνθην**, inf. **εὐφρανθῆναι**) *make glad, cheer up;* pass. *rejoice, be glad, celebrate*

Εὐφράτης, ου m *Euphrates* (1 E–3, 4 H–2)

εὐφροσύνη, ης f *gladness, joy*

εὐχαριστέω *t h a n k , g i v e thanks; be thankful, be grateful* (Ro 16.4)

εὐχαριστία, ας f *thanksgiving, thanks; gratitude, thankfulness*

εὐχάριστος, ον *thankful, grateful*

εὐχή, ῆς f *vow, oath; prayer*

εὔχομαι (aor. opt. **εὐξαίμην**) *pray; wish, long*

εὔχρηστος, ον *useful, beneficial*

εὐψυχέω *be encouraged, be cheered*

εὐωδία, ας f *sweet smell, fragrant aroma*

εὐώνυμος, ον *left* (opposite right)

ἔφαγον aor. of **ἐσθίω**

ἐφάλλομαι (aor. **ἐφαλόμην**) *jump on*

ἐφάνην aor. pass. of **φαίνω**

ἐφάπαξ adv. *once for all time; at one time* (1 Cor 15.6)

Ἐφέσιος, α, ον *Ephesian*

Ἔφεσος, ου f *Ephesus* (3 B–2, 4 E–3)

ἐφέστηκα pf. of **ἐφίστημι**

ἐφεστώς pf. ptc. of **ἐφίστημι**

ἐφευρετής, οῦ m *one who schemes* or *plans*

ἔφη impf. (and perhaps aor.) 3 sg. of **φημί**

ἐφημερία, ας f *division* (of priests for daily temple duties)

ἐφήμερος, ον *daily*

ἐφικνέομαι (aor. inf. **ἐφικέσθαι**) *reach, come* (ἄχρι) *as far as*

ἐφίστημι (aor. **ἐπέστην**, subj. **ἐπιστῶ**, impv. **ἐπίστηθι**, ptc. **ἐπιστάς**; pf. **ἐφέστηκα**, ptc. **ἐφεστώς**) used in pres. and aor. *come up, to* or *before, approach; stand by* or *near; appear; attack* (Ac 17.5); perhaps *be insistent* or *be busy at one's job* (2 Tm 4.2); used in pf. *stand by, be present; be imminent* (of death); *set in* (of rain)

έφοράω (aor. **ἐπεῖδον**, impv.
ἔπιδε) *concern oneself with;
take notice of*
Ἐφραίμ m *Ephraim* (**2** C-6)
ἔφυγον aor. of **φεύγω**
εφφαθα (Aramaic word) *be
opened!*
ἐχάρην aor. of **χαίρω**
ἐχθές adv. *yesterday*
ἔχθρα, ας f *hostility, ill will,
hatred*
ἐχθρός, ά, όν *enemy; hated*
ἔχιδνα, ης f *snake, viper*
ἔχω (impf. **εἶχον**; fut. **ἕξω**;
aor. **ἔσχον**, subj. **σχῶ**; pf.
ἔσχηκα) trans. *have, hold,
possess; keep; receive, get;
regard, consider, think; can,
be able, must* (with inf.);
be married to; wear (of
clothes); *be situated* (σαββάτου ἔχον ὁδόν a Sab-
bath day's journey away Ac
1.12); *τὸ νῦν ἔχον for the
present* (Ac 24.25); intrans.
be, feel; impers. *it is* (οὕτως

ἔχει *it is so);* midd. ptc.
next, neighboring (τῇ ἐχο-
μένῃ *the next day* Lk 13.33)
ἐῶν ptc. of **ἐάω**
ἑώρακα and **ἑόρακα** pf. of
ὁράω
ἑώρων impf. 3 pl. of **ὁράω**
ἕως: (1) conj. (and *ἕως ὅτου*
or *ἕως οὗ*) *until* (with any
tense); *while* (with pres. ind.
only); (2) prep. with gen.
*to, until, as far as, to the
point of* (ἕως τέλους *to the
end, fully;* ἕως τοῦ νῦν
until now; ἕως τούτου cf.
ἐάω); *as many as* (of numerals); (3) *ἕως ἄνω to the
brim* (Jn 2.7); *ἕως ἄρτι
until now, so far, still; ἕως
ἐπί to* (Ac 17.14); *ἕως ἔξω
outside* (Ac 21.5); *ἕως καὶ
εἰς even into* (Ac 26.11);
*ἕως πότε how long? ἕως
πρός as far as* (Lk 24.50);
ἕως ὧδε as far as this place
(Lk 23.5)

Z

Ζαβουλών m *Zebulun:* (1)
an Israelite tribe; (2) and
its territory (**1** C-3, **2**
C-3)
Ζακχαῖος, ου m *Zacchaeus*
(Lk 19.2, 5, 8)

Ζάρα m *Zerah* (Mt 1.3)
Ζαχαρίας, ου m *Zechariah:*
(1) father of John the Baptist; (2) OT prophet (Mt
23.35; Lk 11.51)
ζάω (contracted to **ζῶ**; impf.

ἔζην) *live, be alive; remain alive; come back to life*

Ζεβεδαῖος, ου m *Zebedee* (father of James and John)

ζεστός, ή, όν *hot*

ζεῦγος, ους n *yoke, team; pair*

ζευκτηρία, ας f *rope(s)*

Ζεύς gen. **Διός** acc. **Δία** m *Zeus*

ζέω *boil* (ζέων τῷ πνεύματι *with enthusiasm* Ac 18.25; *with a heart full of devotion* Ro 12.11)

ζηλεύω *be zealous, be earnest*

ζῆλος, ου m and **ους** n *zeal; jealousy*

ζηλόω *be jealous (of); set one's heart on, be deeply concerned about; have* or *show a great interest in;* perhaps *covet* (Jas 4.2)

ζηλωτής, οῦ m *one who is zealous* or *eager; Zealot* (member of a Jewish nationalistic sect)

ζημία, ας f *loss*

ζημιόω pass. only with mng. *lose, forfeit, suffer loss; be punished* (1 Cor 3.15)

Ζηνᾶς acc. **ᾶν** m *Zenas* (Tt 3.13)

ζητέω *seek, search* or *look for; try, attempt, strive for* (ζ. τὸ ἐμαυτοῦ or ζ. τὰ ἐμαυτοῦ *strive for one's own interest* or

advantage); want, ask, ask for; demand, require, expect; consider, deliberate, examine, investigate

ζήτημα, τος n *controversial question, point of disagreement*

ζήτησις, εως f *discussion, debate; controversy, controversial issue; investigation*

ζιζάνιον, ου n *weed* (resembling wheat)

Ζοροβαβέλ m *Zerubbabel* (Mt 1.12; Lk 3.27)

ζόφος, ου m *gloom, darkness*

ζυγός, οῦ m *yoke; balance scales* (Re 6.5)

ζύμη, ης f *yeast* (used to make bread rise)

ζυμόω *cause to rise* (pass. *rise*)

ζωγρέω *catch, capture*

ζωή, ῆς f *life;* ψυχὴ ζωῆς *living thing* (Re 16.3)

ζώνη, ης f *belt; money belt* (Mt 10.9; Mk 6.8)

ζώννυμι and **ζωννύω** (impf. 2 sg. ἐζώννυες; fut. ζώσω; aor. midd. impv. ζῶσαι) *fasten, fasten one's belt; dress*

ζῳογονέω *save life; give life to* (of God); pass. *stay alive*

ζῷον, ου n *living creature; animal*

ζῳοποιέω *give life to, make alive*

H

ἤ particle *or* (ἤ . . . ἤ *either* . . .
or; ἤ καί *or even;* with
negatives *nor, or*); *than* (of
comparison); πρὶν ἤ *before;*
ἀλλ᾽ ἤ *but rather* (Lk
12.51)

ἤγαγον aor. of ἄγω

ἠγάπομεν alt. impf. 1 pl. of
ἀγαπάω

ἤγγειλα aor. of ἀγγέλλω

ἡγεμονεύω *be governor, rule*

ἡγεμονία, ας f *reign, rule*

ἡγεμών, όνος m *governor;
ruler, prince*

ἡγέομαι *consider, regard,
think; lead, rule* (ὁ ἡ. *leader,
ruler;* ὁ ἡ. τοῦ λόγου *the
chief speaker* Ac 14.12)

ἠγέρθην aor. pass. of ἐγείρω

ᾔδειν plpf. of οἶδα

ἡδέως adv. *gladly*

ἤδη adv. *now, already;* ἤδη
ποτέ *now at last*

ἤδιστα (superl. of ἡδέως)
most gladly

ἡδονή, ῆς f *pleasure; passion,
lust*

ἠδυνάσθην and ἠδυνήθην
aor. of δύναμαι

ἡδύοσμον, ου n *mint* (plant)

ἤθελον impf. of θέλω

ἦθος, ους n *habit;* pl. *morals*

ἥκω (pres. 3 pl. ἥκασιν) *have
come, be present; come*

ἠλάμην aor. of ἅλλομαι

ἦλθον and ἦλθα aor. of ἔρχομαι

ηλι (Hebrew word) *my God*

Ἠλί m *Heli* (Lk 3.23)

Ἠλίας, ου m *Elijah*

ἡλικία, ας f *age, span of life,
years* (ἡλικίαν ἔχω *be of
age* Jn 9.21, 23; καὶ παρὰ
καιρὸν ἡ. *though she was
past age for childbirth* He
11.11); *height* (Lk 19.3; Mt
6.27 = *years* or *height*); *maturity* (Eph 4.13)

ἡλίκος, η, ον *how great, how
large; how small*

ἥλιος, ου m *the sun*

ἧλος, ου m *nail*

ἤλπισα, ἤλπικα aor. and. pf.
of ἐλπίζω

ἡμάρτηκα pf. of ἁμαρτάνω

ἥμαρτον and ἡμάρτησα aor.
of ἁμαρτάνω

ἡμέρα, ας f *day* (καθ᾽ ἡμέραν
daily; διὰ τριῶν ἡ. *in three
days;* δι᾽ ἡμερῶν *some days
later*); *time; legal day* (ἀνθρωπίνη ἡ. *human court*
1 Cor 4.3)

ἡμέτερος, α, ον *our*

ἡμιθανής, ές *half dead*

ἥμισυς, εια, υ gen. ἡμίσους
half; τὸ ἥ. *one half*

ἡμίωρον, ου n *half an hour*

ἠμφίεσμαι pf. pass. of ἀμφιέννυμι

ἤνεγκα aor. of φέρω

ἠνέχθην aor. pass. of φέρω

ἠνέῳγμαι pf. pass. of ἀνοίγω

ἠνέῳξα and ἤνοιξα aor. of ἀνοίγω

ἠνεῴχθην, ἠνοίγην and ἠνοίχθην aor. pass. of ἀνοίγω

ἡνίκα when; ἡ. ἄν whenever

ἠντληκώς pf. ptc. of ἀντλέω

ἤπερ than (strengthened form of ἤ)

ἤπιος, α, ον gentle, kind

Ἤρ m Er (Lk 3.28)

ἦρα, ἤρθην aor. and aor. pass. of αἴρω

ἠργασάμην aor. of ἐργάζομαι

ἤρεμος, ον quiet, peaceful

ἤρεσα aor. of ἀρέσκω

ἡρπάγην aor. pass. of ἁρπάζω

ἠρχόμην impf. of ἔρχομαι

Ἡρῴδης, ου m Herod: (1) Herod I, the Great; (2) Herod Antipas; (3) Herod Agrippa I

Ἡρῳδιανοί, ῶν m Herodians (partisans of the Herodian family)

Ἡρῳδιάς, άδος f Herodias (granddaughter of Herod the Great)

Ἡρῳδίων, ωνος m Herodion (Ro 16.11)

Ἠσαΐας, ου m Isaiah

Ἠσαῦ m Esau

ἡσσάομαι alt. form of ἡττάομαι

ἥσσων, ον gen. ονος less; εἰς τὸ ἥ. for the worse (1 Cor 11.17)

ἡσυχάζω be silent or quiet; cease, rest; live a quiet life (1 Th 4.11)

ἡσυχία, ας f silence, quietness; παρέχω ἡσυχίαν be quiet (Ac 22.2)

ἡσύχιος, ον quiet, peaceful

ἤτοι or; ἤτοι . . . ἤ either . . . or

ἡττάομαι be defeated or overcome; be treated worse (ὑπέρ) than (2 Cor 12.13)

ἥττημα, τος n defeat; failure

ἤτω impv. 3 sg. of εἰμί

ηὐξήθην aor. pass. of αὐξάνω

ηὔξησα aor. of αὐξάνω

ηὐφράνθην aor. pass. of εὐφραίνω

ἤφιεν impf. 3 sg. of ἀφίημι

ἠχέω be noisy

ἤχθην aor. pass. of ἄγω

ἦχος, ου m sound, noise; report, news

ἦχος, ους n roar (Lk 21.25)

ἡψάμην aor. midd. of ἅπτω

Θ

Θαδαῖος alt. form of **Θαδδαῖος**
Θαδδαῖος, ου m *Thaddaeus*
(Mt 10.3; Mk 3.18)
θάλασσα, ης f *sea; lake*
θάλπω *take care of*
Θαμάρ f *Tamar* (Mt 1.3)
θαμβέομαι *be amazed* or
shocked
θάμβος, ους n *amazement,
wonder*
θανάσιμον, ου n *deadly poison*
θανατηφόρος, ον *deadly,
causing death*
θάνατος, ου m *death;* ἔσφαγ-
μαι εἰς θ. *be struck a deadly
blow* (Re 13.3); πρὸς θ.
leading to death (1 Jn 5.16f);
ἐν θανάτοις *near death, in
danger of death* (2 Cor 11.23)
θανατόω *kill, put to death; put
in danger of death* (Ro
8.36)
θάπτω (aor. pass. **ἐτάφην**)
bury
Θάρα m *Terah* (Lk 3.34)
θαρρέω *be full of courage; act
boldly; be confident*
θαρσέω (only in impv.) *Courage! Take courage! Cheer up!*
θάρσος, ους n *courage*
θαῦμα, τος n *a wonder, miracle; amazement*
θαυμάζω intrans. *marvel, wonder, be amazed* (θ. ὀπίσω

follow with amazement Re
13.3); trans. *marvel* or *wonder at, admire* (θ. πρόσωπα
flatter people Jd 16)
θαυμάσιος, α, ον *wonderful*
θαυμαστός, ή, όν *marvelous,
wonderful; extraordinary, as-
tonishing*
θεά, ᾶς f *goddess*
θεάομαι *see, look at; notice,
observe; visit* (Ro 15.24)
θεατρίζω *expose to public
shame*
θέατρον, ου n *theatre; spectacle*
θεῖναι aor. inf. of **τίθημι**
θεῖον, ου n *sulphur, brim-
stone*
θεῖος, α, ον *divine;* τὸ θεῖον
the deity or *the divine nature*
(Ac 17.29)
θειότης, ητος f *deity, divine
nature*
θείς aor. ptc. of **τίθημι**
θειώδης, ες *sulphur-yellow*
θέλημα, τος n *will; wish,
desire*
θέλησις, εως f *will*
θέλω (impf. **ἤθελον**) *wish,
desire, want; will; like;* τί
θέλει τοῦτο εἶναι *what
does this mean?* (Ac 2.12;
cf. 17.20)
θεμέλιον, ου n *foundation*

θεμέλιος, ου m *foundation; foundation stone* (Re 21.14, 19)

θεμελιόω *found; establish firmly*

θεοδίδακτος, ον *taught by God*

θεομάχος, ον *opposing God*

θεόπνευστος, ον *inspired by God*

θεός, οῦ m *God* (κατὰ θεόν *according to God's will, godly; after the likeness of God* Eph 4.24); *god;* f *goddess* (Ac 19.37)

θεοσέβεια, ας f *religion, piety*

θεοσεβής, ές *devout, pious, god-fearing*

θεοστυγής, ές *hating God; hateful to God*

θεότης, ητος f *deity, godhead*

Θεόφιλος, ου m *Theophilus* (Lk 1.3; Ac 1.1)

θεραπεία, ας f *healing; household servants* (Lk 12.42)

θεραπεύω *heal, cure; serve* (Ac 17.25)

θεράπων, οντος m *servant*

θερίζω *reap, harvest, gather*

θερισμός, οῦ m *harvest; crop*

θεριστής, οῦ m *reaper*

θερμαίνομαι *warm oneself, keep warm*

θέρμη, ης f *heat*

θέρος, ους n *summer*

θέσθε aor. midd. impv. 2 pl. of τίθημι

Θεσσαλονικεύς, έως m *a Thessalonian*

Θεσσαλονίκη, ης f *Thessalonica* (4 D–2)

θέτε aor. impv. 2 pl. of τίθημι

Θευδᾶς, ᾶ m *Theudas* (Ac 5.36)

θεωρέω *see; watch, look on, observe; perceive, notice; experience* (death)

θεωρία, ας f *sight* (of something seen), *spectacle*

θήκη, ης f *sheath* (of a sword)

θηλάζω *nurse* (of a mother breast feeding her child); *nurse* (of a child feeding at the breast; ὁ θ. *unweaned child* Mt 21.16)

θῆλυς, εια, υ *female; woman*

θήρα, ας f *trap*

θηρεύω *catch, pounce on*

θηριομαχέω *fight wild beasts*

θηρίον, ου n *animal, beast; wild animal; snake* (Ac 28.4, 5)

θησαυρίζω *store up, save; put aside*

θησαυρός, οῦ m *treasure; store; treasure box, storeroom*

θήσω fut. of τίθημι

θιγγάνω (aor. subj. θίγω) *touch*

θλίβω (pf. pass. ptc. τεθλιμμένος) *press hard, crush* (of a crowd); pass. *experience trouble* or *difficulty;* pf. pass. ptc. *narrow* (Mt 7.14)

θλῖψις, εως f *trouble, distress, hard circumstances, suffering*

θνήσκω (pf. τέθνηκα) die; pf. be dead

θνητός, ή, όν mortal

θορυβάζω trouble, bother, distract

θορυβέω set in an uproar; pass. be stirred up, confused or worried

θόρυβος, ου m confusion, disturbance; riot

θραύω oppress

θρέμμα, τος n domesticated animal; pl. cattle, herds, flocks

θρηνέω intrans. mourn, weep; trans. mourn or weep for

θρῆνος, ου m dirge, song of grief

θρησκεία, ας f religion, worship

θρησκός, όν religious

θριαμβεύω lead (someone) as a prisoner in a victory procession; triumph over (someone); perhaps cause (someone) to triumph

θρίξ, τριχός f hair

θροέομαι be alarmed or startled

θρόμβος, ου m drop, clot

θρόνος, ου m throne

θρύπτω break in pieces

Θυάτιρα, ων n Thyatira (4 E–2)

θυγάτηρ, τρός f daughter; any

female descendant; female inhabitant, woman; θ. Σιών Zion, Jerusalem

θυγάτριον, ου n little daughter

θύελλα, ης f wind storm, whirlwind

θύϊνος, η, ον citron, scented (wood)

θυμίαμα, τος n incense; incense offering (Lk 1.10, 11)

θυμιατήριον, ου n altar of incense

θυμιάω offer incense

θυμομαχέω be very angry

θυμόομαι be furious

θυμός, οῦ m anger, rage, fury; intense feeling

θύρα, ας f door, gate (ἐπὶ θ. at the very door); entrance (of a tomb); opportunity

θυρεός, οῦ m shield

θυρίς, ίδος f window

θυρωρός, οῦ m and f doorkeeper

θυσία, ας f sacrifice, offering; act of offering

θυσιαστήριον, ου n altar

θύω (aor. pass. ἐτύθην) slaughter; sacrifice; kill, murder (Jn 10.10)

θῶ aor. subj. of τίθημι

Θωμᾶς, ᾶ m Thomas

θώραξ, ακος m breastplate; chest

I

’Ιάϊρος, ου m *Jairus* (Mk
5.22; Lk 8.41)
’Ιακώβ m *Jacob:* (1) son of
Isaac; (2) father of Joseph
(Mt 1.15, 16)
’Ιάκωβος, ου m *James:* (1)
brother of John, son of Zebedee; (2) brother of Jesus;
(3) son of Alphaeus and one
of the twelve; (4) father of
Judas (Lk 6.16; Ac 1.13);
(5) tax-collector (Mk 2.14)
ἴαμα, τος n *healing*
’Ιαμβρῆς m *Jambres* (2 Tm
3.8)
’Ιανναί m *Jannai* (Lk 3.24)
’Ιάννης m *Jannes* (2 Tm 3.8)
ἰάομαι *heal, cure; restore*
’Ιάρετ m *Jared* (Lk 3.37)
ἴασις, εως f *healing*
ἴασπις, ιδος f *jasper* (a semiprecious stone of varying
colors, but the jasper of the
NT was probably green)
’Ιάσων, ονος m *Jason:* (1) a
Christian of Thessalonica;
(2) another Christian (Ro
16.21)
ἰατρός, οῦ m *physician, doctor*
ἴδε *Look! See! Listen!; here is;
here are*
ἴδετε aor. impv. of ὁράω
ἴδιος, α, ον *one's own, belonging to one, personal;* τὰ

ἴδια *home, possessions, property;* κατ’ ἰδίαν *privately,
alone, apart;* ἰδίᾳ *individually, separately* (1 Cor 12.11)
ἰδιώτης, ου m *untrained* or
*unskilled man, layman; un-
gifted* (of spiritual gifts)
ἰδού *Look! See! Listen!; there*
or *here is* (are), *there* or
here was (were); *there* or
here comes (came); *then, suddenly; even, yet* (of emphasis)
’Ιδουμαία, ας f *Idumea* (2
B–7)
ἱδρώς, ῶτος m *sweat, per-
spiration*
ἰδών aor. ptc. of ὁράω
ἰδώς alt. form of εἰδώς
’Ιεζάβελ f *Jezebel* (Re 2.20)
‘Ιεράπολις, εως f *Hierapolis*
(4 E–2)
ἱερατεία, ας f *priestly office*
ἱεράτευμα, τος n *priesthood*
ἱερατεύω *serve as a priest*
’Ιερεμίας, ου m *Jeremiah*
ἱερεύς, έως m *priest*
’Ιεριχώ f *Jericho* (1 C–6,
li C–1, 2 C–6)
ἱερόθυτος, ον *offered in sacrifice*
ἱερόν, οῦ n *temple; temple
precincts*
ἱεροπρεπής, ές *reverent*
ἱερός, ά, όν *sacred, holy; per-*

taining to the temple (of
service and sacrifice)

ʿΙεροσόλυμα n pl. and f sg.
and **ʾΙερουσαλήμ** f *Jerusalem* (1 C–6, 1i A–1, 2 C–6,
3 C–4, 4 G–4)

ʿΙεροσολυμίτης, ου m *an
inhabitant of Jerusalem*

ἱεροσυλέω *commit sacrilege;
rob temples*

ἱερόσυλος, ου m *a sacrilegious
person; a temple robber*

ἱερουργέω *serve as a priest*

ἱερωσύνη, ης f *priesthood*

ʾΙεσσαί m *Jesse* (father of
David)

ʾΙεφθάε m *Jephthah* (He
11.32)

ʾΙεχονίας, ου m *Jechoniah*
(Mt 1.11f)

ʾΙησοῦς gen. **οῦ** dat. **οῦ**
acc. **οῦν** m (1) *Jesus:* (a) of
the Lord; (b) Jesus Barabbas; (c) Jesus Justus (Col
4.11); (d) in the genealogy
of Jesus (Lk 3.29); (2)
Joshua (Ac 7.45; He 4.8)

ἱκανός, ή, όν *worthy, fit;
sufficient, able* (ἱκανόν ἐστιν
it is enough! Lk 22.38; τὸ
ἱ. ποιῶ *satisfy* Mk 15.15;
τὸ ἱ. *security, peace bond*
Ac 17.9); *large, great, much,*
pl. *many* or *some* (ἐν λό-
γοις ἱ. *at some length* Lk
23.9; ἀπὸ ἱ. ἐτῶν *for many
years* Ro 15.23); *long, con-
siderable* (ἐφʾ ἱ. *for a long
while* Ac 20.11)

ἱκανότης, ητος f *capacity,
capability*

ἱκανόω *make capable, make fit*

ἱκετηρία, ας f *request, plea*

ἱκμάς, άδος f *moisture*

ʾΙκόνιον, ου n *Iconium* (4
F–2)

ἱλαρός, ά, όν *cheerful*

ἱλαρότης, ητος f *cheerfulness*

ἱλάσκομαι *bring about forgiveness for, take away, deal
mercifully with;* pass. *be
merciful, have mercy*

ἱλασμός, οῦ m *means by which
sins are forgiven*

ἱλαστήριον, ου n *means by
which sins are forgiven* (Ro
3.25); *place where sins are
forgiven* (He 9.5)

ἵλεως, ων *merciful* (ἵλεώς
σοι *May God be merciful to
you!* or *God forbid!* Mt 16.22)

ʾΙλλυρικόν, οῦ n *Illyricum*
(4 C–1)

ἱμάς, άντος m *strap* (of a
sandal); perhaps *lash, whip*
(Ac 22.25)

ἱματίζω *clothe, dress*

ἱμάτιον, ου n *garment, clothing; coat, robe, cloak* (of
outer garments)

ἱματισμός, οῦ m *clothing,
apparel*

ἵνα conj. *in order that* (of
purpose); *so that* (of result);
that (indirect statement);
with subj. sometimes =
impv. (e.g. ἡ δὲ γυνὴ ἵνα
φοβῆται τὸν ἄνδρα *the*

wife must respect her husband
Eph 5.33)
ἰνατί conj. *why? for what*
reason?
Ἰόππη, ης f *Joppa, Jaffa*
(1 B-5, 2 B-5, 3 C-4)
Ἰορδάνης, ου m *Jordan River*
(1 D-5, 2 D-5)
ἰός, οῦ m *poison, venom; rust*
Ἰουδαία, ας f *Judea* (2 C-6)
ἰουδαΐζω *live according to Jewish religious regulations*
Ἰουδαϊκός, ή, όν *Jewish*
Ἰουδαϊκῶς adv. *like a Jew*
Ἰουδαῖος, α, ον *a Jew; Jewish; Judean*
Ἰουδαϊσμός, οῦ m *Judaism*
(of the Jewish religion and
way of life)
Ἰούδας, α m (1) *Judah:* (a)
son of Jacob, his tribe, his
territory (1 C-6); (b) person
in the genealogy of Jesus
(Lk 3.30); (2) *Judas:* (a) the
betrayer of Jesus; (b) a
brother of Jesus; (c) an
apostle, the son of James;
(d) member of the Jerusalem
church, called Barsabbas;
(e) a disciple in Damascus
(Ac 9.11); (f) revolutionary
leader (Ac 5.37)
Ἰουλία, ας f *Julia* (Ro 16.15)
Ἰούλιος, ου m *Julius* (Ac
27.1, 3)
Ἰουνία, ας f *Junia* (Ro
16.15)
Ἰουνιᾶς, ᾶ m *Junias* (Ro
16.7)

Ἰοῦστος, ου m *Justus:* (1)
surname of Joseph Barsab-
bas (Ac 1.23); (2) Titius
Justus (Ac 18.7); (3) companion of Paul (Col 4.11)
ἱππεύς, έως m *horseman,
cavalryman*
ἱππικόν, οῦ n *cavalry, horse-
men*
ἵππος, ου m *horse*
ἶρις, ιδος f *rainbow; vari-
colored halo*
Ἰσαάκ m *Isaac*
ἰσάγγελος, ον *like or equal
to an angel*
ἴσασι 3 pl. of οἶδα
ἴσθι impv. of εἰμί
Ἰσκαριώθ and Ἰσκαριώ-
της, ου m *Iscariot*
ἴσος, η, ον *equal, the same; in
agreement* (Mk 14.56, 59);
ἴσα adv. *equally* (τὸ εἶναι
ἴσα *equality* Php 2.6)
ἰσότης, ητος f *equality* (ἐξ
ἰσότητος *as a matter of
equality* 2 Cor 8.13); *fairness*
(of treatment)
ἰσότιμος, ον *equally valuable,
of the same kind, of equal
privilege*
ἰσόψυχος, ον *sharing the
same feelings*
Ἰσραήλ m *Israel*
Ἰσραηλίτης, ου m *an Israelite*
Ἰσσαχάρ m *Issachar* (Re 7.7)
ἴστε ind. or impv. 2 pl. of
οἶδα
ἵστημι and ἱστάνω (fut.

στήσω; 1 aor. ἔστησα; 2
aor. ἔστην, impv. στῆθι,
inf. στῆναι, ptc. στάς; pf.
ἔστηκα, inf. ἑστάναι, ptc.
ἑστηκώς and ἑστώς; plpf.
εἱστήκειν; fut. midd. στήσομαι; aor. pass. ἐστάθην,
inf. σταθῆναι, ptc. σταθείς;
fut. pass. σταθήσομαι)
trans. (in all act. tenses
except 2 aor., pf. and plpf.)
set, place, put; establish, set
up, make stand; put for-
ward; fix (a day of judg-
ment); pay, count out (money); hold against (Ac 7.60);
intrans. (in 2 aor., pf., plpf.
act.; all midd. and pass.
forms) stand; stop, stand
still; be confirmed or established; stand firm, hold one's
ground; be, exist; stand up;
be moored (of boats)
ἱστορέω visit, get to know
ἰσχυρός, ά, όν strong, mighty,
powerful; loud (cry or thunder); severe (famine)
ἰσχύς, ύος f strength, might
ἰσχύω be able, can, have resources (εἰς οὐδέν i. be
worthless Mt 5.13); win over,
defeat; be strong, grow strong
(Ac 19.20; on Jas 5.16 cf.
ἐνεργέω); ὁ. i. a well person
ἴσως adv. perhaps, it may be
Ἰταλία, ας f Italy (4 A–1)
Ἰταλικός, ή, όν Italian
Ἰτουραῖος, α, ον Ituraean
(Ituraea 2 D–2)

ἰχθύδιον, ου n small fish, fish
ἰχθύς, ύος m fish
ἴχνος, ους n footstep, step;
example
Ἰωαθάμ m Jotham (Mt 1.9)
Ἰωακείμ m Jehoiakim (Mt
1. 1)
Ἰωανάν m Joanan (Lk 3.27)
Ἰωάννα, ας f Joanna (Lk
8.3; 24.10)
Ἰωαννᾶς and Ἰωανᾶς, ᾶ
alt. form of Ἰωάννης
Ἰωάννης, ου m John: (1)
the Baptist; (2) son of
Zebedee, one of the twelve;
(3) author of Revelation;
(4) John Mark; (5) father
of Peter and Andrew; (6)
member of the Jewish coun-
cil (Ac 4.6)
Ἰώβ m Job (Jas 5.11)
Ἰωβήδ m Obed (Mt 1.5;
Lk 3.32)
Ἰωδά m Joda (Lk 3.26)
Ἰωήλ m Joel (Ac 2.16)
Ἰωναθάς, ου m Jonathas
(Ac 4.6)
Ἰωνάμ m Jonam (Lk 3.30)
Ἰωνᾶς, ᾶ m Jonah: (1) OT
prophet; (2) father of Peter
and Andrew
Ἰωράμ m Joram (Mt 1.8)
Ἰωρίμ m Jorim (Lk 3.29)
Ἰωσαφάτ m Jehoshaphat (Mt
1.8)
Ἰωσῆς, ῆ or ῆτος m Joses:
(1) brother of Jesus; (2)
brother of James the young-
er (Mk 15.40, 47)

'Ιωσήφ m *Joseph:* (1) son of Jacob the patriarch; (2) husband of Mary, mother of Jesus; (3) of Arimathea, member of the Sanhedrin; (4) brother of Jesus (Mt 13.55); (5) surnamed Barnabas; (6) son of a Mary (Mt 27.56); (7, 8) persons in the genealogy of Jesus (Lk 3.24, 30)

'Ιωσήχ m *Josech* (Lk 3.26)

'Ιωσίας, ου m *Josiah* (Mt 1.10f)

ἰῶτα n *iota* (= *yod,* the smallest letter in the Hebrew alphabet)

K

κἀγώ (from καὶ ἐγώ) dat. κἀμοί acc. κἀμέ *and I, but I; I also; I myself*

καθά conj. or adv. *as, just as*

καθαίρεσις, εως f *destruction, tearing down*

καθαιρέω (fut. καθελῶ; aor. καθεῖλον, ptc. καθελών) *take down; pull down, destroy, overthrow;* pass. *be brought down from, suffer the loss of* (Ac 19.27)

καθαίρω *clean, prune* (branches)

καθάπερ conj. or adv. *as, just as, like*

καθάπτω (aor. καθῆψα) *fasten on*

καθαρίζω (fut. καθαριῶ) *cleanse, make clean, purify; declare ritually acceptable*

καθαρισμός, οῦ m *cleansing, purification; purification rites*

καθαρός, ά, όν *pure, clean; innocent*

καθαρότης, ητος f *purification, purity*

καθέδρα, ας f *seat, chair*

καθέζομαι *sit; sit down; stay, remain*

καθεῖλον aor. of καθαιρέω

καθελῶ fut. of καθαιρέω

καθελών aor. ptc. of καθαιρέω

καθεξῆς adv. *in order* or *sequence (from place to place* Ac 18.23); ἐν τῷ κ. *afterward* (Lk 8.1); οἱ κ. *the successors* (Ac 3.24)

καθεύδω *sleep; be dead* (1 Th 5.10)

καθηγητής, οῦ m *teacher, leader, master*

καθῆκα aor. of καθίημι

καθήκει impers. *it is fitting;*

τὸ μὴ καθῆκον *what is improper* (Ro 1.28)

κάθημαι (2 sg. **κάθῃ**, impv. **κάθου**) *sit; sit down; live, stay, be*

καθημερινός, ή, όν *daily*

καθῆψα aor. of **καθάπτω**

καθίζω intrans. *sit down, sit, take one's seat* (midd. Mt 19.28); *stay* (Ac 18.11); trans. *cause to sit, set* (Ac 2.30; Eph 1.20); *select* (someone) *as a judge* (1 Cor 6.4)

καθίημι (pass. ptc. **καθιέμενος**; aor. **καθῆκα**) *let down, lower*

καθίστημι and **καθιστάνω** (fut. **καταστήσω**; aor. **κατέστησα**; aor. pass. **κατεστάθην**; fut. pass. **κατασταθήσομαι**) *put in charge; make* (someone to be something); *appoint; accompany* (Ac 17.15); midd. *prove to be, be* (Jas 3.6; 4.4)

καθό adv. *as, according as; in so far as, to the degree that*

καθόλου adv. *completely, altogether;* κ. μή *under no condition* (Ac 4.18)

καθοπλίζω *arm fully* (pf. midd. ptc. *fully armed* Lk 11.21)

καθοράω *perceive clearly*

καθότι *because, for; as, in so far as*

κάθου impv. of **κάθημαι**

καθώς adv. *as, just as; inasmuch as, because; in so*

far as, to the degree that; how, that (of indirect discourse)

καθώσπερ adv. *as, just as*

καί conj. *and, also, but, even; that is, namely;* καὶ ... καί *both ... and, not only ... but also;* frequently used merely to mark the beginning of a sentence

Καϊάφας, α m *Caiaphas* (high priest)

Κάϊν m *Cain*

Καϊνάμ m *Cainan:* (1) son of Arphaxad (Lk 3.36); (2) son of Enos (Lk 3.37)

καινός, ή, όν *new; of new quality; unused; unknown, unheard of;* τι καινότερον *the latest thing* (Ac 17.21)

καινότης, ητος f *newness;* κ. ζωῆς, κ. πνεύματος *new life, new spirit* (Ro 6.4; 7.6)

καίπερ conj. *though, although*

καιρός, οῦ m *time* (viewed as an occasion rather than an extent), *appointed* or *proper time, season, age* (ἄχρι κ. *for a while;* ἐν παντὶ κ. *always, at all times;* ἐν ᾧ κ. *at this time* Ac 7.20; πρὸς κ. or πρὸς κ. ὥρας *for a brief while;* κατὰ κ. *at the right time* Ro 5.6, *from time to time* Jn 5.4; κατὰ τὸν κ. τοῦτον [ἐκεῖνον] *about this* [*that*] *time* Ro 9.9; Ac 19.23); *opportunity; the last times*

Καῖσαρ, ος m *Caesar, emperor* (of Rome)

Καισάρεια, ας f *Caesarea:* (1) on the coast (2 B-4, 4 G-4); (2) *Caesarea Philippi* (2 D-2)

καίτοι *yet, and yet, although*

καίτοιγε *although, and yet*

καίω (pf. pass. **κέκαυμαι**; fut. pass. **καυθήσομαι** and **καυθήσωμαι**) *light, keep burning* (pass. *be lit, burn); burn, burn up*

κἀκεῖ adv. *and there; there also*

κἀκεῖθεν adv. *and from there; and then* (Ac 13.21)

κἀκεῖνος, η, ο *and that one, and he; that one also, he also*

κακία, ας f *evil, wickedness; hateful feelings; trouble, worry* (Mt 6.34)

κακοήθεια, ας f *meanness, evil done for the sake of evil*

κακολογέω *speak evil of, curse*

κακοπάθεια, ας f *suffering; endurance*

κακοπαθέω *suffer, undergo hardship; endure hardship patiently*

κακοποιέω *do evil or wrong; harm, injure*

κακοποιός, οῦ m *wrongdoer, criminal*

κακός, ή, όν *evil, bad, wrong; injury, harm* (as a noun); *foul, troublesome* (sore)

κακοῦργος, ου m *criminal*

κακουχέομαι *be ill-treated*

κακόω *treat badly, harm; be*

cruel and force (someone to do something) (Ac 7.19); *κακῶ τὴν ψυχήν τινος κατά poison someone's mind against* (another) (Ac 14.2)

κακῶς adv. *badly, severely* (κ. ἔχω *be sick); wrongly, with wrong motive*

κάκωσις, εως f *cruel suffering, oppression*

καλάμη, ης f *straw; stubble*

κάλαμος, ου m *reed, cane; measuring rod* (Re 11.1; 21.15f); *pen* (3 Jn 13)

καλέω (pf. **κέκληκα**; aor. pass. **ἐκλήθην**; fut. pass. **κληθήσομαι**) *call, name, address; invite; summon, call in*

καλλιέλαιος, ου f *cultivated olive tree*

κάλλιον (comp. of **καλῶς**) *very well*

καλοδιδάσκαλος, ον *teaching what is good*

Καλοὶ Λιμένες m *Fair Havens* (4 D-4)

καλοποιέω *do what is good*

καλός, ή, όν *good; right, proper, fitting; better; honorable, honest; fine, beautiful, precious*

κάλυμμα, τος n *veil*

καλύπτω *cover, hide*

καλῶς adv. *well* (οὐ κ. *for no good purpose* Ga 4.17); *rightly, correctly; very well, well enough; please* (Jas 2.3); *κ. ἔχω be well; κ. ποιῶ do* *good* (Mt 12.12; Lk 6.27), *be kind* (Ac 10.33; Php 4.14)

κάμηλος, ου m and f *camel*

κάμινος, ου f *furnace, oven*

καμμύω *close* (eyes)

κάμνω (aor. subj. 2 pl. **κάμητε**) *be sick;* ἐν ψυχῇ κ. *be discouraged* (He 12.3)

κάμπτω trans. and intrans. *bend, bow* (of the knee)

κἄν (καὶ ἐάν) *even if, and if* (κἄν . . . κἄν *if . . . or* Lk 12.38); *even, at least*

Κανά f *Cana* (2 C-3)

Καναναῖος, ου m *Cananaean* (= *Zealot,* member of a Jewish nationalistic sect)

Κανανίτης, ου m *man of Cana*

Κανδάκη, ης f *Candace* (a royal title, Ac 8.27)

κανών, όνος m *limits, sphere, area; rule, principle* (Ga 6.16)

καπηλεύω *peddle for profit*

καπνός, οῦ m *smoke*

Καππαδοκία, ας f *Cappadocia* (4 G-2)

καρδία, ας f *heart, inner self; mind; will, desire, intention; interior* (of the earth)

καρδιογνώστης, ου m *knower of hearts*

καρπός, οῦ m *fruit, grain; harvest; result, outcome; deed, action; return, gain, advantage; tribute, praise* (of the lips); *offspring* (Lk 1.42); *descendant* (Ac 2.30)

Κάρπος, ου m *Carpus* (2 Tm 4.13)

καρποφορέω *bear fruit, be productive*

καρποφόρος, ον *fruitful*

καρτερέω *endure, persevere*

κάρφος, ους n *speck, small splinter*

κατά prep. with: (1) acc. *according to, corresponding to, with reference to, just as* (τὰ κ. τινα *one's case* or *circumstances;* κ. τὰ αὐτά *so, in the same way;* κ. ἐμέ *my;* κ. τὸ αὐτό *together* Ac 14.1; κ. τί *how* Lk 1.18); used distributively with numerals and places; *in; for; for the purpose of; at, about,* (of time); *on, upon, along, through, to, toward; off, opposite, near, bordering on; with, by means of, because of;* (2) gen. *against; down, down from; throughout; by* (of oaths); *over* (of authority)

καταβαίνω (fut. **καταβήσομαι**; aor. **κατέβην**, impv. **κατάβηθι** and **κατάβα**, inf. **καταβῆναι**, ptc. **καταβάς**; pf. **καταβέβηκα**) *come* or *go down, descend; fall, fall down; be brought down* (Mt 11.23; Lk 10.15); *get out* (Mt 14.29)

καταβάλλω *knock down;* midd. *lay* (a foundation)

καταβαπτίζομαι *wash oneself*

καταβαρέω *be a burden to*
καταβαρύνομαι *be very heavy*
(ὀφθαλμοὶ κ. *be unable to
keep one's eyes open* Mk
14.40)
κατάβασις, εως f *descent,
slope*
καταβιβάζω *throw down, bring
down*
καταβολή, ῆς f *beginning,
creation;* δύναμιν εἰς κ.
σπέρματος ἔλαβεν (Abra-
ham) *became able to become
a father* or (Sarah) *became
able to conceive* (He 11.11)
καταβραβεύω (lit. *rule
against*) *cheat*
καταγαγεῖν aor. inf. of κατάγω
καταγγελεύς, έως m *pro-
claimer, herald*
καταγγέλλω (aor. κατήγ-
γειλα; aor. pass. κατηγ-
γέλην) *proclaim, make
known, preach; teach, advo-
cate* (customs)
καταγεινώσκω alt. form of
καταγινώσκω
καταγελάω (impf. κατεγέ-
λων) *laugh at*
καταγινώσκω (pf. pass. κατέγνωσμαι) *condemn*
κατάγνυμι (fut. κατεάξω;
aor. κατέαξα; aor. pass.
κατεάγην. subj. 3 pl. κατεαγῶσιν) *break*
καταγράφω *write*
κατάγω (aor. κατήγαγον, inf.
καταγαγεῖν; aor. pass. κα-

τήχθην, ptc. καταχθείς)
bring down; bring (Lk 5.11);
pass. *put in* (εἰς) *at* (Ac
27.3; 28.12)
καταγωνίζομαι *conquer, defeat*
καταδέω *bandage, bind up*
κατάδηλος, ον *very evident*
καταδικάζω *condemn*
καταδίκη, ης f *sentence, condemnation*
καταδιώκω *search for diligently*
καταδουλόω *make a slave of;
take advantage of*
καταδυναστεύω *oppress*
κατάθεμα, τος n *something
under God's curse*
καταθεματίζω *curse; place
oneself under a curse* (if one
fails to speak truth)
καταθέσθαι aor. midd. inf. of
κατατίθημι
καταισχύνω *put to shame,
humiliate, disgrace; disap-
point*
κατακαίω (fut. κατακαύσω;
aor. inf. κατακαῦσαι; aor.
pass. κατεκάην; fut. pass.
κατακαήσομαι and κατα-
καυθήσομαι) *burn, burn up,
consume*
κατακαλύπτομαι *cover one's
head*
κατακαυχάομαι (impv. 2 sg.
κατακαυχῶ) *boast against,
despise; be proud; triumph
over* (Jas 2.13)
κατάκειμαι *lie* (in bed), *be*

sick; sit (lit. recline) at table,
dine
κατακλάω break in pieces
κατακλείω shut up, put in
(prison)
κατακληρονομέω make (someone) the owner
κατακλίνω (aor. pass. **κα-
τεκλίθην**) cause to sit down;
pass. sit down, sit (lit. recline) at table, dine
κατακλύζω deluge, flood
κατακλυσμός, οῦ m flood,
deluge
κατακολουθέω follow, accompany
κατακόπτω beat, bruise, cut
κατακρημνίζω throw down
from a cliff
κατάκριμα, τος n condemnation
κατακρίνω (aor. pass. **κατεκρίθην**) condemn, pass
judgment on
κατάκρισις, εως f condemnation; perhaps doom, punishment
κατακύπτω bend down
κατακυριεύω have power over;
overpower (Ac 19.16); try to
show one's authority over
(1 Pe 5.3)
καταλαλέω speak evil of, say
bad things against, slander
καταλαλιά, ᾶς f slander, insult
κατάλαλος, ου m slanderer,
one who speaks evil of another
καταλαμβάνω (aor. **κατέλα-**

βον; pf. **κατείληφα**; pf.
pass. **κατείλημμαι**; aor.
pass. **κατελήμφθην**) act.
and pass. obtain, make one's
own, attain; come upon, over-
take (Jn 12.35; 1 Th 5.4);
attack, seize (Mk 9.18); catch
(Jn 8.3, 4); perhaps put out
(Jn 1.5); midd. realize, understand, learn; see, find (Ac
25.25)
καταλέγω enroll, place on the
list (for financial aid by the
church)
καταλείπω (aor. **κατέλιπον**
and **κατέλειψα**; pf. pass.
καταλέλειμμαι) leave, leave
behind (pass. often remain);
neglect, forsake, abandon;
keep (ἐμαυτῷ) for oneself
(Ro 11.4)
καταλιθάζω stone
καταλλαγή, ῆς f being put
into friendship with God;
leading others to be put into
friendship with God
καταλλάσσω (aor. pass. **κατηλλάγην**, ptc. **καταλλα-
γείς**) put (someone) into
friendship with God; reconcile (of man and wife)
κατάλοιπος, ον rest, remaining
κατάλυμα, τος n room, guest
room; inn
καταλύω trans. destroy, tear
down; stop (Ac 5.39; pass.
come to naught Ac 5.38);
do away with (Mt 5.17);

intrans. *find lodging; be* (someone's) *guest*

καταμανθάνω (aor. impv. 2 pl. **καταμάθετε**) *consider, observe*

καταμαρτυρέω *testify against*

καταμένω *stay, live*

καταναλίσκω *consume, devour*

καταναρκάω *be a* (financial) *burden to*

κατανεύω *signal, motion to*

κατανοέω *consider, think of; notice, observe, see; look; see through, be aware of* (Lk 20.23)

καταντάω *come; arrive, reach; attain*

κατάνυξις, εως f *stupor, numbness*

κατανύσσομαι (aor. **κατενύγην**) *be stabbed* (κ. τὴν καρδίαν *be deeply troubled* Ac 2.37)

καταξιόω *count worthy; make worthy*

καταπατέω *trample on; trample under foot, despise* (He 10.29)

κατάπαυσις, εως f *place of rest; rest*

καταπαύω trans. *cause to rest; prevent;* intrans. *rest, cease*

καταπέτασμα, τος n *curtain*

καταπίμπρημι (aor. **κατέπρησα**) *burn to ashes, destroy by fire*

καταπίνω (aor. **κατέπιον**, inf. **καταπιεῖν, καταπεῖν, καταπῖν**, subj. 3 sg. **καταπίει**

and **καταπίῃ**; aor. pass. **κατεπόθην**, subj. **καταποθῶ**) *swallow; swallow up, devour, overwhelm* (pass. *be drowned* He 11.29)

καταπίπτω (aor. **κατέπεσον**, ptc. **καταπεσών**) *fall, fall down*

καταπλέω (aor. **κατέπλευσα**) *sail* (εἰς) *to*

καταπονέω *mistreat; trouble*

καταποντίζομαι *sink, be drowned*

κατάρα, ας f *curse; something accursed*

καταράομαι (aor. 2 sg. **κατηράσω**; pf. **κατήραμαι**) *curse, place a curse upon*

καταργέω *render ineffective, nullify, cancel; destroy, abolish, do away with* (pass. *pass away, cease);* *use up* (Lk 13.7); pass. with ἀπό *be released from* (Ro 7.2, 6); *be cut off from* (Ga 5.4)

καταριθμέω *number;* pass. with ἐν *be numbered among, be one of*

καταρτίζω *mend, restore, set right, make complete* (midd. *strive for perfection* 2 Cor 13.11); act. and midd. *make, prepare, supply* (κατηρτισμένος *fully trained* Lk 6.40)

κατάρτισις, εως f *being made complete*

καταρτισμός, οῦ m *equipping, training*

κατασείω motion, make a sign, give a signal (κ. τὴν χεῖρα motion with the hand Ac 19.33)

κατασκάπτω demolish, destroy

κατασκευάζω prepare; build, construct; furnish, equip

κατασκηνόω nest; live, dwell

κατασκήνωσις, εως f nest

κατασκιάζω overshadow

κατασκοπέω spy on, spy out

κατάσκοπος, ου m spy

κατασοφίζομαι take advantage of by deception or trickery

κατασταθήσομαι fut. pass. of **καθίστημι**

καταστέλλω (aor. ptc. **καταστείλας**; pf. pass. **κατέσταλμαι**) quieten, silence; κατεσταλμένους ὑπάρχειν to keep quiet (Ac 19.36)

κατάστημα, τος n behavior, way of life

καταστήσω fut. of **καθίστημι**

καταστολή, ῆς f manner of dress, deportment

καταστρέφω overturn

καταστρηνιάω be drawn away by one's own sensuous impulses

καταστροφή, ῆς f ruin, destruction

καταστρώννυμι (aor. pass. **κατεστρώθην**) strike down, put to death

κατασύρω drag, take by force

κατασφάζω slay, slaughter

κατασφραγίζω seal

κατάσχεσις, εως f possession,

act of possessing; κ. τῶν ἐθνῶν taking possession of (i.e. dispossessing) the nations (Ac 7.45)

κατάσχω aor. subj. of **κατέχω**

κατατίθημι (aor. **κατέθηκα**; aor. midd. inf. **καταθέσθαι**) lay, place; midd. κ. χάριν, κ. χάριτα gain favor with or do a favor for

κατατομή, ῆς f mutilation

κατατρέχω (aor. **κατέδραμον**) run down

καταφάγομαι fut. of **κατεσθίω**

καταφέρω (aor. **κατήνεγκα**; aor. pass. ptc. **κατενεχθείς**) bring (charges), cast against (of votes); pass. be overcome (with sleep)

καταφεύγω (aor. **κατέφυγον**, ptc. **καταφυγών**) flee; flee for safety

καταφθείρω (pf. pass. **κατέφθαρμαι**) corrupt, deprave, ruin

καταφιλέω kiss

καταφρονέω despise, treat with contempt, look down on; think nothing of (He 12.2)

καταφρονητής, οῦ m scoffer, scorner

καταχέω (aor. 3 sg. **κατέχεεν**) pour over

καταχθείς aor. pass. pct. of **κατάγω**

καταχθόνιος, ον under the earth, subterranean

καταχράομαι *use, make full use of*

καταψύχω *cool, refresh*

κατεάγην aor. pass. of κατάγνυμι

κατεαγῶσιν aor. pass. subj. 3 pl. of κατάγνυμι

κατέαξα aor. of κατάγνυμι

κατεάξω fut. of κατάγνυμι

κατέβην aor. of καταβαίνω

κατεγέλων impf. of καταγελάω

κατέγνωσμαι pf. pass. of καταγινώσκω

κατέδραμον aor. of κατατρέχω

κατέθηκα aor. of κατατίθημι

κατείδωλος, ον *full of idols*

κατείλημμαι pf. pass. of καταλαμβάνω

κατείληφα pf. of καταλαμβάνω

κατεκάην aor. pass. of κατακαίω

κατεκρίθην aor. pass. of κατακρίνω

κατέλαβον aor. of καταλαμβάνω

κατελήμφθην aor. pass. of καταλαμβάνω

κατελθεῖν aor. inf. of κατέρχομαι

κατέλιπον aor. of καταλείπω

κατέναντι: (1) prep. with gen. *opposite, before; in the sight of;* (2) adv. *opposite*

κατενεχθείς aor. pass. ptc. of καταφέρω

κατενύγην aor. of κατανύσσομαι

κατενώπιον prep. with gen. *before, in the presence of*

κατεξουσιάζω *rule over*

κατέπεσον aor. of καταπίπτω

κατεπέστησαν aor. 3 pl. of κατεφίστημι

κατέπιον aor. of καταπίνω

κατέπλευσα aor. of καταπλέω

κατεπόθην aor. pass. of καταπίνω

κατεργάζομαι *do, accomplish; produce, bring about, work out; prepare, make ready; overcome, conquer* (Eph 6.13)

κατέρχομαι (aor. κατῆλθον, inf. κατελθεῖν) *come* or *go down; arrive, land*

κατεσθίω and κατέσθω (fut. καταφάγομαι; aor. κατέφαγον) *eat up, devour, consume; exploit, prey upon*

κατεστάθην aor. pass. of καθίστημι

κατέσταλμαι pf. pass. of καταστέλλω

κατέστησα aor. of καθίστημι

κατεστρώθην aor. pass. of καταστρώννυμι

κατευθύνω (aor. opt. 3 sg. κατευθύναι, inf. κατευθῦναι) *direct, guide*

κατευλογέω *bless*

κατέφαγον aor. of κατεσθίω

κατέφθαρμαι pf. pass. of καταφθείρω

κατεφίστημι (aor. 3 pl. **κατεπέστησαν**) *attack, set upon*

κατέφυγον aor. of **καταφεύγω**

κατέχεεν aor. 3 sg. of **καταχέω**

κατέχω (aor. subj. **κατάσχω**) trans. *hold fast, keep; take, possess; hold back, restrain, suppress;* intrans. κ. εἰς *head for* (Ac 27.40)

κατήγαγον aor. of **κατάγω**

κατήγγειλα aor. of **καταγγέλλω**

κατηγγέλην aor. pass. of **καταγγέλλω**

κατηγορέω *accuse, bring charges against* (someone)

κατηγορία, ας f *charge, accusation*

κατήγορος, ου m *accuser*

κατήγωρ, ορος m *accuser*

κατηλλάγην aor. pass. of **καταλλάσσω**

κατήνεγκα aor. of **καταφέρω**

κατήραμαι pf. of **καταράομαι**

κατηράσω aor. 2 sg. of **καταράομαι**

κατήφεια, ας f *gloom, depression*

κατηχέω *inform, tell; instruct, teach*

κατήχθην aor. pass. of **κατάγω**

κατιόομαι (pf. 3 sg. **κατίωται**) *rust*

κατισχύω *have strength; over-*

come, overpower (Mt 16.18); *win, prevail* (Lk 23.23)

κατοικέω (aor. **κατῴκησα**) intrans. *live, settle;* trans. *inhabit, live in*

κατοίκησις, εως f *home* (ἔχω κ. *live* Mk 5.3)

κατοικητήριον, ου n *house, home; haunt* (of demons)

κατοικία, ας f *place in which one lives*

κατοικίζω (aor. **κατῴκισα**) *place, put*

κατοπτρίζομαι *behold; reflect*

κάτω adv. *down; below, beneath;* ἀπ' ἄνωθεν ἕως κάτω *from top to bottom*

κατώτερος, α, ον *lower*

κατωτέρω adv. *under, less* (of age)

Καῦδα *Cauda* (4 D–4)

καυθήσομαι and **καυθήσωμαι** fut. pass. of **καίω**

καῦμα, τος n *heat*

καυματίζω *scorch, burn*

καῦσις, εως f *burning*

καυσόομαι *be burned up*

καυστηριάζω *burn with a hot iron so as to deaden to feeling*

καύσων, ωνος m *(scorching) heat*

καυχάομαι *boast, boast about, take pride in; rejoice, be glad*

καύχημα, τος n *ground for boasting, object of boasting; boasting, pride*

καύχησις, εως f *boasting; pride, object of boasting*

Καφαρναούμ f *Capernaum* (2 D–3)

Κεγχρεαί, ὧν f *Cenchreae* (4 D–3)

Κεδρών m *Kidron* (a valley between Jerusalem and the Mt. of Olives)

κεῖμαι *lie, be laid; be, exist; stand, be standing; be destined or appointed; store up* (Lk 12.19)

κειρία, ας f *strip of cloth* (used to wrap the dead)

κείρω *shear* (sheep); midd. *cut one's hair, have one's hair cut*

κέκαυμαι pf. pass. of **καίω**

κεκέρασμαι pf. pass. of **κεράννυμι**

κέκληκα pf. of **καλέω**

κέκλικα pf. of **κλίνω**

κεκόρεσμαι pf. pass. of **κορέννυμι**

κέκραγα pf. of **κράζω**

κέκρικα pf. of **κρίνω**

κέκρυμμαι pf. pass. of **κρύπτω**

κέλευσμα, τος n *shout of command, command*

κελεύω *order, command*

κενοδοξία, ας f *conceit, cheap desire to boast*

κενόδοξος, ον *conceited, boastful*

κενός, ή, όν *empty, empty-handed; to no purpose, without result* (εἰς κ. *in vain*); *foolish, senseless*

κενοφωνία, ας f *foolish talk*

κενόω *deprive of power, make*

of no meaning or effect; ἐμαυτὸν κ. give up or lay aside what one possesses

κέντρον, ου n *sting; goad*

κεντυρίων, ωνος m *centurion* (Roman officer commanding about a hundred men)

κενῶς adv. *in vain, to no purpose*

κεραία, ας f *stroke* (part of a letter)

κεραμεύς, έως m *potter*

κεραμικός, ή, όν *earthen, made of clay*

κεράμιον, ου n *jar* (made of clay)

κέραμος, ου m *roof tile*

κεράννυμι (aor. **ἐκέρασα**; pf. pass. **κεκέρασμαι**) *mix; pour*

κέρας, ατος n *horn* (perhaps *corner* Re 9.13); *might, power* (κ. σωτηρίας *a mighty Savior* Lk 1.69)

κεράτιον, ου n *pod* (of the carob tree)

κερδαίνω (fut. **κερδήσω**; aor. **ἐκέρδησα**, subj. **κερδήσω** and **κερδάνω**, inf. **κερδῆσαι**) *gain, profit; win, win over; avoid, spare oneself* (a loss)

κέρδος, ους n *gain*

κέρμα, τος n *coin*

κερματιστής, οῦ m *money-changer*

κεφάλαιον, ου n *main point, summary; sum of money*

κεφαλή, ῆς f *head* (κατὰ κ. ἔχω *have one's head covered*

1 Cor 11.4); *lord, head* (of
superior rank, etc.); κ. γωνίας *main corner-stone*
κεφαλιόω *beat over the head*
κεφαλίς, ίδος f *roll* (of a
scroll or book)
κημόω *muzzle*
κῆνσος, ου m *tax*
κῆπος, ου m *garden*
κηπουρός, οῦ m *gardener*
κηρίον, ου n *honeycomb*
κήρυγμα, τος n *what is
preached, message, proclama-
tion*
κῆρυξ, υκος m *preacher, herald*
κηρύσσω *proclaim, make
known, preach*
κῆτος, ους n *large sea creature*
Κηφᾶς, ᾶ m *Cephas* (Aramaic
equivalent of Greek Πέ-
τρος, *Peter* mng. *rock*)
κιβωτός, οῦ f *ark* (of a ship);
box (**κ. τῆς διαθήκης** *the
covenant box*)
κιθάρα, ας f *harp*
κιθαρίζω *play a harp*
κιθαρῳδός, οῦ m *harpist,
harper*
Κιλικία, ας f *Cilicia* (**4** G–3)
κινδυνεύω *be in danger, run
a risk;* impers. *there is danger*
(Ac 19.27)
κίνδυνος, ου m *danger, peril*
κινέω *move, shake; remove;
stir up, arouse;* midd. *move*
(Ac 17.28)
κίνησις, εως f *movement,
motion*
κιννάμωμον, ου n *cinnamon*

Κίς m *Kish* (Ac 13.21)
κίχρημι (aor. impv. **χρῆσον**)
lend
κλάδος, ου m *branch*
κλαίω (aor. **ἔκλαυσα**) intrans.
weep, cry; trans. *weep for*
(Mt 2.18)
κλάσις, εως f *breaking* (of
bread)
κλάσμα, τος n *fragment, piece*
Κλαῦδα *Clauda* alt. form of
Καῦδα
Κλαυδία, ας f *Claudia* (2 Tm
4.21)
Κλαύδιος, ου m *Claudius:*
(1) Tiberius Claudius, Roman emperor (A.D. 41–54)
(Ac 11.28); (2) Claudius
Lysias, Roman officer in
Jerusalem (Ac 23.26)
κλαυθμός, οῦ m *bitter crying,
wailing*
κλάω *break* (only of bread in
the NT; often of a cere-
monial or religious act at the
beginning of a meal)
κλείς, κλειδός f *key*
κλείω *shut, close; lock*
κλέμμα, τος n *theft, robbery*
Κλεοπᾶς, ᾶ m *Cleopas* (Lk
24.18)
κλέος, ους n *credit, honor*
κλέπτης, ου m *thief*
κλέπτω *steal*
κληθήσομαι fut. pass. of **καλέω**
κλῆμα, τος n *branch*
Κλήμης, εντος m *Clement*
(Php 4.3)

κληρονομέω receive, gain possession of, share (in), be given (something)

κληρονομία, ας f property, possession(s); what is promised or given by God to his people, God's blessing(s); share, part (Ac 7.5)

κληρονόμος, ου m one who receives what God has promised to his people; heir (Mt 21.38 and parallels; Ga 4.1)

κλῆρος, ου m lot (of something thrown or drawn to reach a decision); share, part, place; someone given to another's care (1 Pe 5.3)

κληρόω choose (ἐν ᾧ ἐκληρώθημεν perhaps in whom we were chosen as God's own people Eph 1.11)

κλῆσις, εως f call, calling; station of life (1 Cor 7.20)

κλητός, ή, όν called (of the Christian call); invited (Mt 22.14)

κλίβανος, ου m oven, furnace

κλίμα, τος n region, district

κλινάριον, ου n small bed, cot

κλίνη, ης f bed, couch; cot; stretcher; sickbed (Re 2.22)

κλινίδιον, ου n bed, cot, stretcher

κλίνω (pf. **κέκλικα**) trans. lay; bow; rout, put to flight (He 11.34); intrans. wear away, draw to a close

κλισία, ας f group (of persons eating)

κλοπή, ῆς f theft

κλύδων, ωνος m rough water, wave(s)

κλυδωνίζομαι be tossed by the sea

Κλωπᾶς, ᾶ m Clopas (Jn 19.25)

κνήθομαι feel an itching

Κνίδος, ου f Cnidus (4 E–3)

κοδράντης, ου m quadrans (Roman copper coin worth 1/4 assarion or 1/64 denarius)

κοιλία, ας f stomach, belly (ἐκ τῆς κ. αὐτοῦ from within him Jn 7.38); womb (ἐκ κ. from birth); appetite, bodily desires (Ro 16.18; Php 3.19)

κοιμάομαι sleep, fall asleep; die

κοίμησις, εως f sleep; κ. τοῦ ὕπνου natural sleep (Jn 11.13)

κοινός, ή, όν common, in common; common, profane; defiled, unclean

κοινόω defile, make unclean; call common (Ac 10.15; 11.9)

κοινωνέω share, take part, participate; contribute, give a share

κοινωνία, ας f fellowship, a close mutual relationship; participation, sharing in; partnership; contribution, gift

κοινωνικός, ή, όν liberal, generous

κοινωνός, οῦ m and f *partner, sharer*

κοίτη, ης f *bed; marital relationship* (He 13.4); *sperm* (*κοίτην ἔχω conceive* Ro 9.10); *sexual impurity* (Ro 13.13)

κοιτών, ῶνος m *bedroom; ὁ ἐπὶ τοῦ κ. one who is in charge of the bed-chamber* (Ac 12.20)

κόκκινος, η, ον *scarlet, red*

κόκκος, ου m *seed, grain*

κολάζω (act. and midd.) *punish*

κολακεία, ας f *flattery*

κόλασις, εως f *punishment; κ. ἔχω have to do with punishment* (1 Jn 4.18)

κολαφίζω *beat, strike; harass, trouble*

κολλάομαι *unite oneself with, associate with, join; stick to* (of dust); *hold on to* (Ro 12.9); *pile up to* (Re 18.5); *hire oneself out to* (Lk 15.15)

κολλούριον, ου n *eye salve*

κολλυβιστής, οῦ m *money-changer*

κολοβόω *shorten, cut short*

Κολοσσαί, ῶν f *Colossae* (4 E-3)

κόλπος, ου m *bosom, chest* (*εἰς τὸν κ. close to, near* Jn 1.18; *ἐν τῷ κ. next to* Jn 13.23); *lap* (Lk 6.38); *bay, gulf* (Ac 27.39)

κολ μβάω *swim*

κολυμβήθρα, ας f *pool*

κολωνία, ας f *colony* (i.e. a city with special Roman privileges)

κομάω *wear long hair*

κόμη, ης f *hair*

κομίζω (fut. midd. **κομίσομαι** and **κομιοῦμαι**) *bring, buy;* midd. *receive, obtain; receive back, be paid back*

κομψότερον adv. *better; κ. ἔχω recover* (from an illness)

κονιάω *whitewash*

κονιορτός, οῦ m *dust*

κοπάζω *cease, stop*

κοπετός, οῦ m *weeping, mourning*

κοπή, ῆς f *slaughter, defeat*

κοπιάω *work, work hard, labor* (πολλὰ κ. *work hard* Ro 16.6, 12); *become tired, grow weary*

κόπος, ου m *work, hard work, labor; trouble, hardship; κόπους* (*κόπον*) *παρέχω τινί trouble or bother someone*

κοπρία, ας f *dung-heap, garbage pile*

κόπριον, ου n *manure*

κόπτω *cut;* midd. *mourn, wail, lament*

κόραξ, ακος m *crow, raven*

κοράσιον, ου n *girl*

Κορβᾶν *Corban* (Hebrew term for a gift set apart for God)

κορβανᾶς, ᾶ m *temple treasury*

Κόρε m *Korah* (Jd 11)

κορέννυμι (pf. pass. **κεκόρεσμαι**; aor. pass. ptc. **κορεσθείς**) *fill;* pass. *be full,* *have enough; be fully content*

Κορίνθιος, ου m *a Corinthian*

Κόρινθος, ου f *Corinth* (4 D–3)

Κορνήλιος, ου m *Cornelius*

κόρος, ου m *cor, measure* (a dry measure of about 10–12 bushels)

κοσμέω *adorn, decorate; put in order; trim* (of lamps)

κοσμικός, ή, όν *worldly; man-made, material* (He 9.1)

κόσμιος, ον *well behaved, respectable; befitting, modest*

κοσμοκράτωρ, ορος m *world ruler, ruler*

κόσμος, ου m *world, world order, universe; world inhabitants, mankind* (especially of men hostile to God); *world, realm of existence, way of life* (especially as opposed to the purpose of God); *adornment* (1 Pe 3.3)

Κούαρτος, ου m *Quartus* (Ro 16.23)

κουμ *stand up* (Aramaic word)

κουστωδία, ας f *a guard* (of soldiers)

κουφίζω *lighten, make weigh less*

κόφινος, ου m *basket* (perhaps smaller than the σπυρίς)

κράβαττος, ου m *bed, cot, stretcher*

κράζω (aor. in Ac 24.21

ἐκέκραξα; pf. with pres. mng. **κέκραγα**) *call out, cry out, shout*

κραιπάλη, ης f *drunken dissipation*

κρανίον, ου n *skull*

κράσπεδον, ου n *fringe, edge; tassel*

κραταιόομαι *become strong*

κραταιός, ά, όν *mighty, strong*

κρατέω *hold, hold fast; take, take hold of; seize, arrest; hold back, restrain; hold unforgiven* (Jn 20.23); *carry out, achieve* (Ac 27.13)

κράτιστος, η, ον *most excellent, your excellency* (used in polite address and in addressing nobility)

κράτος, ους n *might, strength, power, dominion; mighty deed* (Lk 1.51); κατὰ κ. *powerfully, effectively* (Ac 19.20)

κραυγάζω *call out, shout*

κραυγή, ῆς f *shout, outcry; clamor, angry shouting; crying* (Re 21.4)

κρέας, κρέατος and **κρέως** acc. pl. **κρέα** n *meat*

κρεῖττον and **κρεῖσσον** adv. *better* (κ. λαλῶ παρά *speak better things* He 12.24)

κρείττων and **κρείσσων, ον** gen. **ονος** *better; greater, superior*

κρεμάννυμι (midd. **κρέμαμαι**; aor. ptc. **κρεμάσας**; aor. pass. ptc. **κρεμασθείς**) trans. *hang;* intrans. (midd.) *hang; depend* (Mt 22.40)

κρημνός, οῦ m *steep bank*

Κρής, ητός m *a Cretan*

Κρήσκης, εντος m *Crescens* (2 Tm 4.10)

Κρήτη, ης f *Crete* (3 A–2, 4 D–3)

κριθή, ῆς f *barley*

κριθήσομαι fut. pass. of **κρίνω**

κρίθινος, η, ον *made of barley*

κρίμα, τος n *judgment; decision, verdict; condemnation, punishment; lawsuit* (1 Cor 6.7); *power* or *authority to judge* (Re 20.4)

κρίνον, ου n *lily, attractive wild flower*

κρίνω (pf. **κέκρικα**; aor. pass. **ἐκρίθην**, inf. **κριθῆναι**; fut. pass. **κριθήσομαι**) *judge, pass judgment on* (midd. and pass. often *stand trial, go to law); condemn; decide, determine; consider, regard, think; prefer*

κρίσις, εως f *judgment, judging; condemnation, punishment; justice;* perhaps *court* (Mt 5.21f)

Κρίσπος, ου m *Crispus* (Ac 18.8; 1 Cor 1.14)

κριτήριον, ου n *court; case* (κ. ἐλαχίστων perhaps *trivial matters* 1 Cor 6.2)

κριτής, οῦ m *judge*

κριτικός, ή, όν *able to judge*

κρούω *knock* (at a door)

κρυβῆναι aor. pass. inf. of **κρύπτω**

κρύπτη, ης f *cellar, hidden place*

κρυπτός, ή, όν *secret, hidden, private; inward, inmost* (ὁ ἐν τῷ κ. Ἰουδαῖος *one who is a Jew inwardly* Ro 2.29)

κρύπτω (pf. pass. **κέκρυμμαι**; aor. pass. **ἐκρύβην**, inf. **κρυβῆναι**) *hide, conceal, cover* (pass. often *hide oneself); keep secret*

κρυσταλλίζω *be clear* or *bright as crystal*

κρύσταλλος, ου m *crystal; ice*

κρυφαῖος, α, ον *secret, hidden*

κρυφῇ adv. *in secret, secretly*

κτάομαι *acquire, gain* (τὸ ἑαυτοῦ σκεῦος κτᾶσθαι *take a wife for himself* or *exercise self control* 1 Th 4.4); *buy*

κτῆμα, τος n *possession, property; piece of land*

κτῆνος, ους n *animal; mount, pack animal;* pl. *cattle* (Re 18.13)

κτήτωρ, ορος m *owner, possessor*

κτίζω *create, make*

κτίσις, εως f *creation, what is created, created order, creature* (of living beings); *act of creation;* ἀνθρωπίνη κτίσις *human authority* (1 Pe 2.13)

κτίσμα, τος n *what is created, creature*

κτίστης, ου m *Creator*

κυβεία, ας f *trickery, cunning*

κυβέρνησις, εως f *ability to lead*

κυβερνήτης, ου m (doubtful mng.) *captain, navigator*

κυκλεύω *surround*

κυκλόθεν: (1) prep. with gen. *round, about;* (2) adv. *all round, all about*

κυκλόω *surround, gather round; march round* (He 11.30)

κύκλῳ: (1) adv. *in a circle, round, round about;* (2) prep. with gen. *round*

κυλίομαι *roll about*

κυλισμός, οῦ m *wallowing*

κυλλός, ή, όν *crippled*

κῦμα, τος n *wave*

κύμβαλον, ου n *cymbal*

κύμινόν, ου n *cummin* (aromatic plant)

κυνάριον, ου n *house dog, dog*

Κύπριος, ου m *a Cyprian*

Κύπρος, ου f *Cyprus* (3 C–3, 4 G–3)

κύπτω *bend* or *stoop down*

Κυρηναῖος, ου m *a Cyrenian*

Κυρήνη, ης f *Cyrene* (4 C–4)

Κυρήνιος, ου m *Quirinius* (Lk 2.2)

κυρία, ας f *lady*

κυριακός, ή, όν *belonging to the Lord*

κυριεύω *have power over, rule over; be lord of; lord it over; dictate the terms of* (2 Cor 1.24)

κύριος, ου m *Lord* (of God and Christ); *master, lord, owner; sir* (of address)

κυριότης, ητος f *(angelic) power* (believed to have some control over human fate); *authority*

κυρόω *put into effect* (of a covenant); κ. εἰς αὐτὸν ἀγάπην *prove your love for him* (2 Cor 2.8)

κύων, κυνός dat. pl. κυσί m *dog*

κῶλον, ου n *dead body, corpse*

κωλύω *hinder, prevent, stop; forbid; withhold, keep back*

κώμη, ης f *village, small town*

κωμόπολις, εως f *country town, town*

κῶμος, ου m *carousing, orgy, revelry*

κώνωψ, ωπος m *gnat, mosquito*

Κώς, Κῶ acc. Κῶ f *Cos* (4 E–3)

Κωσάμ m *Cosam* (Lk 3.28)

κωφός, ή, όν *dumb, mute; deaf*

Λ

λαβεῖν, λαβών aor. inf. and
ptc. of λαμβάνω
λάβοι aor. opt. 3 sg. of λαμβάνω
λαγχάνω (aor. ἔλαχον, subj.
λάχω, ptc. λαχών) receive,
be given; be chosen, fall to
one's lot (Lk 1.9); cast or
draw lots (Jn 19.24)
Λάζαρος, ου m Lazarus: (1)
brother of Mary and Mar-
tha; (2) the beggar in a
parable
λαθεῖν aor. inf. of λανθάνω
λάθρᾳ adv. secretly, quietly
λαῖλαψ, απος f storm, squall
λακάω burst open
λακτίζω kick (λ. πρός kick
against)
λαλέω speak, talk, say; preach,
proclaim; tell; be able to
speak; address, converse
(with); promise (of God);
sound (of thunder)
λαλιά, ᾶς f what is said; accent,
manner of speech
λαμβάνω (fut. λήμψομαι;
aor. ἔλαβον, inf. λαβεῖν,
ptc. λαβών, opt. 3 sg.
λάβοι; pf. εἴληφα; pf. pass.
3 sg. εἴληπται) take, take
hold of; receive, get, obtain;
take away, remove; collect
(of taxes, etc.); choose (He

5.1); put on (Jn 13.12);
catch (Lk 5.5); trap, take
advantage of (2 Cor 11.20;
12.16)
Λάμεχ m Lamech (Lk 3.36)
λαμπάς, άδος f lamp, lantern;
torch
λαμπρός, ά, όν bright, shining;
fine, splendid; clear, transparent
λαμπρότης, ητος f bright-
ness
λαμπρῶς adv. splendidly
λάμπω shine, give light, flash
λανθάνω (aor. ἔλαθον, inf.
λαθεῖν) be hidden, escape
notice; lose sight of, ignore;
be unaware (He 13.2b)
λαξευτός, ή, όν cut out in the
rock
Λαοδίκεια, ας f Laodicea (4
E–2)
Λαοδικεύς, έως m a Laodi-
cean
λαός, οῦ m people; nation;
crowd; often of the Jews or
the church as the people of
God
λάρυγξ, γγος m throat
Λασαία, ας f Lasea (4 D–4)
λατομέω cut, hew (of rock)
λατρεία, ας f service, worship;
pl. rites or duties (He 9.6)
λατρεύω serve, worship

λάχανον, ου n garden-plant, vegetable

λάχω aor. subj. of λαγχάνω

λαχών aor. ptc. of λαγχάνω

Λεββαῖος, ου m Lebbeus (Mt 10.3; Mk 3.18)

Λεββεδαῖος, ου m Lebbedeus (Mt 10.3)

λεγιών, ῶνος f legion (Roman military unit of 5000–6000 men; figurative of a large number)

λέγω (fut. ἐρῶ; aor. εἶπον and εἶπα, inf. εἰπεῖν; pf. εἴρηκα; plpf. 3 sg. εἰρήκει; pf. pass. εἴρημαι; aor. pass. ἐρρέθην, ptc. ῥηθείς) say, speak, tell (λέγων in discourse is often redundant); call, name; maintain, assert, declare; mean, intend; think (to oneself); command, order; answer, ask (dependent on context)

λεῖμμα, τος n remnant, small remainder

λεῖος, α, ον smooth, level

λείπω trans. and intrans. lack, fall short

λειτουργέω serve; worship

λειτουργία, ας f service, ministry; worship; offering, sacrifice

λειτουργικός, ή, όν ministering

λειτουργός, οῦ m servant, minister

λεμα why? (Aramaic word)

λέντιον, ου n towel

λεπίς, ίδος f flake, (fish)scale

λέπρα, ας f leprosy, skin disease

λεπρός, οῦ m leper, a man with a skin disease

λεπτόν, οῦ n lepton (copper coin worth 1/2 quadrans or 1/128 denarius)

λευδορέω alt. form of λοιδορέω

Λευί, Λευίς and Λευεί m Levi: (1) disciple of Jesus; (2) son of Jacob; (3, 4) persons in the genealogy of Jesus (Lk 3.24, 29)

Λευίτης, ου m a Levite (descendant of Levi and an assistant to the priest)

Λευιτικός, ή, όν Levitical

λευκαίνω (aor. ἐλεύκανα, inf. λευκᾶναι) make white; bleach

λευκός, ή, όν white; shining, brilliant

λέων, οντος m lion

λήθη, ης f forgetfulness; λήθην λαμβάνω τινός forget something (2 Pe 1.9)

λῆμψις, εως f receiving

λήμψομαι fut. of λαμβάνω

ληνός, οῦ f wine press

λῆρος, ου m nonsense, empty talk

λῃστής, οῦ m robber; insurrectionist

λίαν adv. exceedingly, greatly, very much; very, quite; λ. ἐκ περισσοῦ utterly, completely (Mk 6.51) λίβα acc. of λίψ

λίβανος, ου m *frankincense; incense*

λιβανωτός, οῦ m *censer, incense container*

Λιβερτῖνος, ου m *Freedman* (either a former slave or a descendant of former slaves)

Λιβύη, ης f *Libya* (3 A–4, 4 D–5)

λιθάζω *stone*

λίθινος, η, ον *made of stone*

λιθοβολέω *stone, throw stones at*

λίθος, ου m *stone; precious stone; stone image* (Ac 17.29)

λιθόστρωτον, ου n *pavement*

λικμάω *crush*

λιμήν, ένος m *harbor*

λίμνη, ης f *lake*

λιμός, οῦ m and f *famine; hunger*

λίνον, ου n *linen; wick*

Λίνος, ου m *Linus* (2 Tm 4.21)

λιπαρός, ά, όν *costly, luxurious*

λίτρα, ας f *pound* (of the Roman pound weighing 11.5 ounces)

λίψ acc. λίβα m *the southwest wind* (κατὰ λ. *facing southwest* Ac 27.12)

λογεία, ας f *contribution, collection*

λόγια, ων n *oracles, words, messages*

λογίζομαι *count, reckon, calculate, take into account; credit, place to one's account; consider, think, suppose; evaluate, look / upon as, class; maintain, claim; think on, reflect upon*

λογικός, ή, όν *rational, spiritual*

λόγιος, α, ον *eloquent; learned*

λογισμός, οῦ m *thought, reasoning; false argument* or *reasoning*

λογομαχέω *fight* or *quarrel about words*

λογομαχία, ας f *fight* or *quarrel about words*

λόγος, ου m *something said* (e.g. *word; saying; message, teaching; talk, conversation; question* after ἐρωτάω; *preaching* 1 Tm 5.17; πολὺς ἡμῖν ὁ λόγος *we have much to say* He 5.11); *Word* (in Johannine Christology); *account, settlement of an account* (πρὸς ὃν ἡμῖν ὁ λόγος *to whom we must render an account* He 4.13); *value* (Ac 20.24); *reason, grounds* (κατὰ λόγον *reasonably, patiently* Ac 18.14); *charge* (Ac 19.38); *matter, thing* (Ac 8.21); *book* (Ac 1.1)

λόγχη, ης f *spear*

λοιδορέω *curse, speak evil of, insult*

λοιδορία, ας f *cursing* or *speaking evil* (of someone)

λοίδορος, ου m *slanderer*

λοιμός, οῦ m *plague, pestilence; trouble maker, nuisance*

λοιπός, ή, όν: (1) adj. *rest, remaining, other;* (2) adv. (τὸ) λοιπόν *finally; from now on, henceforth; still; beyond that, in addition;* τοῦ λοιποῦ *henceforth, in the future; finally;* ὧδε λοιπόν *moreover, in this connection*

Λουκᾶς, ᾶ m *Luke*

Λούκιος, ου m *Lucius:* (1) of Cyrene (Ac 13.1); (2) mentioned by Paul (Ro 16.21)

λουτρόν, οῦ n *washing, cleansing; water*

λούω *wash, bathe*

Λύδδα, ας acc. **Λύδδα** f *Lydda* (2 B–6)

Λυδία, ας f *Lydia* (Ac 16.14, 40)

Λυκαονία, ας f *Lycaonia* (4 F–2)

Λυκαονιστί adv. *in the Lycaonian language*

Λυκία, ας f *Lycia* (4 E–3)

λύκος, ου m *wolf*

λυμαίνομαι *harass, destroy*

λυπέω *pain, grieve, injure;* pass. *be sad, sorrowful* or *distressed; grieve, weep*

λύπη, ης f *grief, sorrow, pain;* ἐκ λύπης *reluctantly, with regret* (2 Cor 9.7)

Λυσανίας, ου m *Lysanias* (Lk 3.1)

Λυσίας, ου m *Lysias* (Ac 23.26; 24.7, 22)

λύσις, εως f *separation, divorce*

λυσιτελεῖ impers. *it is advantageous* or *better*

Λύστρα dat. **Λύστροις** acc. **Λύστραν** f and n *Lystra* (4 F–2)

λύτρον, ου n *means of release, means of redeeming*

λυτρόομαι *redeem, set free, liberate*

λύτρωσις, εως f *redemption, liberation, setting free*

λυτρωτής, οῦ m *liberator, deliverer*

λυχνία, ας f *lampstand, stand*

λύχνος, ου m *lamp*

λύω *loose, untie; release, set free; break, set aside; destroy, pull down; break up; allow* (Mt 16.19; 18.18)

Λωΐς, ΐδος f *Lois* (2 Tm 1.5)

Λώτ m *Lot*

M

Μάαθ m *Maath* (Lk 3.26)

Μαγαδάν f *Magadan* (location uncertain)

Μαγδαλά f *Magdala* (**2** C–3)

Μαγδαληνή, ῆς f *woman of Magdala*

Μαγεδάλ alt. of **Μαγαδάν**

μαγεία, ας f *magic, magical art*

μαγεύω *practice magic*

μάγος, ου m *wise man* (of one trained in astrology and dream interpretation); *magician, sorcerer*

Μαγώγ m *Magog* (cryptic name)

Μαδιάμ m *Midian* (**3** C–4)

μαθεῖν aor. inf. of **μανθάνω**

μαθητεύω trans. *make a disciple of;* intrans. (or pass.) *be a disciple*

μαθητής, οῦ m *disciple, pupil, follower*

μαθήτρια, ας f *woman disciple*

Μαθθαῖος, ου m *Matthew*

Μαθθίας, ου m *Matthias* (Ac 1.23, 26)

Μαθουσαλά m *Methuselah* (Lk 3.37)

μαίνομαι *be out of one's mind, be insane*

μακαρίζω *consider fortunate or happy*

μακάριος, α, ον *blessed, fortunate, happy;* μ. θεός

God who is worthy of all praise (1 Tm 1.11; 6.15)

μακαρισμός, οῦ m *happiness, blessing*

Μακεδονία, ας f *Macedonia* (**4** C–2)

Μακεδών, όνος m *a Macedonian*

μάκελλον, ου n *meat market*

μακράν adv. *far, far off, at some distance;* εἰς μακράν *far away* (Ac 2.39)

μακρόθεν adv. *far off, at a distance;* ἀπὸ μακρόθεν *at a distance, from a distance, in the distance*

μακροθυμέω *be patient, wait patiently;* μ. ἐπ' αὐτοῖς *perhaps be slow to help them* or *delay to help them* (Lk 18.7)

μακροθυμία, ας f *patience*

μακροθύμως adv. *patiently*

μακρός, ά, όν *long; distant, far off*

μακροχρόνιος, ον *long-lived*

μαλακία, ας f *sickness*

μαλακός, ή, όν *soft, fancy, luxurious; homosexual pervert* (1 Cor 6.9)

Μαλελεήλ m *Maleleel* (Lk 3.37)

μάλιστα adv. *especially, above all, most of all*

μᾶλλον adv. *more* (πολλῷ μ. *much more, all the more;* πόσῳ μ. *how much more;* καλόν ἐστιν μ. *it is better;* μ. διαφέρω *be of more value than;* πολλῷ μ. κρεῖσσον *better by far* Php 1.23; μ. περισσότερον *all the more* Mk 7.36); *rather, instead* (μ. ἤ *rather than, more than); all the more, more than ever, more than that*

Μάλχος, ου m *Malchus* (Jn 18.10)

μάμμη, ης f *grandmother*

μαμωνᾶς, ᾶ m *money, wealth, property*

Μαναήν m *Manaen* (Ac 13.1)

Μανασσῆς, ῆ acc. ῆ m *Manasseh:* (1) son of Joseph, founder of an Israelite tribe (Re 7.6); (2) in the genealogy of Jesus (Mt 1.10)

μανθάνω (aor. ἔμαθον, inf. μαθεῖν; pf. μεμάθηκα) *learn; find out, discover; learn by experience; attend a rabbinic school* (Jn 7.15)

μανία, ας f *madness, insanity*

μάννα n *manna*

μαντεύομαι *tell fortunes, predict the future*

μαραίνομαι (fut. μαρανθήσομαι) *wither away*

μαρανα θα (in Aramaic) *our Lord, come!* or μαραν αθα *our Lord has come!*

μαργαρίτης, ου m *pearl*

Μάρθα, ας f *Martha*

Μαρία, ας and Μαριάμ f *Mary:* (1) mother of Jesus; (2) sister of Martha and Lazarus; (3) Mary Magdalene; (4) mother of James and Joseph; (5) wife of Clopas (Jn 19.25); (6) mother of John Mark (Ac 12.12); (7) Christian in Ro 16.6

Μᾶρκος, ου m *Mark*

μάρμαρος, ου m *marble*

μαρτυρέω *bear witness, testify, be a witness; attest, affirm, confirm; speak well of, approve* (pass. *be well spoken of, receive approval*)

μαρτυρία, ας f *testimony, witness, evidence; reputation* (1 Tm 3.7)

μαρτύριον, ου n *testimony, witness; evidence, proof; opportunity to testify* (Lk 21.13)

μαρτύρομαι *testify, address solemnly; insist, urge*

μάρτυς, μάρτυρος dat. pl. μάρτυσιν m *witness; martyr*

μασάομαι *gnaw, bite*

μαστιγόω *beat with a whip; discipline, punish* (He 12.6)

μαστίζω *beat with a whip, whip*

μάστιξ, ιγος f *whip; beating with a whip; illness, disease*

μαστός, οῦ m *breast; chest*

ματαιολογία, ας f *empty talk*

ματαιολόγος, ου m *empty talker*

ματαιόομαι *be given to worthless or futile speculation*

μάταιος, α, ον *worthless, futile, useless*

ματαιότης, ητος f *worthlessness, futility*

μάτην adv. *in vain, to no purpose*

Ματθάν m *Matthan* (Mt 1.15)

Ματθάτ m *Matthat:* (1) father of Eli (Lk 3.24); (2) father of Jorim (Lk 3.29)

Ματταθά m *Mattatha* (Lk 3.31)

Ματταθίας, ου m *Mattathias:* (1) son of Amos (Lk 3.25); (2) son of Semein (Lk 3.26)

μάχαιρα, ης f *sword; war* (Mt 10.34); *violent death* (Ro 8.35)

μάχη, ης f *quarrel, fight*

μάχομαι *quarrel, fight*

μεγαλεῖον, ου n *mighty act or deed*

μεγαλειότης, ητος f *majesty, greatness*

μεγαλοπρεπής, ές *majestic* (μ. δόξα *Majestic Glory* as a name for God 2 Pe 1.17)

μεγαλύνω *enlarge, extend* (μ. ἔλεος *show great kindness* Lk 1.58); *praise; hold in high honor*

μεγάλως adv. *greatly*

μεγαλωσύνη, ης f *majesty, greatness; Majesty* (name for God)

μέγας, μεγάλη, μέγα *large, great* (of a *loud* sound;

strong wind; *high* fever; etc.); *greatest; surprising* (2 Cor 11.15)

μέγεθος, ους n *greatness*

μεγιστάν, ᾶνος m *person of high status*

μέγιστος, η, ον (superl. of μέγας) *very great, greatest*

μεθερμηνεύω *translate*

μέθη, ης f *drunkenness*

μεθίστημι and μεθιστάνω (aor. μετέστησα, ptc. μεταστήσας; aor. pass. subj. μετασταθῶ) *remove; mislead; bring* (εἰς) *into;* pass. μ. ἐκ τῆς οἰκονομίας *lose one's job as a steward* (Lk 16.4)

μεθοδεία, ας f *trickery;* pl. *tricks*

μεθύσκομαι *get drunk*

μέθυσος, ου m *drunkard*

μεθύω *be drunk;* perhaps *drink freely* (Jn 2.10)

μείζων, ον and μειζότερος, α, ον (comp. of μέγας) *greater* (*older* Ro 9.12); often =superl. *greatest;* adv. μεῖζον *all the more* (Mt 20.31)

μεῖναι, μεῖνον aor. inf. and impv. of μένω

μέλας, αινα, αν gen. ανος, αίνης, ανος *black;* τὸ μ. *ink*

Μελεά m *Melea* (Lk 3.31)

μέλει impers. *it is of concern;* μή σοι μελέτω *never mind* (1 Cor 7.21)

μελετάω *practice, cultivate; plot, think about* (Ac 4.25)

μέλι, ιτος n *honey*

μελίσσιος, ον *belonging to bees; μελίσσιον κηρίον honeycomb* (Lk 24.42)

Μελίτη, ης f *Malta* (4 A–3)

μέλλω (before an inf.) *be going, be about, intend; must, be destined;* (ptc. without inf.) *coming, future;* (finite verb without inf.) *delay, wait (τί μέλλεις what are you waiting for?* Ac 22.16)

μέλος, ους n *a bodily part, member*

Μελχί m *Melchi:* (1) father of Levi (Lk 3.24); (2) father of Neri (Lk 3.28)

Μελχισέδεκ m *Melchizedek*

μεμάθηκα pf. of μανθάνω

μεμβράνα, ης f *parchment* (a document or material to write on)

μεμενήκεισαν plpf. 3 pl. of μένω

μεμίαμμαι pf. pass. of μιαίνω

μέμνημαι pf. of μιμνήσκομαι

μέμφομαι *find fault with, blame*

μεμψίμοιρος, ον *complaining, dissatisfied with life*

μέν particle indicating contrast, emphasis or continuation; *μὲν ... δέ on the one hand ... on the other hand; μὲν ... ἀλλά or μὲν ... πλήν indeed ... but; ὃς μὲν ... καὶ ἄλλος (ἕτερος) one*

... another; μὲν οὖν so, then; now, indeed

Μεννά m *Menna* (Lk 3.31)

μενοῦν and μενοῦνγε *rather, on the contrary; indeed, much more*

μέντοι *but, nevertheless, however*

μένω (aor. ἔμεινα, impv. μεῖνον, inf. μεῖναι; plpf. 3 pl. μεμενήκεισαν) intrans. *remain, stay, abide; live, dwell; last, endure, continue;* trans. *await, wait for*

μερίζω *divide* (midd. *share* Lk 12.13); *give, assign, apportion; be of divided interest* (1 Cor 7.34)

μέριμνα, ης f *care, concern; anxiety, worry*

μεριμνάω *be anxious, worry about; care for, be concerned about*

μερίς, ίδος f *part, portion, share (τίς μερὶς πιστῷ μετὰ ἀπίστου what does a believer have in common with an unbeliever?* 2 Cor 6.15); *district* (Ac 16.12)

μερισμός, οῦ m *distribution, distributing; division, separation*

μεριστής, οῦ m *divider* (of one who settles property disputes)

μέρος, ους n *part, piece (ἀνὰ μέρος one at a time* 1 Cor 14.27; *ἀπὸ μέρους partially, partly* 2 Cor 1.14; *at*

times, at some points Ro
15.15; *for a while* Ro 15.24;
to some degree 2 Cor 2.5;
πώρωσις ἀπὸ μέρους *a partial hardening* Ro 11.25; ἐκ
μέρους *individually* 1 Cor
12.27; *partially, imperfectly*
1 Cor 13.9ff; τὸ ἐκ μέρους
the partial or *incomplete*
1 Cor 13.10; κατὰ μέρος *in
detail* He 9.5); *place, region,
district; share, portion; case,
matter, circumstance* (ἐν μέ-
ρει ἑορτῆς *with regard to a
festival* Col 2.16); *trade, business* (Ac 19.27); *party, sect*
(Ac 23.9); *side* (Jn 21.6)

μεσημβρία, ας f *noon, midday;
south;* κατὰ μ. *toward the
south* or *about noon* (Ac 8.26)

μεσιτεύω *confirm, guarantee*

μεσίτης, ου m *mediator, in-
termediary*

μεσονύκτιον, ου n *midnight*

Μεσοποταμία, ας f *Mesopo-
tamia* (3 E-2)

μέσος, η, ον: (1) adj. *middle,
in the middle* (ἀνὰ μέσον
among Mt 13.25; *between*
1 Cor 6.5; *through* Mk 7.31;
at the center Re 7.17; ἐν
μέσῳ or εἰς μέσον *in the
middle, in the midst, among;*
ἐν τῷ μέσῳ *before the guests*
Mt 14.6; ἐν μέσῳ αὐτῆς *inside the city* Lk 21.21; ἐκ
μέσου *from, from among;*
αἴρω ἐκ τοῦ μέσου *set aside*
Col 2.14; γίνομαι ἐκ μέσου

be removed, disappear 2 Th
2.7; διέρχομαι διὰ μέσον
cross the borderland between
Lk 17.11; σχίζω μέσον *tear
in two* Lk 23.45); (2) prep.
with gen. *in the middle, in
the midst* (Mt 14.24; Php
2.15)

μεσότοιχον, ου n *dividing
wall*

μεσουράνημα, τος n *mid-
heaven, high in the sky*

μεσόω *be in the middle, be half
over*

Μεσσίας, ου m *Messiah* (Aramaic and Hebrew equivalent
of Greek Χριστός)

μεστός, ή, όν *full*

μεστόω *fill* (pf. pass. *be full*)

μετά prep. with: (1) gen. *with,
in company with, among; by,
in; on the side of; against;*
(2) acc. *after, behind* (μετὰ
τό with inf. *after*)

μεταβαίνω (fut. μεταβήσο-
μαι; aor. μετέβην, impv.
μετάβα and μετάβηθι, ptc.
μεταβάς; pf. μεταβέβηκα)
leave, move, go, cross over

μεταβάλλομαι (aor. ptc. με-
ταβαλόμενος) *change one's
mind*

μετάγω *guide, direct, control*

μεταδίδωμι (inf. μεταδιδό-
ναι, ptc. μεταδιδούς; aor.
subj. μεταδῶ, impv. 3 sg.
μεταδότω, inf. μεταδοῦ-
ναι) *share, give, impart*

μετάθεσις, εως f removal; change; taking up (of Enoch)

μεταίρω (aor. μετῆρα) go away, leave

μετακαλέομαι send for, summon, invite

μετακινέω shift, move, dislodge

μεταλαμβάνω (aor. inf. μεταλαβεῖν) receive, share in; have, take (opportunity)

μετάλημψις, εως f receiving, accepting

μεταλλάσσω. (aor. μετήλλαξα) exchange

μεταμέλομαι regret, be sorry; change one's mind

μεταμορφόομαι be changed in form, be transformed

μετανοέω repent, have a change of heart, turn from one's sins, change one's ways

μετάνοια, ας f repentance, change of heart, turning from one's sins, change of way

μεταξύ: (1) prep. with gen. between, among (μ. ἀλλήλων τῶν λογισμῶν their conflicting thoughts or their thoughts which argue the case on either side Ro 2.15); (2) adv. meanwhile (Jn 4.31); after (τὸ μ. σάββατον the next Sabbath Ac 13.42)

μεταπέμπομαι (aor. impv. μετάπεμψαι) send for, summon

μετασταθῶ aor. pass. subj. of μεθίστημι

μεταστήσας aor. ptc. of μεθίστημι

μεταστρέφω (fut. pass. μεταστραφήσομαι) turn, alter, change; distort

μετασχηματίζω change, transform (midd. disguise); apply (1 Cor 4.6)

μετατίθημι (aor. μετέθηκα; aor. pass. μετετέθην) remove, take back; take up (of Enoch); change (of priesthood); distort (Jd 4); midd. desert, turn away (Ga 1.6)

μετατρέπω (aor. pass. impv. 3 sg. μετατραπήτω) turn, change, alter

μετέβην aor. of μεταβαίνω

μετέπειτα adv. afterwards

μετέστησα aor. of μεθίστημι

μετέχω (aor. μετέσχον; pf. μετέσχηκα) share in (something); eat (food), live on (milk); have (authority); belong to (He 7.13)

μετεωρίζομαι worry, be upset

μετήλλαξα aor. of μεταλλάσσω

μετῆρα aor. of μεταίρω

μετοικεσία, ας f carrying off

μετοικίζω (fut. μετοικιῶ; aor. μετῴκισα) make to move; send off

μετοχή, ῆς f partnership

μέτοχος, ου m one who shares in, partner; companion, comrade

μετρέω measure; deal out, give

μετρητής, οὖ m *measure* (a liquid measure of about 9 or 10 gallons)

μετριοπαθέω *be gentle* (*with*), *have feeling* (*for*)

μετρίως adv. *measurably* (οὐ μετρίως *immeasurably, greatly* Ac 20.12)

μέτρον, ου n *measure, degree, quantity* (οὐκ ἐκ μέτρου *without measure* Jn 3.34; κατὰ τὸ μέτρον τοῦ κανόνος οὗ ἐμέρισεν ἡμῖν ὁ θεὸς μέτρου, ἐφικέσθαι ἄχρι καὶ ὑμῶν *within the limits God assigned us, which allowed us to come as far as you* 2 Cor 10.13; κατ᾽ ἐνέργειαν ἐν μέτρῳ ἑνὸς ἑκάστου μέρους *by the proper working of each part* Eph 4.16)

μετῴκισα aor. of μετοικίζω

μέτωπον, ου n *forehead*

μέχρι and μέχρις: (1) prep. with gen. *until, to* (μέχρι τέλους *to the end*); *to the extent, to the point; as far as* (Ro 15.19); (2) conj. *until* (μέχρι οὗ *until*)

μή *not* (generally used with non-indicative verbs); used in questions when a negative answer is expected; · used with οὐ for emphasis or solemn assertion

μήγε in the combination εἰ δὲ μήγε *otherwise, for then; but if not*

μηδαμῶς adv. *no, by no means*

μηδέ negative particle *nor, and not* (μηδέ . . . μηδέ *neither . . . nor); not even*

μηδείς, μηδεμία, μηδέν: (1) *no one, nothing;* (2) adj. *no;* (3) μηδέν adv. *not at all, in no way*

μηδέποτε adv. *never*

μηδέπω adv. *not yet*

Μῆδος, ου m *Mede* (*Media* 3 G–3)

μηθέν = μηδέν

μηκέτι adv. *no longer, no more*

μῆκος, ους n *length*

μηκύνομαι *grow*

μηλωτή, ῆς f *sheepskin*

μήν intensive particle *indeed, surely* (εἰ μήν *surely* He 6.14)

μήν, μηνός m *month* (κατὰ μῆνα ἕκαστον *each month* Re 22.2)

μηνύω *make known, disclose; inform, report*

μήποτε: (1) conj. *lest, that . . . not, otherwise;* (2) interrog. particle *whether perhaps, perhaps;* (3) *never* (He 9.17)

μήπου (μή που) conj. *that . . . somewhere, that*

μήπω adv. *not yet*

μήπως (μή πως) conj. *that perhaps, lest somehow*

μηρός, οῦ m *thigh, leg*

μήτε *and not* (μήτε . . . μήτε *neither . . . nor*)

μήτηρ, τρός f *mother*

μήτι used in qu stions to indicate the expectation of a negative answer; sometimes

used to indicate that the
questioner is in doubt regarding the answer (Mt
12.23; Jn 4.29); εἰ μήτι
unless (Lk 9.13)

μήτιγε how much more, not to
speak of

μήτρα, ας f womb (πᾶν ἄρσεν
διανοῖγον μ. every firstborn
male Lk 2.23)

μητρολῴας, ου m one who
murders his mother

μιαίνω (pf. pass. **μεμίαμμαι**;
aor. pass. subj. **μιανθῶ**) defile, contaminate (of ritual
defilement Jn 18.28)

μίασμα, τος n corruption, defilement

μιασμός, οῦ m corruption, defilement

μίγμα, τος n mixture

μίγνυμι (aor. **ἔμιξα**; pf. pass.
μέμιγμαι) mix, mingle

μικρός, ά, όν little, small; of
least importance, insignificant, humble (ἀπὸ μικροῦ
ἕως μεγάλου from the least to
the greatest Ac 8.10; He
8.11); younger (Mk 15.40);
adv. μικρόν a little while, a
little farther (ἔτι μ. a little
longer Jn 13.33; 14.19; μετὰ
μ. a little later Mt 26.73);
μικρότερος least, smallest

Μίλητος, ου f Miletus (4 E–3)

μίλιον, ου n mile (of the
Roman mile which was 8
στάδια or about 1618
yards)

μιμέομαι imitate, follow another's example

μιμητής, οῦ m imitator, i. e.
one who is like another

μιμνήσκομαι (aor. **ἐμνήσθην**, impv. **μνήσθητι**; fut.
μνησθήσομαι; pf. **μέμνημαι**) remember, keep in mind,
call to mind; be concerned
about; be remembered (Ac
10.31; Re 16.19)

μισέω hate, despise; disregard,
be indifferent to (Mt 6.24;
Lk 16.13)

μισθαποδοσία, ας f reward;
retribution, punishment

μισθαποδότης, ου m rewarder

μίσθιος, ου m hired man,
laborer

μισθόομαι hire

μισθός, οῦ m pay, wages;
reward, recompense, gain; retribution, punishment

μίσθωμα, τος n expense, rent;
rented quarters

μισθωτός, οῦ m hired man,
laborer

Μιτυλήνη, ης f Mitylene (4
E–2)

Μιχαήλ m Michael (archangel)

μνᾶ, ᾶς f mina (Greek coin
worth 100 denarii or 1/60
of a talent)

Μνάσων, ωνος m Mnason
(Ac 21.16)

μνεία, ας f remembrance, mention

μνῆμα, τος n grave, tomb

μνημεῖον, ου n grave, tomb; monument (Lk 11.47)

μνήμη, ης f remembrance, memory

μνημονεύω remember, keep in mind, think of; make mention of (He 11.22)

μνημόσυνον, ου n memorial, something done to arouse the memory of another

μνησθήσομαι fut. of μιμνήσκομαι

μνήσθητι aor. impv. of μιμνήσκομαι

μνηστεύομαι be engaged, be promised in marriage

μογγιλάλος, ον either (1) a variant form of μογιλάλος or (2) an independent word mng. speaking in a hoarse voice

μογιλάλος, ον having difficulty in speaking; mute, dumb

μόγις adv. hardly, scarcely

μόδιος, ου m basket, bucket (a grain-measuring container of about 8 quarts)

μοιχαλίς, ίδος f adulteress; unfaithful (of men and women Jas 4.4); γενεὰ μ. unfaithful or godless people

μοιχάομαι commit adultery

μοιχεία, ας f adultery

μοιχεύω commit adultery

μοιχός, οῦ m adulterer

μόλις adv. with difficulty, hardly, scarcely

Μολόχ m Moloch (Canaanite god)

μολύνω defile, make unclean

μολυσμός, οῦ m defilement

μομφή, ῆς f cause for complaint, complaint

μονή, ῆς f room; μονὴν ποιῶ live (Jn 14.23)

μονογενής, ές only, unique

μονόομαι be left alone

μόνος, η, ον: (1) adj. only, alone (Mt 12.4; Php 4.15), κατὰ μόνας alone; (2) adv. μόνον only, alone

μονόφθαλμος, ον one-eyed

μορφή, ῆς f nature, form

μορφόω form (μέχρις οὗ μ. Χριστὸς ἐν ὑμῖν until Christ's nature be formed in you Ga 4.19)

μόρφωσις, εως f outward form (2 Tm 3.5); content, full content (Ro 2.20)

μοσχοποιέω make a calf

μόσχος, ου m calf, young bull

μουσικός, οῦ m musician

μόχθος, ου m labor, hardship

μυελός, οῦ m marrow (of bones)

μυέομαι learn the secret of

μῦθος, ου m myth, fanciful story

μυκάομαι roar

μυκτηρίζω mock, make a fool of

μυλικός, ή, όν pertaining to a mill (λίθος μ. millstone)

μύλινος, η, ον pertaining to a mill, millstone

μύλος, ου m *mill; millstone*
(μ. ὀνικός *large millstone
drawn by a donkey*)
Μύρα, ων n *Myra* (4 F–3)
μυριάς, άδος f *group of ten
thousand, myriad; countless
thousands*
μυρίζω *pour perfume on*
μύριοι, αι, α *ten thou-
sand*
μυρίος, α, ον *countless, thousands*
μύρον, ου n *ointment, perfume, oil*
Μυσία, ας f *Mysia* (4 E–2)
μυστήριον, ου n *secret, mys-
tery* (of something formerly
unknown but now revealed)

Μυτιλήνη alt. form of Μιτυλήνη
μυωπάζω *be shortsighted*
μώλωψ, ωπος m *wound*
μωμάομαι *find fault with;* aor.
pass. *be found fault with*
μῶμος, ου m *blemish,* i. e. *a
disgrace*
μωραίνω (aor. ἐμώρανα; aor.
pass. subj. μωρανθῶ) *make
foolish; make tasteless* (pass.
become tasteless)
μωρία, ας f *foolishness*
μωρολογία, ας f *foolish talk*
μωρός, ά, όν *foolish* (μωρέ
you worthless fool! Mt 5.22);
τὸ μ. *foolishness*
Μωϋσῆς, έως m *Moses*

N

Ναασσών m *Nahshon* (Mt 1.4;
Lk 3.32)
Ναγγαί m *Naggai* (Lk 3.25)
Ναζαρά, Ναζαρέθ and Ναζα-
ρέτ f *Nazareth* (2 C–3)
Ναζαρηνός, οῦ m *inhabitant
of Nazareth, Nazarene*
Ναζωραῖος, ου m *inhabitant
of Nazareth, Nazarene*
Ναθάμ m *Nathan* (Lk 3.31)
Ναθαναήλ m *Nathanael*
ναί *yes; yes indeed, indeed, cer-
tainly; certainly so, surely*
Ναιμάν m *Naaman* (Lk 4.27)

Ναΐν f *Nain* (2 C–4)
ναός, οῦ m *temple, inner part
of Jewish temple, sanctuary;
model of a temple* or *shrine*
(Ac 19.24)
Ναούμ m *Nahum* (Lk
3.25)
Ναραῖος alt. form of Ναζωραῖος
νάρδος, ου f *oil of nard* (an
aromatic plant)
Νάρκισσος, ου m *Narcissus*
(Ro 16.11)
ναυαγέω *be shipwrecked*

ναύκληρος, ου m *ship-owner; captain*

ναῦς acc. ναῦν f *ship*

ναύτης, ου m *sailor*

Ναχώρ m *Nahor* (Lk 3.34)

νεανίας, ου m *young man*

νεανίσκος, ου m *young man*

Νέα Πόλις f *Neapolis* (4 D–2)

νεῖκος, ους n alt. form of νῖκος

νεκρός, ά, όν *dead, lifeless* (ὁ ν. *a dead person, corpse;* ἐπὶ ν. *in the case of dead persons or at death* He 9.17); *useless, ineffective*

νεκρόω *put to death* (pf. pass. ptc. *as good as dead*)

νέκρωσις, εως f *death; barrenness* (of the womb of a woman who has no children)

νεομηνία, ας f *new moon festival*

νέος, α, ον *new, fresh; young;* νεώτερος *young, younger, youngest*

νεότης, ητος f *youth, youthfulness*

νεόφυτος, ον *recently converted*

νεύω *motion, nod*

νεφέλη, ης f *cloud*

Νεφθαλίμ m *Naphtali:* (1) an Israelite tribe; (2) and its territory (1 C–3, 2 C–3)

νέφος, ους n *cloud*

νεφρός, οῦ m (lit. *kidney*) *mind, thought*

νεωκόρος, ου m *temple keeper*

νεωτερικός, ή, όν *youthful, associated with youth*

νή *by* (with the acc. to denote a solemn oath)

νήθω *spin*

νηπιάζω *be a child*

νήπιος, α, ον *baby, infant, child; immature; innocent; under age* (Ga 4.1)

Νηρεύς, έως m *Nereus* (Ro 16.15)

Νηρί m *Neri* (Lk 3.27)

νησίον, ου n *small island*

νῆσος, ου f *island*

νηστεία, ας f *fasting, going without food as a religious duty; hunger, starvation; the Fast* (of the Day of Atonement Ac 27.9)

νηστεύω *fast, go without food as a religious duty*

νῆστις, ιδος acc. pl. νήστεις m and f *hungry, without food*

Νήφα alt. form of Νύμφα

νηφάλιος, α, ον *temperate, sober*

νήφω *be sober; be self-controlled*

Νίγερ m *Niger* (Ac 13.1)

νίθω alt. form of νήθω

Νικάνωρ, ορος m *Nicanor* (Ac 6.5)

νικάω intrans. and trans. *conquer, overcome; win the verdict* (Ro 3.4)

νίκη, ης f *victory*

Νικόδημος, ου m *Nicodemus*

Νικολαΐτης, ου m *Nicolaitan* (Re 2.6, 15)

Νικόλαος, ου m *Nicolaus* (Ac 6.5)

Νικόπολις, εως f *Nicopolis* (4 C–2)

νῖκος, ους n *victory*

Νινευίτης, ου m *inhabitant of Nineveh* (*Nineveh* 3 E–2)

νιπτήρ, ῆρος m *washbasin*

νίπτω (aor. midd. impv. **νίψαι**) *wash;* midd. *wash oneself, wash for oneself*

νοέω *understand, perceive, discern; think over, consider; imagine, think* (Eph 3.20)

νόημα, τος n *mind, thought; method, design, plot* (2 Cor 2.11)

νόθος, η, ον *illegitimate* (as of children)

νομή, ῆς f *pasture; spreading* (ν. ἔχω *spread, eat away* 2 Tm 2.17)

νομίζω *think, suppose, assume* (οὗ ἐνομίζομεν προσευχὴν εἶναι *where we thought there would be a place of prayer* Ac 16.13); pass. *be the custom* (οὗ ἐνομίζετο προσευχὴ εἶναι *where it was customary for a place of prayer to be* Ac 16.13)

νομικός, ή, όν *pertaining to the law;* ὁ ν. *lawyer*

νομίμως adv. *lawfully, legitimately, according to the rules*

νόμισμα, τος n *coin, money*

νομοδιδάσκαλος, ου m *teacher* or *interpreter of the law*

νομοθεσία, ας f (God's) *giving of the law* (to Israel)

νομοθετέομαι *be given the law* (ὁ λαὸς γὰρ ἐπ᾽ αὐτῆς νε. *on the basis of it,* i. e. *the Levitical priesthood, the people were given the law* He 7.11); *be based on* (He 8.6)

νομοθέτης, ου m *lawgiver*

νόμος, ου m *law* (often of the Jewish sacred tradition; ὁ νόμος καὶ οἱ προφῆται *the Old Testament;* νόμος τοῦ ἀνδρός *marriage law* Ro 7.2); *principle, rule*

νοσέω *have an unhealthy desire* (περί) *for*

νόσημα, τος n *disease, illness*

νόσος, ου f *disease, illness*

νοσσιά, ᾶς f *brood*

νοσσίον, ου n *young bird* (pl. *brood*)

νοσσός, οῦ m *young* (of a bird)

νοσφίζομαι *keep back for oneself; pilfer, embezzle*

νότος, ου m *south wind; south*

νουθεσία, ας f *instruction; warning*

νουθετέω *instruct, teach; warn*

νουνεχῶς adv. *wisely, sensibly*

νοῦς, νοός, νοΐ, νοῦν m *mind,*

thought, reason; attitude, intention, purpose; understanding, discernment

Νύμφα, ας f *Nympha* or **Νυμφᾶς, ᾶ** m *Nymphas* (Col 4.15)

νύμφη, ης f *bride; daughter-in-law*

νυμφίος, ου m *bridegroom*

νυμφών, ῶνος m *wedding hall* (υἱὸς τοῦ ν. *bridegroom's attendant, wedding guest*)

νῦν adv. *now, at the present* (often with article as equivalent of adj. *now, present* or noun *the present, the present time,* e.g. ἀπὸ τοῦ νῦν *from now on;* τὰ νῦν *but now, and now;* τὸ νῦν ἔχον *for the present* Ac 24.25); *now, then, indeed;* ἄγε νῦν cf. ἄγω

νυνί adv. (originally an emphatic form of *νῦν*) *now*

νύξ, νυκτός f *night*

νύσσω (aor. ἔνυξα) *prick, stab*

νυστάζω *grow drowsy; be asleep, be idle*

νυχθήμερον, ου n *a night and a day*

Νῶε m *Noah*

νωθρός, ά, όν *lazy, sluggish; hard* (of hearing)

νῶτος, ου m *back*

Ξ

ξαίνω *comb, clean* (of wool)

ξενία, ας f *place of lodging, room, guest room*

ξενίζω *entertain as a guest* (pass. *live, stay*); *surprise, astonish*

ξενοδοχέω *show hospitality*

ξένος, η, ον *strange, foreign, unusual;* ὁ ξ. *stranger, foreigner; host* (Ro 16.23)

ξέστης, ου m *jug, pitcher, pot*

ξηραίνω (aor. ἐξήρανα; aor. pass. ἐξηράνθην; pf. pass. ἐξήραμμαι) *dry up, scorch;* pass. *wither; cease* (of a hemorrhage); *be ripe* (of a harvest); *become stiff* (Mk 9.18)

ξηρός, ά, όν *dry* (ἡ ξηρά *land* Mt 23.15); *withered, paralyzed*

ξύλινος, η, ον *wooden*

ξύλον, ου n *wood, tree; club; cross; stocks* (Ac 16.24)

ξυράομαι *shave, have oneself shaved*

Ο

ὁ, ἡ, τό pl. οἱ, αἱ, τά the; this, that; he, she, it; τοῦ with inf. in order that, so that, with the result that, that

ὀγδοήκοντα eighty

ὄγδοος, η, ον eighth

ὄγκος, ου m impediment, something that gets in one's way

ὅδε, ἥδε, τόδε this; he, she, it; εἰς τήνδε τὴν πόλιν into such and such a city (Jas 4.13)

ὁδεύω travel, be on a journey

ὁδηγέω lead, guide

ὁδηγός, οῦ m guide, leader

ὁδοιπορέω travel, be en route

ὁδοιπορία, ας f journey

ὁδός, οῦ f way, road; journey (σαββάτου ἔχον ὁδόν a Sabbath day's journey away, i. e. about half a mile Ac 1.12); way of life, conduct; Way (of the Christian faith and life)

ὀδούς, ὀδόντος m tooth

ὀδυνάομαι be in great pain; be deeply distressed or worried

ὀδύνη, ης f pain, sorrow

ὀδυρμός, οῦ m mourning, grieving

Ὀζίας, ου m Uzziah (Mt 1.8, 9)

ὄζω give off an odor, stink

ὅθεν adv. where, from where; and so, therefore, for which reason

ὀθόνη, ης f large piece of cloth

ὀθόνιον, ου n linen cloth, wrapping

οἶδα (pf. with pres. mng. ἴστε may be 2 pl. ind. or impv., ind. 3 pl. οἴδασι and ἴσασι, subj. εἰδῶ, inf. εἰδέναι, masc. ptc. εἰδώς, fem. ptc. εἰδυῖα; plpf. ᾔδειν; fut. εἰδήσω) know, understand, perceive (τοῦτο γὰρ ἴστε γινώσκοντες be very sure of this or you know this very well Eph 5.5); experience, learn, know how; be acquainted with, recognize, acknowledge; remember (1 Cor 1.16); pay proper respect to (1 Th 5.12)

οἰέσθω impv. 3 sg. of οἶμαι

οἰκεῖος, ου m member of the household; member of a family (1 Tm 5.8)

οἰκετεία, ας f household (of slaves)

οἰκέτης, ου m house servant, servant

οἰκέω intrans. live, dwell; trans. live in (1 Tm 6.16)

οἴκημα, τος n prison cell

οἰκητήριον, ου n dwelling, home

οἰκία, ας f house, home, property; family, household

οἰκιακός, οῦ m member of a household

οἰκοδεσποτέω run the household

οἰκοδεσπότης, ου m householder, landowner, master

οἰκοδομέω build, erect; build up, encourage, strengthen, edify; rebuild, restore

οἰκοδομή, ῆς f upbuilding, strengthening, encouragement; building, structure

οἰκοδόμος, ου m builder

οἰκονομέω be manager, be steward

οἰκονομία, ας f management of a household; task, work, responsibility; (divine) plan (Eph 1.10; 3.9; 1 Tm 1.4)

οἰκονόμος, ου m steward, manager; treasurer (of a city); trustee (Ga 4.2)

οἶκος, ου m house, home (κατ' οἶκον or κατὰ τοὺς οἴκους from house to house; ἡ κατ' οἶκον αὐτῶν ἐκκλησία the church in their house); family, household; nation, people; temple, sanctuary

οἰκουμένη, ης f world; inhabited earth; mankind; Roman Empire

οἰκουργός, όν devoted to home duties

οἰκτιρμός, οῦ m compassion, mercy, pity

οἰκτίρμων, ον merciful, compassionate

οἰκτίρω (fut. **οἰκτιρήσω**) have compassion on

οἶμαι (contracted from **οἴο-μαι**; impv. 3 sg. **οἰέσθω**, ptc. **οἰόμενος**) suppose, think

οἰνοπότης, ου m drinker, drunkard

οἶνος, ου m wine

οἰνοφλυγία, ας f drunkenness

οἷος, α, ον relative pro. such as, as, of what kind; οἷος ... τοιοῦτος as ... so; such as (Mk 13.19); οὐχ οἷον δὲ ὅτι but it is not as though or perhaps it is not possible (Ro 9.6); indicating exclamation (e. g. οἴους διωγμοὺς ὑπήνεγκα the terrible persecutions I endured! 2 Tm 3.11); οἷος δήποτ' οὖν whatever, whatever kind of (Jn 5.4)

οἴσω fut. of **φέρω**

ὀκνέω delay, hesitate

ὀκνηρός, ά, όν lazy; troublesome, irksome (Php 3.1)

ὀκταήμερος, ον on the eighth day

ὀκτώ eight

ὄλεθρος, ου m destruction, ruin

ὀλιγοπιστία, ας f littleness of faith

ὀλιγόπιστος, ον of little faith

ὀλίγος, η, ον little, small, pl. few (ἐν ὀλίγῳ in a short while, briefly; πρὸς ὀλίγον for a *little while, in only a small way;* δι᾿ ὀλίγων *briefly*); adv.

ὀλίγον *a little, only a little*

ὀλιγόψυχος, ον *fainthearted, discouraged*

ὀλιγωρέω *think lightly of*

ὀλίγως adv. *barely, just*

ὀλοθρευτής, οῦ m *destroying angel*

ὀλοθρεύω *destroy* (ὁ ὀλοθρεύων = ὀλοθρευτής)

ὀλοκαύτωμα, τος n *whole burnt offering*

ὀλοκληρία, ας f *full health, soundness*

ὀλόκληρος, ον *sound, whole, complete*

ὀλολύζω *wail, moan*

ὅλος, η, ον *whole, all, complete, entire* (δι᾿ ὅλου *throughout); altogether, wholly* (Jn 9.34; 13.10)

ὀλοτελής, ές *wholly, in every part*

᾿Ολυμπᾶς, ᾶ m *Olympas* (Ro 16.15)

ὅλυνθος, ου m *late fig, unripe fig*

ὅλως adv. *at all; actually*

ὄμβρος, ου m *shower, rainstorm*

ὀμείρομαι *yearn for, long for*

ὀμιλέω *talk, converse*

ὀμιλία, ας f *company, association*

ὄμιλος, ου m *crowd, multitude, people*

ὀμίχλη, ης f *mist, fog*

ὄμμα, τος n *eye*

ὀμνύω and **ὄμνυμι** (inf. ὀμνύναι; aor. ὤμοσα, inf. ὀμόσαι) *swear, vow, make an oath*

ὀμοθυμαδόν adv. *with one mind, by common consent, together* (γινόμενοι ὁ. *unanimously* Ac 15.25)

ὀμοιάζω *be like, resemble*

ὀμοιοπαθής, ές *like in every way*

ὅμοιος, α, ον *of the same nature as, like*

ὀμοιότης, ητος f *likeness, similarity;* κατὰ πάντα καθ᾿ ὁ. *in everything the same way* (*we are*) (He 4.15)

ὀμοιόω *make like* (pass. resemble, be like; ὀμοιωθεὶς ἀνθρώπῳ *in human form* Ac 14.11); *compare*

ὀμοίωμα, τος n *likeness* (ἐν ὁ. ἀνθρώπων γενόμενος *being born like a man* Php 2.7); *appearance* (Re 9.7); *something made to look like, image* (Ro 1.23)

ὀμοίως adv. *in the same way, likewise, too, so*

ὀμοίωσις, εως f *likeness*

ὀμολογέω *confess; admit; declare, say plainly; promise; claim* (Tt 1.16); *give thanks to* or *praise* (He 13.15)

ὀμολογία, ας f *confession, profession*

ὀμολογουμένως adv. *undeniably*

ὀμόσαι aor. inf. of **ὀμνύω**

ὁμότεχνος, ον *of the same trade*

ὁμοῦ adv. *together*

ὁμόφρων, ον *of one mind*

ὅμως adv. *even; nevertheless*

ὀναίμην aor. opt. of ὀνίναμαι

ὄναρ n *dream* (κατ' ὄναρ *in a dream*)

ὀνάριον, ου n *(young) donkey*

ὀνειδίζω *reproach, denounce, insult*

ὀνειδισμός, οῦ m *reproach, insult, abuse; disgrace, shame*

ὄνειδος, ους n *disgrace*

'Ονήσιμος, ου m *Onesimus* (Col 4.9; Phm 10)

'Ονησίφορος, ου m *Onesiphorus* (2 Tm 1.16; 4.19)

ὀνικός, ή, όν *of a donkey* (cf. μύλος)

ὀνίναμαι (aor. opt. ὀναίμην) *benefit, profit, have joy*

ὄνομα, τος n *name* (κατ' ὄ. *by name); title; person; authority, power; status, category* (e. g. εἰς ὄ. προφήτου *because he is a prophet;* ἐν ὀ. ὅτι Χριστοῦ ἐστε *because you are followers of Christ* Mk 9.41); *reputation* (Mk 6.14; Re 3.1)

ὀνομάζω *name, call* (pass. *be known* or *heard of* Ro 15.20); *pronounce* (Ac 19.13); *mention, talk about* (Eph 5.3)

ὄνος, ου m and f *donkey*

ὄντως adv. *really, certainly, indeed; real* (used as attributive adj.)

ὄξος, ους n *sour wine*

ὀξύς, εῖα, ύ *sharp; swift* (Ro 3.15)

ὀπή, ῆς f *opening, hole, cave*

ὄπισθεν: (1) adv. *behind, from behind; on the back, outside* (Re 5.1); (2) prep. with gen. *behind; after* (Mt 15.23)

ὀπίσω: (1) prep. with gen. *after* (after ἔρχομαι or related verbs often *follow, be a disciple); behind; away from* (Mt 16.23; Mk 8.33); (2) adv. *back, behind* (εἰς τὰ ὀπίσω *back; around* Jn 20.14; τὰ ὀπίσω *what lies behind* Php 3.13)

ὁπλίζομαι *arm oneself with*

ὅπλον, ου n *weapon; tool, instrument*

ὁποῖος, α, ον correlative pro. *of what sort, as, such as* (ὁποῖός ποτε *whatever* Ga 2.6)

ὁπότε adv. *when*

ὅπου adv. *where* (ὅπου ἄν or ὅπου ἐάν *wherever, whenever); whereas, while*

ὀπτάνομαι *appear, be seen*

ὀπτασία, ας f *vision*

ὀπτός, ή, όν *broiled, baked*

ὀπώρα, ας f *fruit*

ὅπως (or ὅπως ἄν) *that, in order that*

ὅραμα, τος n *vision; sight, something seen* (Ac 7.31)

ὅρασις, εως f *vision; appearance*

ὁρατός, ή, όν *visible*

ὁράω (impf. 3 pl. ἑώρων; fut. ὄψομαι; aor. εἶδα and εἶδον, ptc. ἰδών, impv. ἴδετε; pf. ἑώρακα and ἑόρακα; aor. pass. ὤφθην, ptc. ὀφθείς; fut. pass. ὀφθήσομαι) trans. see, observe, notice (pass. appear); perceive, understand, recognize; experience; visit, come to see (He 13.23); intrans. make sure, see to, take care (ὅρα μή do not do that)

ὀργή, ῆς f wrath, anger; retribution, punishment; revenge

ὀργίζομαι be angry, be furious

ὀργίλος, η, ον quick-tempered

ὀργυιά, ᾶς f fathom (six feet)

ὀρέγομαι be eager for, long for, desire

ὀρεινή, ῆς f hill country

ὄρεξις, εως f lustful passion

ὀρθοποδέω be consistent (πρός) with or make progress (πρός) towards

ὀρθός, ή, όν straight; upright, erect

ὀρθοτομέω use or interpret correctly

ὀρθρίζω come early in the morning

ὀρθρινός, ή, όν early in the morning

ὄρθρος, ου m early morning (cf. βαθύς Lk 24.1; ὑπὸ τὸν ὄρθρον at daybreak Ac 5.21)

ὀρθῶς adv. rightly, correctly, properly; plainly, without any trouble (Mk 7.35)

ὁρίζω decide, determine; appoint, designate

ὅριον, ου n territory, region; neighborhood, vicinity

ὁρκίζω beg (someone) τὸν θεόν in the name of God; command (someone) τὸν Ἰησοῦν in the name of Jesus

ὅρκος, ου m oath, vow

ὁρκωμοσία, ας f oath, taking an oath

ὁρμάω rush

ὁρμή, ῆς f impulse, attempt; mind, will

ὅρμημα, τος n violence

ὄρνεον, ου n bird

ὄρνις, ιθος f hen

ὁροθεσία, ας f limit, boundary

ὄρος, ους n mountain, hill, mount

ὅρος, ου m limit, boundary

ὀρύσσω (aor. ὤρυξα) dig; dig a hole in

ὀρφανός, ή, όν orphaned (noun orphan Mk 12.40); alone, friendless (Jn 14.18)

ὀρχέομαι dance

ὅς, ἥ, ὅ relative pro. who, which, what, that (ὃς ἄν or ὃς ἐάν whoever; ὃς μὲν ... ὃς δέ one ... another); he, she

ὁσάκις adv. as often as, whenever

ὅσιος, α, ον holy (τὰ ὅσια sacred promises or blessings Ac 13.34); devout, pious

ὁσιότης, ητος f holiness

ὁσίως adv. in a manner pleasing to God

ὀσμή, ῆς f *fragrance* (ὀσμὴ
εὐωδίας *sweet-smelling offering* or *fragrant scent* Php
4.18)

ὅσος, η, ον *correlative pro. as
much as, how much; as great
as, how great; as far as, how
far; whoever* (= ὅσος ἄν, ὅσος
ἐάν); pl. *as many as, all,
everyone;* ἐφ' ὅσον *inasmuch
as, while;* καθ' ὅσον *just as,
as* (καθ' ὅσον . . . κατὰ το-
σοῦτο or ὅσα . . . τοσοῦτον
*to the degree that . . . to the
same degree;* κατὰ πάντα ὅσα
ἄν *whatever* Ac 3.22); ὅσῳ
as, just as, to the degree that
(He 8.6); ὅσον . . . μᾶλλον
περισσότερον *the more . . .
the more* (Mk 7.36); το-
σούτῳ . . . ὅσῳ (*by*) *as much
. . . as* (He 1.4); ὅσον χρόνον
as long as (Mk 2.19); ἔτι
γὰρ μικρὸν ὅσον ὅσον *for
in a very short while* (He
10.37)

ὅσπερ, ἥπερ, ὅπερ *who, which*

ὀστέον, ου and ὀστοῦν, οῦ n
bone

ὅστις, ἥτις, ὅ τι *who, which;
whoever, whichever; anyone,
someone*

ὀστράκινος, η, ον *made of
baked clay, pottery*

ὄσφρησις, εως f *sense of
smell, nose*

ὀσφῦς, ύος f *waist; reproduc-
tive organs* (καρπὸς τῆς ὀ.
descendant Ac 2.30; ἐξέρ-

χομαι ἐκ τῆς ὀ. *be descended
from* He 7.5)

ὅταν *when, whenever, as often
as* (εἰ μὴ ὅταν *until* Mk 9.9)

ὅτε conj. *when, at which time;
while, as long as*

ὅτι conj. *that* (τί ὅτι *why?* ὡς
ὅτι *that* generally introducing the subjective opinion of
the writer, e.g. 2 Cor 5.19;
11.21; 2 Th 2.2); *because,
for, since;* may mark the
beginning of direct discourse

οὗ adv. *where* (οὗ ἐάν *wherever); to which*

οὔ *no*

οὐ (οὐκ, οὐχ) *not* (generally
used with indicative verbs);
used in questions when an
affirmative answer is ex-
pected

οὐά interj. *aha! ha!*

οὐαί: (1) interj. *how horrible
it will be!* (2) f noun *horror,
disaster, calamity*

οὐδαμῶς adv. *by no means,
not at all*

οὐδέ *neither, nor, and not*
(οὐδὲ . . . οὐδέ *neither . . .
nor;* ἀλλ' οὐδέ *neither, not
even); not, not even*

οὐδείς, οὐδεμία, οὐδέν *no
one, nothing; no; worth nothing;* οὐδέν *not at all, in no
respect*

οὐδέποτε adv. *never*

οὐδέπω adv. *not yet* (οὐδέπω
οὐδείς *no one ever before)*

οὐθείς = οὐδείς

οὐκέτι adv. *no longer, no more* (οὐκέτι οὐ μή *never again*)

οὐκοῦν adv. *so, then*

οὖν *therefore, then; thus, so, accordingly*

οὔπω adv. *not yet* (οὐδεὶς οὔπω *no one ever before*)

οὐρά, ᾶς f *tail*

οὐράνιος, ον *heavenly, in heaven, from heaven*

οὐρανόθεν adv. *from heaven*

οὐρανός, οῦ m *heaven* (also used of God to avoid mention of the sacred name); *sky*

Οὐρβανός, οῦ m *Urbanus* (Ro 16.9)

Οὐρίας, ου m *Uriah* (Mt 1.6)

οὖς, ὠτός n *ear* (πρὸς τὸ οὖς λαλέω *whisper* Lk 12.3); *hearing*

οὐσία, ας f *property, money, wealth*

οὔτε adv. *not, no, nor* (οὔτε . . . οὔτε *neither . . . nor*)

οὗτος, αὕτη, τοῦτο demonstrative pro. and adj. *this, this one; he, she, it;* τοῦτ᾽ ἔστιν *that is, which means*

οὕτω and **οὕτως**: (1) adv. *in this way, thus, so, in the same way, like this* (ἔχειν οὕτως often *be so* or *true*; τὸ οὕτως εἶναι *to remain as one is* 1 Cor 7.26); *as follows;* (2) adj. *such, of such kind* (ὁ μὲν οὕτως, ὁ δὲ οὕτως *one of one kind and one of another* 1 Cor 7.7)

οὐχί (emphatic form of **οὐ**) *not; no, no indeed;* used in questions when an affirmative answer is expected

ὀφειλέτης, ου m *one who is under obligation, debtor; one who is guilty, offender, sinner*

ὀφειλή, ῆς f *debt; what is due* (with specific reference to conjugal rights 1 Cor 7.3)

ὀφείλημα, τος n *debt* (κατὰ ὀ. *as a debt* Ro 4.4); *wrong, sin, guilt*

ὀφείλω *owe; ought, must, be bound* or *obligated; sin against, wrong* (Lk 11.4)

ὄφελον (fixed form introducing an unattainable wish) *would that, I wish*

ὄφελος, ους n *gain, benefit* (τί τὸ ὄφελος *what good is it?* Jas 2.14, 16)

ὀφθαλμοδουλία, ας f *service rendered merely for the sake of impressing others*

ὀφθαλμός, οῦ m *eye* (ὀφθαλμὸς πονηρός *envy, jealousy* Mk 7.22; οἷς κατ᾽ ὀφθαλμούς *before whose eyes* Ga 3.1); *sight* (Ac 1.9)

ὀφθείς aor. pass. ptc. of **ὁράω**

ὀφθήσομαι fut. pass. of **ὁράω**

ὄφις, εως m *snake, serpent*

ὀφρῦς, ύος f *brow* (of a hill)

ὀχλέομαι *trouble, harass*

ὀχλοποιέω *gather a crowd* or *mob*

ὄχλος, ου m *crowd, multitude; (common) people; mob*

ὀχύρωμα, τος n *stronghold, fortress*

ὀψάριον, ου n *fish*

ὀψέ: (1) adv. *late in the day, evening;* (2) prep. with gen. *after*

ὀψία, ας f *evening*

ὄψιμος, ου m *late rain* (of the rain that comes late in the season), *spring rain*

ὄψιος, α, ον *late*

ὄψις, εως f *face;* κατ᾽ ὄψιν *by outward appearances, by external standards*

ὄψομαι fut. of **ὁράω**

ὀψώνιον, ου n *pay, wages, compensation; support* (2 Cor 11.8); *expense* (1 Cor 9.7)

Π

παγιδεύω *trap, entangle*

παγίς, ίδος f *snare, trap*

παθεῖν aor. inf. of **πάσχω**

πάθημα, τος n *suffering; passion, desire* (Ro 7.5; Ga 5.24)

παθητός, ή, όν *subject to suffering, must suffer*

πάθος, ους n *lustful passion*

παθών, παθοῦσα aor. masc. and fem. ptc. of **πάσχω**

παιδαγωγός, οῦ m *instructor, teacher, guide*

παιδάριον, ου n *boy*

παιδεία, ας f *discipline; instruction, training*

παιδευτής, οῦ m *teacher; one who disciplines or corrects*

παιδεύω *instruct, train, teach; discipline, correct; whip, scourge, beat*

παιδιόθεν adv. *from childhood*

παιδίον, ου n *child; infant*

παιδίσκη, ης f *maid, slave-girl, slave*

παίζω *dance, play*

παῖς, παιδός m and f *servant, slave; child, boy, girl*

παίω *strike, hit; sting* (Re 9.5)

πάλαι adv. *long ago; formerly; all this time* (2 Cor 12.19); *already* (Mk 15.44)

παλαιός, ά, όν *old; former*

παλαιότης, ητος f *age, oldness* (δουλεύω ἐν π. γράμματος *serve in the old way of a written law* Ro. 7.6)

παλαιόω *make or declare old or obsolete;* pass. *become old or obsolete, wear out*

πάλη, ης f *struggle, fight*

παλιγγενεσία, ας f *rebirth, new birth; new age, next world*

πάλιν adv. *again, once more* (εἰς τὸ πάλιν = πάλιν 2 Cor 13.2); *back; furthermore; on the other hand, yet*

παμπληθεί adv. *together, one and all*

Παμφυλία, ας f *Pamphylia* (4 F-3)

πανδοχεῖον, ου n *inn*

πανδοχεύς, έως m *inn-keeper*

πανήγυρις, εως f *festal gathering, joyful gathering*

πανοικεί adv. *with one's entire household*

πανοπλία, ας f *armor*

πανουργία, ας f *trickery, deceit, craftiness, cunning*

πανοῦργος, ον *tricky, crafty, cunning*

πανταχῇ adv. *everywhere*

πανταχοῦ adv. *everywhere*

παντελής, ές *complete;* εἰς τὸ π. *fully* or *at all* (Lk 13.11), *forever, completely* (He 7.25)

πάντῃ adv. *in every way*

πάντοθεν adv. *on all sides, entirely; from every quarter, from all directions*

παντοκράτωρ, ορος m *the Almighty* (of God)

πάντοτε adv. *always, at all times*

πάντως adv. *by all means, surely, certainly, doubtless;* οὐ π. *not at all, by no means; I did not mean* (1 Cor 5.10)

παρά prep. with: (1) gen. *from, of* (τὰ παρά τινος *one's provisions, money* or *gift;* οἱ

παρ᾽ αὐτοῦ *his family* Mk 3.21); *by, with;* (2) dat. *with, in the presence of, before; in the judgment of; near, beside; for;* (3) acc. *beside, by, at; on, along; to; than, more than, above; rather than; contrary to;* παρὰ τοῦτο *because of this* (1 Cor 12.15, 16); παρὰ μίαν *less one* (2 Cor 11.24)

παραβαίνω (aor. παρέβην) trans. *break, disobey;* intrans. *turn away, leave*

παραβάλλω (aor. παρέβαλον) *arrive, come near*

παράβασις, εως f (lit. *overstepping*) *disobedience, sin; breaking, violation*

παραβάτης, ου m *one who breaks* or *disobeys* (God's Law)

παραβιάζομαι *urge; persuade*

παραβολεύομαι *risk*

παραβολή, ῆς f *parable, proverb; figure, symbol* (ἥτις π. εἰς *this is a figure which refers to* He 9.9; ἐν π. *so to speak* He 11.19)

παραγγελία, ας f *order, command; instruction*

παραγγέλλω (aor. παρήγγειλα, ptc. παραγγείλας) *command, order* (παραγγελίᾳ παραγγέλλω *give strict orders* Ac 5.28)

παραγίνομαι (aor. παρεγενόμην, subj. παραγένωμαι) *come, arrive; appear;*

come to one's defense, stand
by (2 Tm 4.16)
παράγω pass by, pass on;
pass. (and sometimes act.)
pass away, disappear
παραδειγματίζω expose to
public ridicule
παράδεισος, ου m paradise
παραδέχομαι accept, receive;
welcome; acknowledge, recognize
παραδίδωμι (pres. 2 sg. **παρα-
δίδως**, subj. 3 sg. **παρα-
διδῷ** and **παραδιδοῖ**, inf.
παραδιδόναι, ptc. **παραδι-
δούς**; impf. 3 sg. **παρεδίδου**, 3 pl. **παρεδίδουν**
and **παρεδίδοσαν**; fut. **πα-
ραδώσω**; aor. **παρέδωκα**,
3 pl. **παρέδωκαν** and **παρέδοσαν**, subj. 3 sg. **παραδῷ**
and **παραδοῖ**, inf. **παρα-
δοῦναι**, ptc. **παραδούς**; pf.
ptc. **παραδεδωκώς**; plpf. 3
pl. **παραδεδώκεισαν**; pf.
midd. **παραδέδομαι**; aor.
pass. **παρεδόθην**, subj. **πα-
ραδοθῶ**, inf. **παραδοθῆναι**,
ptc. **παραδοθείς**; fut. pass.
παραδοθήσομαι) hand or
give over, deliver up (pass.
often be arrested); betray,
deliver (to death); deliver,
entrust, commit, give; hand
down, pass on; commend
(Ac 14.26; 15.40); risk (Ac
15.26); permit (ὅταν παραδοῖ ὁ καρπός when the crop
permits, i. e. is ripe Mk 4.29)

παράδοξος, ον incredible, unusual
παράδοσις, εως f tradition (of
teachings, etc. handed down
from one group or genera-
tion to another)
παραδῷ aor. subj. 3 sg. of
παραδίδωμι
παραζηλόω make jealous
παραθαλάσσιος, α, ον by the
sea or lake
παραθεῖναι aor. inf. of **παρατίθημι**
παραθεωρέω overlook, neglect
παραθήκη, ης f what is entrusted to one's care
παραθήσω fut. of **παρατίθημι**
παράθου aor. midd. impv. of
παρατίθημι
παραινέω (impf. 3 sg. **παρή-
νει**) advise, urge
παραιτέομαι (impf. **παρητούμην**; pf. ptc. **παρῃτη-
μένος**) ask for, request; excuse (ἔχε με π. please accept
my apologies Lk 14.18b, 19);
keep away from, have nothing
to do with; ask to escape
(death); do not include
(1 Tm 5.11); refuse to hear
(He 12.25); beg (He 12.19)
παρακαθέζομαι sit, seat oneself
παρακαλέω (pf. pass. **παρα-
κέκλημαι**; aor. pass. **παρεκλήθην**, subj. **παρακληθῶ**;
fut. pass. **παρακληθήσομαι**)
beg, urge; encourage, speak
words of encouragement; re-

quest, ask, appeal to; console, comfort, cheer up; invite, summon

παρακαλύπτομαι be hidden or concealed

παράκειμαι be present, be at hand

παράκλησις, εως f encouragement, help; comfort; appeal, request (μετὰ πολλῆς π. most insistently 2 Cor 8.4); salvation, setting free (Lk 2.25)

παράκλητος, ου m Helper, Intercessor (refers to the Holy Spirit and in 1 Jn 2.1 to Jesus Christ)

παρακοή, ῆς f disobedience, disloyalty

παρακολουθέω follow closely, give careful attention to; accompany, attend

παρακούω refuse to listen; pay no attention to or overhear (Mk 5.36)

παρακύπτω look into; stoop, bend over

παραλαμβάνω (fut. **παραλήμψομαι**; aor. **παρέλαβον**, impv. **παράλαβε**; fut. pass. **παραλημφθήσομαι**) take, take along; receive, accept (often of a tradition); learn (1 Th 4.1); take charge of (Jn 19.16b)

παραλέγομαι sail or coast along

παράλιος, ου f coastal district

παραλλαγή, ῆς f variation, change

παραλογίζομαι deceive, lead astray

παραλύομαι be paralyzed (ὁ παραλελυμένος paralytic); be weak (He 12.12)

παραλυτικός, οῦ m paralytic, cripple

παραμένω (aor. ptc. **παραμείνας**) stay, remain; continue in office (He 7.23); stand by, serve (Php 1.25)

παραμυθέομαι console, comfort; encourage, cheer up

παραμυθία, ας f comfort

παραμύθιον, ου n comfort; incentive

παρανομέω act contrary to the law

παρανομία, ας f offense, wrongdoing

παραπικραίνω (aor. **παρεπίκρανα**) rebel

παραπικρασμός, οῦ m rebellion (during the time of Israel's wandering in the wilderness)

παραπίπτω (aor. ptc. **παραπεσών**) fall away, commit apostasy

παραπλέω (aor. inf. **παραπλεῦσαι**) sail past

παραπλήσιον adv. nearly, almost

παραπλησίως adv. likewise

παραπορεύομαι pass by, go through, go

παράπτωμα, τος n sin; wrongdoing

παραρρέω (aor. pass. subj. παραρυῶ) drift away

παράσημος, ον marked with a figurehead (of a ship)

παρασκευάζω prepare a meal; midd. prepare oneself, get ready (pf. be ready)

παρασκευή, ῆς f day of preparation (before a sacred day)

παραστήσομαι fut. midd. of παρίστημι

παραστήσω fut. of παρίστημι

παρασχών aor. ptc. of παρέχω

παρατείνω (aor. παρέτεινα) prolong

παρατηρέω (used in act. and midd.) watch, watch closely; observe, keep (Ga 4.10)

παρατήρησις, εως f óbservation, watching for something

παρατίθημι (fut. παραθήσω; aor. παρέθηκα, inf. παραθεῖναι; aor. midd. παρεθέμην, impv. παράθου) place or put before; give, distribute; midd. commit, entrust; point out, prove (Ac 17.3)

παρατυγχάνω happen to be present

παραυτίκα (adv. used as adj.) momentary

παραφέρω (aor. impv. παρένεγκε) take away, remove; carry or lead away; drive along (by wind)

παραφίημι (aor. inf. παραφιέναι) neglect, put aside

παραφρονέω be out of one's mind

παραφρονία, ας f madness, insanity

παραχειμάζω spend the winter

παραχειμασία, ας f wintering

παραχρῆμα adv. immediately, at once

πάρδαλις, εως f leopard

παρέβαλον aor. of παραβάλλω

παρέβην aor. of παραβαίνω

παρεγενόμην aor. of παραγίνομαι

παρεδίδοσαν impf. 3 pl. of παραδίδωμι

παρεδίδου impf. 3 sg. of παραδίδωμι

παρεδίδουν impf. 3 pl. of παραδίδωμι

παρεδόθην aor. pass. of παραδίδωμι

παρέδοσαν aor. 3 pl. of παραδίδωμι

παρεδρεύω serve, wait upon

παρέδωκα aor. of παραδίδωμι

παρεθέμην aor. midd. of παρατίθημι

παρέθηκα aor. of παρατίθημι

παρειμένος pf. pass. ptc. of παρίημι

πάρειμι (inf. παρεῖναι (Ac 24.19; Ga 4.18, 20), ptc. παρών, παροῦσα, παρόν; impf. 3 pl. παρῆσαν) be present or here (πρὸς τὸ π. for the moment He 12.11; τὰ π. what one has He 13.5; ἡ π. ἀλήθεια the truth which you have 2 Pe 1.12); come

παρεῖναι aor. inf. of **παρίημι** (Lk 11.42) and the inf. of *πάρειμι* (Ac 24.19; Ga 4,18, 20)

παρεισάγω *bring in under false pretenses, bring in*

παρείσακτος, ον *brought in under false pretenses*

παρεισδύω *sneak in under false pretenses* or *slip in unnoticed*

παρεισέρχομαι (aor. **παρεισῆλθον**) *come in, slip in*

παρειστήκειν plpf. of **παρίστημι**

παρεισφέρω (aor. ptc. **παρεισενέγκας**) *exert* (*σπουδὴν πᾶσαν π. do one's best* 2 Pe 1.5)

παρεκλήθην aor. pass. of **παρακαλέω**

παρεκτός: (1) prep. with gen. *except, apart from;* (2) adv. used as adj. *external, unmentioned* (*χωρὶς τῶν π. apart from these external things* or *apart from those things left unmentioned* 2 Cor 11.28)

παρέλαβον aor. of **παραλαμβάνω**

παρελεύσομαι fut. of **παρέρχομαι**

παρεληλυθέναι pf. inf. of **παρέρχομαι**

παρεληλυθώς pf. ptc. of **παρέρχομαι**

παρελθεῖν aor. inf. of **παρέρχομαι**

παρεμβάλλω (fut. **παρεμβαλῶ**) *set up*

παρεμβολή, ῆς f *barracks; camp; army*

παρένεγκε aor. impv. of **παραφέρω**

παρενοχλέω *add extra difficulties*

παρέξῃ fut. midd. 2 sg. of **παρέχω**

παρεπίδημος, ου m *temporary resident; refugee*

παρεπίκρανα aor. of **παραπικραίνω**

παρέρχομαι (fut. **παρελεύσομαι**; aor. **παρῆλθον**, inf. **παρελθεῖν**; pf. inf. **παρεληλυθέναι**, ptc. **παρεληλυθώς**) *pass, pass by* (perhaps *pass through* Ac 16.8); *pass away, disappear; neglect, break; come, arrive*

πάρεσις, εως f *passing by, overlooking*

παρέστηκα pf. of **παρίστημι**

παρέστην 2 aor. of **παρίστημι**

παρέστησα 1 aor. of **παρίστημι**

παρεστώς and **παρεστηκώς** pf. ptc. of **παρίστημι**

παρέχω (fut. midd. 2 sg. **παρέξῃ**; aor. **παρέσχον**, ptc. **παρασχών**) used in act. and midd. *cause, bring about, do* (*π. κόπους trouble*); *grant, give, offer, present*

παρήγγειλα aor. of **παραγγέλλω**

παρηγορία, ας f *comfort*

παρῆλθον aor. of **παρέρχομαι**

παρῆνει impf. 3 sg. of **παραινέω**

παρῆσαν impf. 3 pl. of πάρ
ειμι

παρητημένος pf. ptc. of παρ
αιτέομαι

παρητούμην impf. of παραι
τέομαι

παρθενία, ας f virginity (ἀπὸ
τῆς π. αὐτῆς from the time
of her marriage Lk 2.36)

παρθένος, ου f virgin, unmarried girl; m undefiled
man or unmarried man (Re
14.4)

Πάρθοι, ων m Parthians

παρίημι (aor. inf. παρεῖναι
(Lk 11.42); pf. pass. ptc.
παρειμένος) neglect; pf.
pass. ptc. drooping, weakened (Heb 12.12)

παρίστημι and παριστάνω
(fut. παραστήσω; 1 aor.
παρέστησα; 2 aor. παρέ
στην; pf. παρέστηκα, ptc.
παρεστώς and παρεστη
κώς; plpf. παρειστήκειν;
fut. midd. παραστήσομαι)
trans. present, bring into
one's presence, show; offer,
yield, dedicate; provide, send;
prove (Ac 24.13); intrans.
(pf., plpf., 2 aor. act.; all
midd.) stand by, be present,
stand; come; stand before;
stand together (Ac 4.26)

Παρμενᾶς, ᾶ acc. ᾶν m Parmenas (Ac 6.5)

πάροδος, ου f passage; ἐν π.
in passing

παροικέω live in; make a

temporary home, live as a
stranger

παροικία, ας f stay (among
strangers)

πάροικος, ου m alien, stranger, exile

παροιμία, ας f parable, figure
of speech, proverb

πάροινος, ου m drunkard,
given to strong drink

παροίχομαι (pf. παρῴχημαι)
go by, pass (pf. ptc. past
Ac 14.16)

παρομοιάζω be like, resemble

παρόμοιος, ον like, similar

παροξύνομαι be irritable; be
greatly upset (Ac 17.16)

παροξυσμός, οῦ m encouragement; sharp argument or
disagreement

παροργίζω (fut. παροργιῶ)
make angry, make resentful

παροργισμός, οῦ m anger

παροτρύνω (aor. παρώτρυ
να) incite, stir up

παρουσία, ας f coming, arrival;
presence

παροψίς, ίδος f plate, dish

παρρησία, ας f openness,
frankness (παρρησίᾳ openly,
plainly, freely); boldness, confidence, assurance; before the
public (ἐν π. εἶναι to be
known publicly Jn 7.4; δειγ
ματίζω ἐν π. make a public
example of Col 2.15)

παρρησιάζομαι speak boldly
or freely; have courage (1 Th
2.2)

παρών, παροῦσα, παρόν ptc. of πάρειμι

παρώτρυνα aor. of παρο-τρύνω

παρῴχημαι pf. of παροίχο-μαι

πᾶς, πᾶσα, πᾶν gen. παντός, πάσης, παντός: (1) without the article each, every (pl. all); every kind of; all, full, absolute, greatest; (2) with the article entire, whole; all (πᾶς ὁ with ptc. everyone who); (3) everyone, everything (διὰ παντός always, continually, forever; κατὰ πάντα in everything, in every respect)

πάσχα n Passover (festival); Passover meal; Passover lamb

πάσχω (aor. ἔπαθον, inf. παθεῖν, ptc. παθών, fem. ptc. παθοῦσα; pf. πέπονθα) suffer, endure, undergo; experience

Πάταρα, ων n Patara (4 E–3)

πατάσσω strike; strike down; tap, touch (Ac 12.7)

πατέω trans. trample (π. ληνόν squeeze out the grapes); intrans. walk (Lk 10.19)

πατήρ, πατρός m father (sometimes as an honorary title for a noted person); Father (of God); forefather, ancestor

Πάτμος, ου m Patmos (4 E–3)

πατριά, ᾶς f family; nation, people

πατριάρχης, ου m patriarch (one of the noted ancestors of the Jewish nation)

πατρικός, ή, όν coming from one's (fore)fathers

πατρίς, ίδος f homeland; home town

Πατροβᾶς, ᾶ m Patrobas (Ro 16.14)

πατρολῴας, ου m one who murders his father

πατροπαράδοτος, ον handed down from one's ancestors

πατρῷος, α, ον belonging to one's ancestors, coming from one's ancestors

Παῦλος, ου m Paul: (1) the apostle; (2) Sergius Paulus, governor of Cyprus (Ac 13.7)

παύω stop, keep from (1 Pe 3.10); midd. stop, cease; cease from, be done with

Πάφος, ου f Paphos (4 F–3)

παχύνομαι grow dull or insensitive

πέδη, ης f chain (for feet)

πεδινός, ή, όν level (ground)

πεζεύω travel by land

πεζῇ adv. on foot; by land

πειθαρχέω obey; listen to (Ac 27.21)

πειθοῖς perhaps a dat. masc. pl. of πειθός

πειθός, ή, όν persuasive; skillful

πειθώ, οῦς dat. sg. πειθοῖ f persuasiveness, persuasive power πείθω (aor. ἔπεισα; pf. πέποιθα; plpf. ἐπεποίθειν; pf. pass. πέπεισμαι; fut. pass. πεισθήσομαι) persuade, convince, win over; conciliate, satisfy (Mt 28.14); seek favor or approval from (Ga 1.10); reassure (1 Jn 3.19); pass. obey, pay attention to, listen to; be a follower (Ac 5.36, 37); pf. act. and pass. trust, rely on; have confidence, be confident; be certain or sure

πεῖν aor. inf. of πίνω

πεινάω be hungry, hunger

πεῖρα, ας f attempt (λαμβάνω π. attempt He 11.29); experience (ἐμπαιγμῶν π. λαμβάνω undergo ridicule He 11.36)

πειράζω (aor. pass. ἐπειράσθην and ἐπιράσθην) test, put to the test; tempt; try, attempt

πειράομαι try, attempt

πειρασμός, οῦ m period or process of testing, trial, test (πύρωσις πρὸς π. fiery ordeal 1 Pe 4.12); temptation, enticement

πεισθήσομαι fut. pass. of πείθω

πεισμονή, ῆς f persuasion

πέλαγος, ους n depths (of the sea); sea, open sea

πελεκίζω behead

πέμπτος, η, ον fifth

πέμπω send; commission, appoint

πένης, ητος m poor or needy person

πενθερά, ᾶς f mother-in-law

πενθερός, οῦ m father-in-law

πενθέω intrans. mourn, be sad, experience sorrow; trans. mourn or grieve over (2 Cor 12.21)

πένθος, ους n mourning, sorrow

πενιχρός, ά, όν poor, needy

πεντάκις adv. five times

πεντακισχίλιοι, αι, α five thousand

πεντακόσιοι, αι, α five hundred

πέντε five

πεντεκαιδέκατος, η, ον fifteenth

πεντήκοντα fifty (κατὰ π. by fifties)

πεντηκοστή, ῆς f Pentecost (Jewish festival celebrated on the fiftieth day after the Passover Feast)

πέπεισμαι pf. pass. of πείθω

πεποιήκεισαν plpf. 3 pl. of ποιέω

πέποιθα pf. of πείθω

πεποίθησις, εως f confidence, trust

πέπονθα pf. of πάσχω

πέπραγμαι pf. pass. of πράσσω

πέπρακα pf. of πιπράσκω

πέπραμαι pf. pass. of πιπράσκω

πέπραχα pf. of πράσσω

πεπρησμένος pf. ptc. of **πίμπραμαι**

πέπτωκα pf. of **πίπτω**

πέπωκα pf. of **πίνω**

περαιτέρω adv. *further*

πέραν: (1) prep. with gen. *beyond, across, to* or *on the other side;* (2) τὸ π. *the other side*

πέρας, ατος n *end, boundary* (of the earth); *end, conclusion* (He 6.16)

Πέργαμος, ου f and **Πέργαμον, ου** n *Pergamum* (4 E–2)

Πέργη, ης f *Perga* (4 F–3)

περί prep. with: (1) gen. *about, concerning, of, with reference to; for, on account of* (π. ἁμαρτίας often *sin offering*); (2) acc. *around, about; near; of, with reference to, regarding* (οἱ π. τὰ τοιαῦτα ἐργάται *workmen of the same trade* Ac 19.25; τὰ π. ἐμέ *how I stand* Php 2.23); *with, in company with*

περιάγω intrans. *go around* or *about; travel over* (Mt 23.15); trans. *take along* (1 Cor 9.5)

περιαιρέω (aor. inf. **περιελεῖν**, ptc. **περιελών**; impf. pass. 3 sg. **περιῃρεῖτο**) *take away, remove; cut away* (of anchors); pass. *be abandoned, be given up* (of hope)

περιάπτω (aor. ptc. **περιάψας**) *kindle*

περιαστράπτω *flash around*

περιβάλλω (fut. **περιβαλῶ**; aor. **περιέβαλον**; aor. midd. impv. **περιβαλοῦ**; pf. pass. **περιβέβλημαι**) *put on, clothe, dress*

περιβλέπομαι *look around*

περιβόλαιον, ου n *cloak, coat; covering*

περιδέω (plpf. pass. 3 sg. **περιεδέδετο**) *wrap, bind*

περιέδραμον aor. of **περιτρέχω**

περιεζωσμένος pf. midd. ptc. of **περιζώννυμι**

περιέθηκα aor. of **περιτίθημι**

περιελεῖν aor. inf. of **περιαιρέω**

περιελθών aor. ptc. of **περιέρχομαι**

περιελών aor. ptc. of **περιαιρέω**

περιέπεσον aor. of **περιπίπτω**

περιεργάζομαι *be a busybody*

περίεργος, ου m *busybody;* τὰ π. *magic* (Ac 19.19)

περιέρχομαι (aor. **περιῆλθον**, ptc. **περιελθών**) *go or travel about* (ptc. *itinerant* Ac 19.13); *sail around* (Ac 28.13)

περιέστησαν aor. 3 pl. of **περιΐστημι**

περιεστώς pf. ptc. of **περιΐστημι**

περιέτεμον aor. of **περιτέμνω**

περιετμήθην aor. pass. of **περιτέμνω**

περιέχω (aor. περιέσχον)
trans. *seize, overcome; contain* (of a document); π.
τάδε as follows (Ac 15.23);
intrans. *stand, say* (in Scripture)

περιζώννυμι and περιζων-
νύω (fut. midd. περιζώ-
σομαι; aor. midd. ptc. πε-
ριζωσάμενος; pf. midd.
ptc. περιεζωσμένος) *wrap
around* (of clothes); midd.
*dress oneself; make oneself
ready*

περιῆλθον aor. of περιέρχομαι

περιῃρεῖτο impf. pass. 3 sg.
of περιαιρέω

περιθείς aor. ptc. of περιτίθημι

περίθεσις, εως f *wearing* (of
jewelry)

περιΐστημι (aor. 3 pl. περιέστησαν; pf. ptc. περι-
εστώς; pres. midd. impv. 2
sg. περιΐστασο) *stand
around;* midd. *avoid, keep
clear of*

περικάθαρμα, τος n *refuse,
rubbish*

περικαλύπτω *cover, conceal;
blindfold; cover over* (with
gold)

περίκειμαι *be placed around;
be bound* (in chains); *be
surrounded* (He 12.1); *be subject to, be beset with* (He 5.2)

περικεφαλαία, ας f *helmet*

περικρατής, ές *in control of*

περικρύβω *keep in seclusion*

περικυκλόω *surround, encircle*

περιλάμπω *shine around*

περιλείπομαι *remain, be left*

περίλυπος, ον *very sad, deeply
distressed*

περιμένω *wait for*

πέριξ adv. *around, in the
vicinity*

περιοικέω *live in the neighborhood of*

περίοικος, ου m *neighbor*

περιούσιος, ον *special, belonging only to oneself*

περιοχή, ῆς f *passage* (of
Scripture)

περιπατέω *walk, go* or *move
about; live, conduct oneself*

περιπείρω *pierce through* (as
with a spike)

περιπίπτω (aor. περιέπε-
σον, ptc. περιπεσών) *encounter* (trials); *fall into the
hands of* (robbers); *strike* (a
reef)

περιποιέομαι *obtain, acquire,
win; preserve, save* (life)

περιποίησις, εως f *obtaining,
gaining; possession, property; saving, preserving*

περιραίνω (pf. pass. περιρέ-
ραμμαι) and περιραντίζω
(pf. pass. περιρεράντισμαι)
sprinkle or *cover with*

περιρήγνυμι (aor. ptc. περι-
ρήξας) *tear off*

περισπάομαι *be distracted* or
worried

περισσεία, ας f abundance, overflow; εἰς π. much greater (2 Cor 10.15)

περίσσευμα, τος n abundance, overflow; pieces left over (from a meal)

περισσεύω intrans. be left over, be more than enough (τὸ π. what is left; wealth, ample possessions); increase, abound, overflow; excel, exceed; have plenty, have more than enough; be better off (1 Cor 8.8); π. μᾶλλον do even more (1 Th 4.1, 10); trans. cause to increase or abound; provide in abundance

περισσός, ή, όν: (1) adj. more (λίαν ἐκ π. utterly, completely Mk 6.51); unnecessary (2 Cor 9.1); (2) adv. to the full (Jn 10.10); (3) τὸ π. advantage (Ro 3.1)

περισσότερος, α, ον: (1) adj. more, greater; much more, even more; severest (judgment); (2) adv. more (He 7.15); more clearly (He 6.17); μᾶλλον π. all the more (Mk 7.36)

περισσοτέρως adv. all the more, even more so, especially, to a greater degree; π. μᾶλλον all the more (2 Cor 7.13)

περισσῶς adv. all the more, even more; even louder; π. ἐμμαίνομαι be insanely furious (Ac 26.11)

περιστερά, ᾶς f dove, pigeon

περιτέμνω (aor. περιέτεμον, inf. περιτεμεῖν; pf. pass. περιτέτμημαι; aor. pass. περιετμήθην, inf. περιτμηθῆναι) circumcise

περιτίθημι (pres. 3 pl. περιτιθέασιν; aor. περιέθηκα, ptc. περιθείς) put around; put on; clothe in; π. τιμήν treat or invest with honor (1 Cor 12.23)

περιτομή, ῆς f circumcision (as a religious rite); those who are circumcised, Jews (also ὁ ἐκ π. = Jew)

περιτρέπω drive (εἰς μανίαν) insane

περιτρέχω (aor. περιέδραμον) run about

περιφέρω carry about; bring, carry; blow about (Eph 4.14)

περιφρονέω lightly esteem, disregard

περίχωρος, ου f surrounding region, neighborhood

περίψημα, τος n scum, dirt

περπερεύομαι be conceited, brag

Περσίς, ίδος f Persis (Ro 16.12)

πέρυσι adv. a year ago (ἀπὸ π. a year ago, since last year)

πεσεῖν aor. inf. of πίπτω

πεσοῦμαι fut. of πίπτω

πεσών aor. ptc. of πίπτω

πετεινόν, οῦ n bird

πέτομαι fly

πέτρα, ας f rock, solid rock;

stone; rocky ground (Lk 8.6, 13)

Πέτρος, ου m *Peter*

πετρῶδες, ους n *rocky ground*

πεφίμωσο pf. pass. impv. of φιμόω

πήγανον, ου n *rue* (a scented herb)

πηγή, ῆς f *spring, fountain; well; flow* (π. τοῦ αἵματος *hemorrhage, severe bleeding* Mk 5.29)

πήγνυμι (aor. ἔπηξα) *put up* (a tent)

πηδάλιον, ου n *rudder*

πηλίκος, η, ον *how large; how great*

πηλός, οῦ m *mud; clay*

πήρα, ας f *bag* (either a traveler's bag or a beggar's bag)

πηρόω *disable, cripple*

πῆχυς, εως m *cubit* (about 18 inches); π. ἐπὶ τὴν ἡλικίαν *foot* (to one's height) or *day* (to one's life)

πιάζω *seize, arrest; catch* (of fish or animals); *take hold of* (Ac 3.7)

πίε aor. impv. of πίνω

πιέζω *press down*

πιεῖν aor. inf. of πίνω

πίεσαι fut. 2 sg. of πίνω

πιθανολογία, ας f *attractive* (but false) *argument*

πιθός alt. form of πειθός

πικραίνω (fut. πικρανῶ; aor. pass. ἐπικράνθην) *make bitter;* pass. *become bitter; be harsh* or *embittered* (Col 3.19)

πικρία, ας f *bitterness* (χολὴ πικρίας perhaps *bitter envy* Ac 8.23); *spite, bitter feeling*

πικρός, ά, όν *bitter*

πικρῶς adv. *bitterly*

Πιλᾶτος, ου m *Pilate*

πίμπλημι (aor. ἔπλησα, ptc. πλήσας; aor. pass. ἐπλήσθην, inf. πλησθῆναι; fut. pass. πλησθήσομαι) *fill; end* (aor. pass. *come to an end*); *fulfill, make come true* (Lk 21.22); *soak* (Mt 27.48)

πίμπραμαι (inf. πίμπρασθαι; aor. ptc. πρησθείς; pf. ptc. πεπρησμένος) *swell up; burn with fever*

πινακίδιον, ου n *writing tablet*

πίναξ, ακος f *plate, platter, dish*

πίννω alt. form of πίνω

πίνω (fut. πίομαι, 2 sg. πίεσαι; aor. ἔπιον, subj. πίω, impv. πίε, inf. πιεῖν and πεῖν; pf. πέπωκα) *drink*

πιότης, ητος f *richness* (of plants)

πιπράσκω (pf. πέπρακα; pf. pass. πέπραμαι; aor. pass. ἐπράθην, inf. πραθῆναι, ptc. neut. πραθέν) *sell; sell as a slave* (Mt 18.25); πεπραμένος ὑπὸ τὴν ἁμαρτίαν *be a slave to sin* (Ro 7.14)

πίπτω (fut. πεσοῦμαι; aor. ἔπεσα, inf. πεσεῖν, ptc. πεσών; pf. πέπτωκα, 2 sg. πέπτωκες) *fall, fall down; fall to one's ruin* or *destruc-*

tion; fall to one's knees, bow (of worship); *be done away with, come to an end* (Lk 16.17; 1 Cor 13.8); *die* (Lk 21.24; 1 Cor 10.8); *strike, beat on* (of the sun's heat); ἔπεσεν ὁ κλῆρος ἐπί *the choice fell upon* (Ac 1.26)

Πισιδία, ας f *Pisidia* (4 F–2)

Πισίδιος, α, ον *Pisidian, of Pisidia*

πιστεύω *believe* (*in*), *have faith* (*in*) (with God or Christ as object); *believe, believe in; have confidence* (in someone or something), *entrust* (something to another); ὃς μὲν π. φαγεῖν πάντα *one man's faith allows him to eat anything* (Ro 14.2)

πιστικός, ή, όν perhaps *pure, genuine*

πίστις, εως f *faith, trust, belief; the Christian faith; conviction, good conscience* (Ro 14.22, 23); perhaps *body of faith, doctrine* (Jd 3, 20); *assurance, proof* (Ac 17.31); *promise* (1 Tm 5.12)

πιστόομαι *firmly believe; be entrusted with*

πιστός, ή, όν *faithful, trustworthy, reliable; believing* (often *believer, Christian;* ὁ ἐκ περιτομῆς π. *Jewish Christian* Ac 10.45); *sure, true, unfailing* (τὰ π. *sure promises* or *blessings* Ac 13.34)

πλανάω *lead astray, mislead,*

deceive; pass. *stray away, go astray; be mistaken; be deceived* or *misled; wander about* (He 11.38)

πλάνη, ης f *error, deceit, deception, delusion; lie* or *deception* (Mt 27.64); perhaps *perversion* (Ro 1.27)

πλανήτης, ου m *wanderer* (ἀστέρες π. *stars out of their orbit* Jd 13)

πλάνος, ον *deceitful;* ὁ π. *deceiver, imposter*

πλάξ, πλακός f *tablet*

πλάσμα, τος n *what is molded* (of clay)

πλάσσω (aor. ptc. **πλάσας;** aor. pass. **ἐπλάσθην**) *mold, form;* perhaps *create* (1 Tm 2.13)

πλαστός, ή, όν *made-up, invented*

πλατεῖα, ας f *wide street*

πλάτος, ους n *breadth, width*

πλατύνω *enlarge, widen; open wide*

πλατύς, εῖα, ύ *wide*

πλέγμα, τος n *elaborate hairstyle*

πλεῖστος, η, ον (superl. of **πολύς**) *most; large;* τὸ π. *at the most* (1 Cor 14.27)

πλείων, πλεῖον or **πλέον** gen. **ονος** nom. pl. **πλείονες** or **πλείους** (comp. of **πολύς**) *more* (*more than* of comparison; πολλῷ π. *many more* Jn 4.41; διὰ τῶν π. *through more and more people*

2 Cor 4.15); *most, the major-ity (a larger amount* Mt 20.10; Lk 7.43); *many, a larger number; greater (great-er than* of comparison); *more acceptable* (sacrifice); ἐπὶ π. *further, more and more, on and on; very far* (2 Tm 3.9); ἐπὶ π. χρόνον *longer* (Ac 18.20); δι' ἐτῶν π. *after some years' absence* (Ac 24.17)

πλέκω *weave, twist together*

πλεονάζω (aor. opt. 3 sg. πλεονάσαι) intrans. *in-crease, grow, become more, be extended; have too much* (2 Cor 8.15); trans. *cause to grow* or *increase* (1 Th 3.12)

πλεονεκτέω *take advantage of, cheat; get the better of* (2 Cor 2.11)

πλεονέκτης, ου m *one who is grasping* or *greedy, one who is covetous*

πλεονεξία, ας f *greed, cov-etousness; something one feels forced to do* (2 Cor 9.5)

πλευρά, ᾶς f *side* (of the body)

πλέω *sail* (ὁ ἐπὶ τόπον πλέων *passenger on a ship* Re 18.17)

πληγή, ῆς f *plague, mis-fortune; blow, beating* (ἐπι-τίθημι π. *beat* Lk 10.30; Ac 16.23); *wound* (λούω ἀπὸ π. *wash one's wounds* Ac 16.33; ἡ π. τοῦ θανάτου *fatal wound* Re 13.3, 12)

πλῆθος, ους n *crowd; quan-tity, number; people, pop-*

ulation; congregation; assem-bly

πληθύνω trans. *increase, mul-tiply, spread* (pass. some-times *grow*); intrans. *grow, increase in number* (Ac 6.1)

πλήκτης, ου m *a quick-tempered* or *violent man*

πλήμμυρα, ης f *flood*

πλήν: (1) conj. *but, yet, never-theless, however* (πλὴν ὅτι *except that, only that* Ac 20.23; Php 1.18); (2) prep. with gen. *except, but, besides*

πλήρης, ες (indeclinable in Jn 1.14; Ac 6.5) *full; com-plete; full-grown* (Mk 4.28); *covered* (with leprosy)

πληροφορέω *accomplish, carry out fully* (τὰ πεπλη-ροφορημένα ἐν ἡμῖν πράγ-ματα *those things that have taken place among us* Lk 1.1); *convince fully, assure fully; proclaim fully* (2 Tm 4.17)

πληροφορία, ας f *full as-surance, conviction, certainty*

πληρόω *fulfill, make come true, bring about* (of Scrip-ture); *fill, make full; bring to completion, complete, ac-complish, finish; make fully known, proclaim fully* (Ro 15.19; Col 1.25); *supply fully* (Php 4.18, 19); pass. *elapse, pass* (of time)

πλήρωμα, τος n *fullness, com-pleteness* (often of the divine being or nature); *fulfilling, fulfillment, completion* (τὸ π. τοῦ χρόνου *the right time* Ga 4.4; cf. Eph 1.10); *that which fills, contents* (τὸ π. τῆς γῆς *everything on the earth* 1 Cor 10.26); *patch* (of cloth); *full number* (Ro 11.12, 25); *full measure* (Ro 15.29)

πλήσας aor. ptc. of **πίμπλημι**

πλησθῆναι aor. pass. inf. of **πίμπλημι**

πλησθήσομαι fut. pass. of **πίμπλημι**

πλησίον: (1) prep. with gen. *near;* (2) ὁ π. *fellow man, neighbor*

πλησμονή, ῆς f *satisfaction* (οὐκ ἐν τιμῇ τινι πρὸς π. τῆς σαρκός either *no value in controlling physical passions* or *no value, except for satisfying physical passions* Col 2.23)

πλήσσω (aor. pass. ἐπλήγην) *strike*

πλοιάριον, ου n *boat, small boat*

πλοῖον, ου n *boat; ship, sailing vessel*

πλοῦς, πλοός acc. **πλοῦν** m *voyage*

πλούσιος, α, ον *rich; well-to-do*

πλουσίως adv. *richly, in full measure*

πλουτέω *be rich; grow rich, prosper; be generous* (Ro 10.12)

πλουτίζω *enrich, make rich*

πλοῦτος, ου m and n *riches, wealth, abundance* (τὸ π. τῆς ἁπλότητος *extreme generosity* 2 Cor 8.2); *rich blessings, enrichment*

πλύνω *wash*

πνεῦμα, τος n *Spirit* (of God); *spirit, inner life, self; disposition, state of mind; spirit, spirit being* or *power, power* (often of evil spirits); *life* (ἀφίημι τὸ π. *die* Mt 27.50); *wind* (He 1.7; perhaps Jn 3.8); *breath* (2 Th 2.8); *ghost, apparition* (Lk 24.37; 39)

πνευματικός, ή, όν *spiritual, pertaining to the spirit; spiritual person; spiritual thing, spiritual gift; supernatural* or *spiritual* (1 Cor 10.3, 4); τὰ π. τῆς πονηρίας *evil spiritual forces* (Eph 6.12)

πνευματικῶς adv. *spiritually, through the guidance of the Spirit; symbolically, allegorically* (Re 11.8)

πνέω (aor. ἔπνευσα) *blow* (of wind)

πνίγω *choke;* pass. *drown* (Mk 5.13)

πνικτός, ή, όν *strangled* (of animals killed for food without draining their blood)

πνοή, ῆς f *wind; breath*

ποδήρης, ους m *long robe*

πόθεν interrog. adv. *from where, where; how, why*

ποιέω (unaugmented plpf.

3 pl. **πεποιήκεισαν**) *make, do, cause, effect, bring about, accomplish, perform, provide; create* (of God); *produce, yield, bear, put forth; give, prepare, keep, celebrate* (of feasts, etc.); *claim, pretend* (to be somebody); *show* (mercy, etc.); *work, be active; live, practice, act* (καλῶς π. *do good, act benevolently or kindly*); *spend, stay* (of time); *exercise* (authority); *wage* (war); *execute* (judgment); *give* (alms); *appoint* (Mk 3.14; He 3.2); *consider, count* (Ac 20.24); often with a noun as a verb equivalent, e.g. π. δέησιν *pray* (Lk 5.33); π. τὸ ἱκανόν *please, satisfy* (Mk 15.15); π. λύτρωσιν *redeem, set free* (Lk 1.68)

ποίημα, τος n *what is created or made*

ποίησις, εως f *doing, undertaking*

ποιητής, οῦ m *one who does or carries out, doer; poet* (Ac 17.28)

ποικίλος, η, ον *various kinds of, all kinds of, varied, diverse*

ποιμαίνω (fut. **ποιμανῶ**; aor. impv. 2 pl. **ποιμάνατε**) *tend like a shepherd; rule; keep sheep* (Lk 17.7); π. ἑαυτόν *care only for oneself* (Jd 12)

ποιμήν, ένος m *shepherd; pastor* (Eph 4.11)

ποίμνη, ης f *flock*

ποίμνιον, ου n *flock*

ποῖος, α, ον interrog. pro. *what, which; what kind of*

πολεμέω *wage war, fight*

πόλεμος, ου m *war, battle; strife, conflict* (Jas 4.1)

πόλις, εως f *city, town* (κατὰ π. *from city to city*); *inhabitants* (of a city)

πολιτάρχης, ου m *city official, member of the city council*

πολιτεία, ας f *citizenship; state, people* (of Israel)

πολίτευμα, τος n *place of citizenship*

πολιτεύομαι *live, conduct one's life*

πολίτης, ου m *citizen; fellowman, fellow-citizen*

πολλάκις adv. *often, repeatedly, frequently*

πολλαπλασίων, ον gen. **ονος** *more* (neut. pl. *many times more*)

πολυλογία, ας f *many words, long prayer*

πολυμερῶς adv. *little by little, many times*

πολυποίκιλος, ον *in varied forms*

πολύς, πολλή, πολύ gen. **πολλοῦ, ῆς, οῦ**: (1) *much, many* (of great crowds; *loud* mourning; *plentiful* harvest; *deep* soil; *late* hour; *long* time; etc.); (2) πολλά *many things*; adv. *often, frequently; strictly; insistently; strongly;*

hard; heartily; etc.; πολύ
much, greatly (ἐπὶ π. a long
time Ac 28.6; μετ' οὐ π. soon
Ac 27.14; π. μᾶλλον much
more, all the more He 12.9,
25); πολλῷ μᾶλλον much
more, all the more; πολλῷ
πλείους many more (Jn
4.41); πολλοῦ for a large sum
(Mt 26.9)

πολύσπλαγχνος, ον very compassionate

πολυτελής, ές expensive, costly; of great value, very precious

πολύτιμος, ον expensive, costly; of great value, very precious

πολυτρόπως adv. in many
ways

πόμα, τος n drink

πονηρία, ας f wickedness, evil;
evil intention

πονηρός, ά, όν evil, bad,
wicked, sinful; (noun evil
person; Evil One [of the
Devil]; τὸ π. what is evil,
evil); guilty (of conscience);
unsound (eye); bad, worthless
(of fruit); malignant or painful (of sores); ὀφθαλμὸς π.
envy, jealousy (Mk 7.22)

πόνος, ου m pain, suffering;
hard work

Ποντικός, ή, όν of Pontus
(Π. τῷ γένει a native of
Pontus Ac 18.2)

Πόντιος, ου m Pontius

Πόντος, ου m Pontus (4 G-1)

πόντος, ου m the sea, the
open sea

Πόπλιος, ου m Publius (Ac
28.7, 8)

πορεία, ας f journey; pursuit
(of business or wealth)

πορεύομαι go, proceed; travel,
journey; leave; live, conduct
one's life; die (Lk 22.22)

πορθέω destroy; try to destroy;
kill

πορισμός, οῦ m gain, means
of gain

Πόρκιος, ου m Porcius (Ac
24.27)

πορνεία, ας f sexual immorality (ἐκ π. οὐκ ἐγεννήθημεν
we are not bastards Jn 8.41);
unfaithfulness (Mt 5.32;
19.9)

πορνεύω commit sexual immorality

πόρνη, ης f prostitute

πόρνος, ου m man who practices sexual immorality

πόρρω adv. far away, far

πόρρωθεν adv. at or from a
distance

πορρώτερον adv. farther

πορφύρα, ας f purple cloth or
garment (often as a symbol
of high position)

πορφυρόπωλις, ιδος f (woman) dealer in purple cloth

πορφυροῦς, ᾶ, οῦν purple;
purple garment

ποσάκις adv. how often?

πόσις, εως f drinking; a
drink

πόσος, η, ον *how much, how many* (πόσῳ μᾶλλον *how much more); how much? how many?* (Mt 15.34; Lk 16.5, 7)

ποταμός, οῦ m *river, stream; river in flood* (Mt 7.25, 27)

ποταμοφόρητος, ον *swept away by a river*

ποταπός, ή, όν *of what sort or kind; what wonderful* (Mk 13.1; 1 Jn 3.1)

ποτέ enclitic particle *once, formerly, at one time; ever, at any time* (οὐ . . . ποτέ *never); at last, after so long* (Ro 1.10; Php 4.10); *when* (Lk 22.32); ὁποῖός ποτε *whoever or whatever* (Ga 2.6)

πότε interrog. adv. *when?* (ἕως πότε *how long?*)

πότερον adv. *whether*

ποτήριον, ου n *cup, drinking vessel*

ποτίζω *give to drink; water*

Ποτίολοι, ων m *Puteoli* (4 A-1)

πότος, ου m *drunken orgy*

ποῦ interrog. adv. *where, at what place; to what place;* οὐκ ἔχω ποῦ *have nowhere* (to do something)

πού enclitic adv. *somewhere; almost* (Ro 4.19)

Πούδης, εντος m *Pudens* (2 Tm 4.21)

πούς, ποδός m *foot* (of the body); perhaps *leg* (Re 10.1)

πρᾶγμα, τος n *matter, thing, affair; event, happening, deed; undertaking, task; dispute, lawsuit* (1 Cor 6.1)

πραγματεῖαι, ῶν f *affairs, pursuits*

πραγματεύομαι *trade, do business*

πραθέν aor. pass. ptc. neut. of πιπράσκω

πραθῆναι aor. pass. inf. of πιπράσκω

πραιτώριον, ου n *headquarters* or *residence* (of an army or governor); *palace guard*

πράκτωρ, ορος m *officer* (of the court)

πρᾶξις, εως f *what one does, deed, action, practice; function* (of body parts); *magical practice* (Ac 19.18)

πραότης alt. form of πραΰτης

πρασιά, ᾶς f (lit. *garden plot*) *group* (πρασιαὶ πρασιαί *in groups* Mk 6.40)

πράσσω (pf. πέπραχα; pf. pass. πέπραγμαι) trans. *do, practice; collect* (of taxes or interest); π. τὰ ἴδια *mind one's own business* (1 Th 4.11); intrans. *act, do; get along* (Eph 6.21)

πραϋπάθεια, ας f *gentleness, humility*

πραΰς, πραεῖα, πραΰ *humble, gentle*

πραΰτης, ητος f *gentleness, humility*

πρέπει impers. *it is fitting* or

proper (πρέπον ἐστίν *it is fitting* or *proper*)

πρεσβεία, ας f *messenger(s), representative(s)*

πρεσβεύω *be an ambassador, be a representative* (for someone)

πρεσβυτέριον, ου n *body of elders* (of the highest Jewish council or of a church council)

πρεσβύτερος, α, ον *elder* (of the Jewish religious leaders and of church leaders); *elder* (of two sons); *eldest* (Jn 8.9); *old man* or *woman* (Ac 2.17; 1 Tm 5.2); παράδοσις τῶν π. *the tradition of pronouncements by earlier Jewish leaders*

πρεσβύτης, ου m *old* or *elderly man*

πρεσβῦτις, ιδος f *old* or *elderly woman*

πρηνής, ές gen. οὖς *headfirst* or perhaps *swollen*

πρίζω (aor. pass. ἐπρίσθην) *saw in two*

πρίν (and πρὶν ἤ) conj. *before*

Πρίσκα and **Πρίσκιλλα, ης** f *Prisca, Priscilla* (wife of Aquila)

πρό prep. with gen. *before* (of time or place); πρὸ ἐτῶν δεκατεσσάρων *fourteen years ago* (2 Cor 12.2); πρὸ ἓξ ἡμερῶν τοῦ πάσχα *six days before the Passover* (Jn 12.1);

πρὸ πάντων *above all else* (Jas 5.12; 1 Pe 4.8)

προάγω (aor. προήγαγον, inf. προαγαγεῖν) intrans. *go before* or *ahead of; come* or *go before* (προάγουσα ἐντολή *former commandment* He 7.18; αἱ π. προφητεῖαι *the prophecies made long ago* 1 Tm 1.18); *go too far* (2 Jn 9); trans. *lead* or *bring out; bring* (ἐπί) *before* (Ac 25.26)

προαιρέομαι (pf. προῄρημαι) *decide*

προαιτιάομαι *accuse beforehand*

προακούω *hear before* or *previously*

προαμαρτάνω (pf. προημάρτηκα) *sin previously* or *in the past*

προαύλιον, ου n *gateway, forecourt*

προβαίνω (aor. ptc. προβάς; pf. προβέβηκα) *go on;* προβέβηκα ἐν ταῖς ἡμέραις *be old* or *advanced in years*

προβάλλω (aor. subj. προβάλω) trans. *put forward;* intrans. *put out leaves*

προβατικός, ή, όν *pertaining to sheep;* ἡ π. *sheep gate*

προβάτιον, ου n *lamb, sheep*

πρόβατον, ου n *sheep*

προβέβηκα pf. of **προβαίνω**

προβιβάζω *prompt, urge, persuade*

προβλέπομαι *have in store, provide*

προγίνομαι *happen previously* (προγεγόνατα ἁμαρτήματα *former sins* Ro 3.25)

προγινώσκω (aor. προέγνων) *know already, know beforehand; choose from the beginning, choose beforehand*

πρόγνωσις, εως f *foreknowledge, purpose*

πρόγονος, ου m or f *parent, forefather*

προγράφω *write in former times* (pf. pass. *be written about* or *marked out* Jd 4); *write above* or *already; put on public display, placard* (Ga 3.1)

πρόδηλος, ον *very obvious* or *evident*

προδίδωμι (aor. προέδωκα) *give first*

προδότης, ου m *traitor, betrayer; treacherous person*

προδραμών aor. ptc. of προτρέχω

πρόδρομος, ου m *forerunner*

προέγνων aor. of προγινώσκω

προέδραμον aor. of προτρέχω

προέδωκα aor. of προδίδωμι

προεθέμην aor. of προτίθεμαι

προεῖπον aor. of προλέγω

προείρηκα pf. of προλέγω

προέλαβον aor. of προλαμβάνω

προελεύσομαι fut. of προέρχομαι

προελθών aor. ptc. of προέρχομαι

προελπίζω (pf. προήλπικα) *be the first to hope*

προενάρχομαι *begin, begin beforehand*

προεπαγγέλλομαι (aor. προεπηγγειλάμην; pf. προεπήγγελμαι) *promise from the beginning, promise long ago*

προέρχομαι (fut. προελεύσομαι; aor. προῆλθον, ptc. προελθών) *go ahead, go on before* (π. τινά *arrive before someone* Mk 6.33); *go before, precede* (lead Lk 22.47); *go, come; pass along* (a street)

προεστώς pf. ptc. of προΐστημι

προετοιμάζω *prepare beforehand*

προευαγγελίζομαι *proclaim the good news beforehand* or *ahead of time*

προέχομαι (if midd.) *be better off, have an advantage;* (if pass.) *be worse off, be at a disadvantage*

προήγαγον aor. of προάγω

προηγέομαι *outdo, lead the way* (τιμῇ ἀλλήλους π. perhaps *be eager to show respect to one another* Ro 12.10)

προῆλθον aor. of προέρχομαι

προήλπικα pf. of προελπίζω

προημάρτηκα pf. of προα-
μαρτάνω

προῄρημαι pf. of προαιρέομαι

πρόθεσις, εως f purpose, plan,
will; perhaps steadfastness,
loyalty (Ac 11.23; 2 Tm
3.10); ἄρτοι τῆς π.
bread
offered to God

προθεσμία, ας f set time

προθυμία, ας f willingness,
readiness, eagerness, zeal

πρόθυμος, ον willing; τὸ π.
eagerness

προθύμως adv. willingly, eagerly

προϊδών aor. ptc. of προοράω

πρόϊμος, ου m early rain (of
the rain that comes early in
the season), autumn rain

προΐστημι (aor. inf. προστῆναι; pf. ptc. προεστώς) be a
leader, have authority over,
manage; care for, give help;
engage in, practice (Tt 3.8,
14)

προκαλέομαι irritate, make
angry

προκαταγγέλλω (aor. προ-
κατήγγειλα) announce be-
forehand or long ago

προκαταρτίζω prepare in advance

προκατέχω have previously
(π. περισσόν have a previous
advantage)

πρόκειμαι be set before; be
present, lie before; π. δεῖγμα
serve as an example (Jd 7)

προκηρύσσω preach before-
hand

προκοπή, ῆς f progress, ad-
vancement

προκόπτω advance, progress,
grow (π. ἐπὶ τὸ χεῖρον go
from bad to worse 2 Tm 3.13);
be far gone (of night)

πρόκριμα, τος n prejudice

προκυρόω make previously (of
a covenant)

προλαμβάνω (aor. προέλα-
βον; aor. pass. subj. προ-
λη"μφθῶ) do (something)
ahead of time; begin (eating)
before (others do); catch
(in sin)

προλέγω (aor. προεῖπον; pf.
προείρηκα) pres. say or
warn; say or warn in ad-
vance; aor. and pf. say or
warn in advance, before or
long ago; predict; quote already or above (He 4.7)

προμαρτύρομαι predict, fore-
tell

προμελετάω prepare ahead of
time

προμεριμνάω worry ahead of
time

προνοέω have in mind to do,
try to do; care for, take care of
(1 Tm 5.8)

πρόνοια, ας f provision, fore-
sight, care, attention

προοράω (aor. ptc. προϊδών)
see ahead of time, see previously; midd. keep one's eyes
on, see before one

προορίζω *decide from the beginning* or *beforehand, predestine; set apart from the beginning* or *beforehand*

προπάσχω (aor. ptc. προπαθών) *suffer previously*

προπάτωρ, ορος m *forefather*

προπέμπω *send* or *help on one's way; escort, accompany* (Ac 20.38; 21.5)

προπετής, ές gen. οῦς *rash, reckless*

προπορεύομαι *go before* or *in front of*

πρός prep. with: (1) acc. *to; toward; for the sake* or *purpose of, in order to, so that* (especially of πρὸς τό with inf.); *for; against; with, in company with; at, about, near, beside* (τὰ πρὸς τὴν θύραν *on the street near the door* Mk 2.2); *pertaining to, with reference to* (τί πρὸς ἡμᾶς *what is it to us?* Mt 27.4; πρὸς οὐδὲ ἓν ῥῆμα *not even one word* Mt 27.14); *before, in the presence of; in comparison with* (Ro 8.18); (2) dat. *at, on, near;* (3) gen. *for, for the sake of* (Ac 27.34)

προσάββατον, ου n *the day before the Sabbath, Friday*

προσαγορεύω *designate, name*

προσάγω (aor. inf. προσαγαγεῖν; aor. pass. προσήχθην) trans. *bring to* or *before;* intrans. *come near* (Ac 27.27)

προσαγωγή, ῆς f *freedom* or *right to enter*

προσαιτέω *beg*

προσαίτης, ου m *beggar*

προσαναβαίνω (aor. impv. προσανάβηθι) *move up*

προσαναλίσκω or προσαναλόω *spend*

προσαναπληρόω *supply, provide*

προσανατίθεμαι (aor. προσανεθέμην) *go* (to someone) *for advice; add to*

προσανέχω *rise up toward* (τινί) *someone*

προσαπειλέομαι *threaten further*

προσαφίημι (fut. pass. προσαφεθήσομαι) *perhaps mng.* *leave* (in addition)

προσαχέω *resound* (of the surf)

προσβιβάζω *persuade*

προσδαπανάω *spend in addition*

προσδέομαι *need, have need*

προσδέχομαι *wait for, expect; receive, welcome; accept, hold* (Ac 24.15)

προσδοκάω *wait for; look for, expect; live in suspense, wait* or *be on watch* (Ac 27.33)

προσδοκία, ας f *expectation; foreboding*

προσδραμών aor. ptc. of προστρέχω

προσεάω *allow to go farther*

προσεγγίζω *come* or *get near*

προσέθηκα aor. of προστί-
θημι

προσεκλίθην aor. of προσ-
κλίνομαι

προσελαβόμην aor. of προσλαμβάνομαι

προσελεύσομαι fut. of προσέρχομαι

προσελήλυθα pf. of προσ-
έρχομαι

πρόσελθε aor. impv. of προσέρχομαι

προσενέγκαι and προσενεγ-
κεῖν aor. inf. of προσφέρω

προσένεγκον and προσένεγ-
κε aor. impv. of προσφέρω

προσενεχθείς aor. pass. ptc.
of προσφέρω

προσενήνοχα pf. of προσ-
φέρω

προσέπεσον aor. of προσ-
πίπτω

προσεργάζομαι make more (of
profit)

προσέρηξα aor. of προσρήγνυμι

προσέρχομαι (fut. προσελ-
εύσομαι; aor. προσῆλθον,
impv. πρόσελθε; pf. προσ-
ελήλυθα) come or go to,
approach; agree with (1 Tm
6.3); associate with (Ac
10.28)

προσέταξα aor. of προστάσσω

προσετέθην aor. pass. of
προστίθημι

προσευχή, ῆς f prayer; place
of prayer (Ac 16.13, 16)

προσεύχομαι pray

προσέχω (aor. προσέσχον;
pf. προσέσχηκα) pay close
attention to, hold on to, give
oneself to (οἴνῳ πολλῷ π. be
addicted to wine, be fond of
much wine 1 Tm 3.8); be on
guard, watch, be careful (π.
ἀπό watch out for, be on
guard against); serve as a
priest (He 7.13)

προσῆλθον aor. of προσ-
έρχομαι

προσηλόω nail to

προσήλυτος, ου m proselyte
(a convert to Judaism)

προσήνεγκα aor. of προσ-
φέρω

προσηνέχθην aor. pass. of
προσφέρω

προσήχθην aor. pass. of
προσάγω

προσθεῖναι aor. inf. of προστίθημι

προσθείς aor. ptc. of προστίθημι

πρόσθες aor. impv. of προστίθημι

προσθῶ aor. subj. of προστίθημι

πρόσκαιρος, ον not lasting,
temporary

προσκαλέομαι (pf. προσκέ-
κλημαι) call to oneself, summon, invite; call (to or for
a Christian task)

προσκαρτερέω devote oneself
to, continue in; keep close
company with (Ac 8.13); be

a personal attendant (Ac
10.7); be in attendance (Ac
2.46); be ready (of a boat)

προσκαρτέρησις, εως f perseverance

προσκεφάλαιον, ου n cushion, pillow

προσκληρόομαι join, join company with

προσκλίνομαι (aor. προσεκλίθην) join

πρόσκλισις, εως f favoritism

προσκολλάομαι be united (in marriage)

πρόσκομμα, τος n that which causes stumbling or offense (ὁ διὰ προσκόμματος ἐσθίων one who eats something that causes someone else to fall into sin Ro 14.20)

προσκοπή, ῆς f cause for offense

προσκόπτω intrans. stumble; take offense, be offended; beat against (of rain); trans. strike (τί) something (πρός) against (Mt 4.6; Lk 4.11)

προσκυλίω roll against or to

προσκυνέω worship; fall down and worship, kneel, bow low, fall at another's feet

προσκυνητής, οῦ m worshiper

προσλαλέω speak to or with

προσλαμβάνομαι (aor. προσελαβόμην, impv. προσλαβοῦ) welcome, accept, receive; take aside; eat (food); gather or take along (Ac 17.5)

προσλέγω answer, reply

πρόσλημψις, εως f acceptance

προσμένω (aor. inf. προσμεῖναι) remain or stay with; remain, stay on; remain faithful to, continue in

προσορμίζομαι moor, tie up (of boats)

προσοφείλω owe, owe besides

προσοχθίζω be angry

πρόσπεινος, ον hungry

προσπήγνυμι (aor. ptc. προσπήξας) crucify

προσπίπτω (aor. προσέπεσον, fem. ptc. προσπεσοῦσα) fall at someone's feet, fall down before someone; beat against (Mt 7.25)

προσποιέομαι act as if, give the impression that

προσπορεύομαι come to, approach

προσρήγνυμι and προσρήσσω (aor. προσέρηξα) burst upon

προστάσσω (aor. προσέταξα; pf. pass. προστέταγμαι) command, order; προστεταγμένοι καιροί designated times or ordered seasons (Ac 17.26)

προστάτις, ιδος f helper, good friend

προστῆναι aor. inf. of προΐστημι

προστίθημι (impf. 3 sg. προσετίθει; aor. προσέθηκα, impv. πρόσθες, inf. προσθεῖναι, ptc. **προσθείς**, subj. **προσθῶ**; aor. midd. **προσεθέμην**; aor. pass. **προσετέθην**, inf. **προστεθῆναι**; fut. pass. **προστεθήσομαι**) add, add to, increase; give, grant; proceed, go ahead, continue, do again; win over (of followers); bury (Ac 13.36)

προστρέχω (aor. ptc. **προσδραμών**) run up (to someone)

προσφάγιον, ου n fish

πρόσφατος, ον new, not previously available

προσφάτως adv. recently

προσφέρω (aor. **προσήνεγκα**, impv. **προσένεγκον** and **προσένεγκε**, inf. **προσενέγκαι** and **προσενεγκεῖν**; pf. **προσενήνοχα**; aor. pass. **προσηνέχθην**, ptc. **προσενεχθείς**) offer, present (especially of gifts and sacrifices); bring; bring (someone) before (an official); perform, do (a service); hold (something) up (Jn 19.29); pass. treat, deal with (He 12.7)

προσφιλής, ές pleasing, lovely

προσφορά, ᾶς f offering, sacrifice, gift; act of offering or sacrificing

προσφωνέω call to, address; call (someone) to oneself

πρόσχυσις, εως f sprinkling (of blood)

προσψαύω touch

προσωπολημπτέω show favoritism, treat one person better than another

προσωπολήμπτης, ου m one who shows favoritism

προσωπολημψία, ας f favoritism, treating one person better than another

πρόσωπον, ου n face, countenance, appearance (τὰ κατὰ π. what is before one's eyes 2 Cor 10.7; ἐν π. καυχῶμαι put on an outward show 2 Cor 5.12; π. τῆς γενέσεως one's natural face Jas 1.23); presence (ἀπὸ π. from, from the presence of; κατὰ π. in the presence of, face to face; πρὸ π. before, ahead of; εἰς π. in the presence of 2 Cor 8.24); person (λαμβάνω π. or βλέπω εἰς π. show favoritism; θαυμάζω π. flatter people Jd 16); surface (of the earth)

προτείνω tie up (with straps) or stretch out (for a beating)

πρότερος, α, ον: (1) adj. former, earlier, past; (2) adv. πρότερον and τὸ π. before, previously, formerly; first, first of all; at first, the first time, originally

προτίθεμαι (aor. **προεθέμην**) plan, purpose, intend; perhaps show openly or publicly (Ro 3.25)

προτρέπομαι encourage

προτρέχω (aor. **προέδραμον**, ptc. **προδραμών**) run

on ahead; π. *τάχιον outrun*
(Jn 20.4)

προϋπάρχω *be* or *exist previously*

πρόφασις, εως f *false motive, pretense, pretext; excuse* (Jn 15.22)

προφέρω *bring out, produce*

προφητεία, ας f *preaching the message of God, the gift of preaching the message of God; an inspired message* or *utterance; intelligible preaching, an intelligible message* (as opposed to speaking in tongues 1 Cor 14.6, 22)

προφητεύω *proclaim God's message, preach; prophesy, predict; speak God's message intelligibly* (as opposed to speaking in tongues 1 Cor 14.1ff); *use prophetic insights to make something known* (Mt 26.68; Mk 14.65; Lk 22.64)

προφήτης, ου m *prophet* (of one who has insight into the divine will and possesses the power of inspired utterance); προφῆται *prophetic books of the OT* (νόμος καὶ π. *the OT*)

προφητικός, ή, όν *prophetic*

προφῆτις, ιδος f *prophetess* (fem. equivalent of προφήτης)

προφθάνω *come before* (π. αὐτὸν ὁ Ἰησοῦς λέγων *Jesus spoke to him first* Mt 17.25)

προχειρίζομαι midd. *choose* or *appoint for oneself;* pass. *be chosen* or *appointed* (Ac 3.20)

προχειροτονέω *choose in advance*

Πρόχορος, ου m *Prochorus* (Ac 6.5)

πρύμνα, ης f *stern* (of a ship)

πρωΐ adv. *early morning, in the morning, morning;* εὐθὺς π. *as soon as morning came* (Mk 15.1); λίαν π. *very early* (Mk 16.2); π. ἔννυχα λίαν *early morning while it was still dark* (Mk 1.35)

πρωΐα, ας f *morning* (π. δὲ ἤδη γενομένης *as day was breaking* Jn 21.4)

πρωϊνός, ή, όν *morning*

πρῷρα, ης f *bow* (of a ship)

πρωτεύω *have first place, be above all else*

πρωτοκαθεδρία, ας f *place of honor*

πρωτοκλισία, ας f *place of honor* (at a feast)

πρῶτον: (1) adv. *first, in the first place; first of all, above all else; to begin with; earlier, before;* τὸ π. *the first time; at first, earlier;* (2) equivalent to prep. with gen. *before* (Jn 15.18)

πρῶτος, η, ον *first; leading, foremost, prominent, most important; earlier, former, before*

πρωτοστάτης, ου m ring-leader

πρωτοτόκια, ων n birthright, rights belonging to the first-born son

πρωτότοκος, ον first-born, first; first-born Son (of Christ); π. πάσης κτίσεως existing before all creation or superior to all creation (Col 1.15)

πρώτως adv. for the first time

πταίω stumble, go wrong, sin

πτέρνα, ης f heel (of a foot)

πτερύγιον, ου n highest point or parapet (of the Temple)

πτέρυξ, υγος f wing

πτηνόν, οῦ n bird

πτοέομαι be terrified or startled

πτόησις, εως f something that causes fear; fear

Πτολεμαΐς, ΐδος f Ptolemais, Acco (2 B–3, 4 G–4)

πτύον, ου n winnowing-shovel

πτύρομαι be frightened or afraid

πτύσμα, τος n saliva, spittle

πτύσσω (aor. ptc. πτύξας) close (a book), roll (a scroll)

πτύω spit

πτῶμα, τος n body, corpse

πτῶσις, εως f fall

πτωχεία, ας f poverty (ἡ κατὰ βάθους π. extreme poverty 2 Cor 8.2)

πτωχεύω become poor

πτωχός, ή, όν poor; perhaps pitiful or inferior (Ga 4.9)

πυγμή, ῆς f fist (πυγμῇ of

doubtful mng. with the fist, to the wrist, carefully or in the proper way Mk 7.3)

Πύθιος, ου m Pythius (Ac 20.4)

πυθόμενος aor. ptc. of πυνθάνομαι

πύθων, ωνος m Python (a spirit of divination); ἔχω πνεῦμα π. be a fortuneteller

πυκνά adv. often, frequently; comp. πυκνότερον often, as often as possible

πυκνός, ή, όν frequent

πυκτεύω box

πύλη, ης f gate, door

πυλών, ῶνος m gate; gateway, entrance; porch, vestibule

πυνθάνομαι (aor. ἐπυθόμην, ptc. πυθόμενος) inquire, ask, question; learn (by inquiry)

πῦρ, ός n fire

πυρά, ᾶς f a fire

πύργος, ου m tower, watchtower

πυρέσσω be sick with fever

πυρετός, οῦ m fever

πύρινος, η, ον fiery red, the color of fire

πυρόομαι burn, be inflamed; burn with sexual desire (1 Cor 7.9); burn with distress (2 Cor 11.29); pf. be refined (of metal)

πυρράζω be red (of the sky)

Πύρρος, ου m Pyrrhus (Ac 20.4)

πυρρός, ά, όν red, fiery red

πύρωσις, εως f *burning; fiery ordeal, painful test*

πωλέω *sell; put on sale*

πῶλος, ου m *colt, young donkey*

πώποτε adv. *ever, at any time*

πωρόω *make stubborn or with-* *out feeling;* pass. *be stubborn or without feeling*

πώρωσις, εως f *stubbornness, lack of feeling*

πῶς interrog. particle *how? in what way? how is it possible?*

πώς enclitic particle *somehow, in some way*

Ρ

Ῥαάβ f *Rahab* (He 11.31; Jas 2.25); alt. form for Ῥαχάβ

ῥαββί *rabbi, teacher, master* (honorary title of address)

ῥαββουνι (Aramaic word) = ῥαββί

ῥαβδίζω *whip, beat (with a stick)*

ῥάβδος, ου f *stick, staff, rod; scepter* (He 1.8)

ῥαβδοῦχος, ου m *policeman*

Ῥαγαύ m *Reu* (Lk 3.35)

ῥᾳδιούργημα, τος n *wrongdoing, crime*

ῥᾳδιουργία, ας f *the lack of principle, unscrupulousness*

ῥαίνω (pf. pass. ἔρραμαι, ῥέραμμαι) *sprinkle* (Re 19.13)

Ῥαιφάν m *Rephan* (pagan god Ac 7.43)

ῥακά *empty-headed fool* (term of strong abuse)

ῥάκος, ους n *piece of cloth*

Ῥαμά f *Ramah* (1 C–6, 1i A–1)

ῥαντίζω (pf. pass. ptc. ἐρραντισμένος and ῥεραντισμένος) *sprinkle;* midd. *wash oneself;* pass. *be washed or purified*

ῥαντισμός, οῦ m *sprinkling*

ῥαπίζω *hit, strike*

ῥάπισμα, τος n *a blow (with a stick); slap (with a hand)*

ῥαφίς, ίδος f *needle*

Ῥαχάβ f *Rahab* (Mt 1.5)

Ῥαχήλ f *Rachel* (Mt 2.18)

Ῥεβέκκα, ας f *Rebecca* (Ro 9.10)

ῥέδη, ης f *(four-wheeled) carriage*

ῥέραμμαι pf. pass. of ῥαίνω

ῥέω (fut. ῥεύσω) *flow*

Ῥήγιον, ου n *Rhegium* (4 B–2)

ῥῆγμα, τος n *ruin, destruction*

ῥήγνυμι and ῥήσσω (fut. ῥήξω; aor. ἔρρηξα, impv.

ῥῆξον) burst, tear in pieces; attack (of animals); dash to the ground (in convulsions); break forth (of a shout)

ῥηθείς aor. pass. ptc. of λέγω

ῥῆμα, τος n what is said, word, saying; thing, matter, event, happening

Ῥησά m Rhesa (Lk 3.27)

ῥήτωρ, ορος m lawyer, attorney, spokesman

ῥητῶς adv. expressly, specifically

ῥίζα, ης f root; descendant; source, cause (of evil)

ῥιζόομαι (pf. ἐρρίζωμαι) be firmly rooted

ῥιπή, ῆς f blinking (of an eye)

ῥιπίζομαι be tossed about

ῥίπτω and ῥιπτέω (aor. ἔρριψα, ptc. ῥίψας; pf. pass. ἔρριμμαι) throw, throw down; let down (anchors); place, put down (Mt 15.30); pf. pass. ptc. perhaps helpless or dejected (Mt 9.36)

Ῥοβοάμ m Rehoboam (Mt 1.7)

Ῥόδη, ης f Rhoda (Ac 12.13)

Ῥόδος, ου f Rhodes (3 B-2, 4 E-3)

ῥοιζηδόν adv. with a loud noise

ῥομφαία, ας f sword; intense pain, sorrow (Lk 2.35)

ῥοπή, ῆς f movement, move

Ῥουβήν m Reuben (Re 7.5)

Ῥούθ f Ruth (Mt 1.5)

Ῥοῦφος, ου m Rufus: (1) son of Simon (Mk 15.21); (2) Christian (Ro 16.13)

ῥύμη, ης f street, alley

ῥύομαι (aor. ἐρρυσάμην, impv. ῥῦσαι, 3 sg. ῥυσάσθω; aor. pass. ἐρρύσθην, subj. ῥυσθῶ) save, rescue, deliver (ὁ ῥυόμενος the Deliverer, the Savior Ro 11.26)

ῥυπαίνομαι (aor. impv. 3 sg. ῥυπανθήτω) be filthy or impure

ῥυπαρία, ας f impurity, filthiness

ῥυπαρός, ά, όν shabby (of clothing); impure, filthy (of persons)

ῥύπος, ου m dirt

ῥύσις, εως f flow (ῥ. αἵματος hemorrhage, severe bleeding)

ῥυτίς, ίδος f wrinkle

Ῥωμαϊκός, ή, όν Roman language (i.e. Latin)

Ῥωμαῖος, ου m Roman

Ῥωμαϊστί adv. in the Latin language

Ῥώμη, ης f Rome (4 A-1)

ῥώννυμαι (pf. impv. ἔρρωσο, 2 pl. ἔρρωσθε) be healthy; pf. impv. (used at the conclusion of a letter) farewell, good-bye

Σ

σαβαχθανι (Aramaic word) *you have forsaken me*

Σαβαώθ (a descriptive name of God in Hebrew, lit. *of the armies*) κίριος Σ. *Lord Almighty*

σαββατισμός, οῦ m *a Sabbath day's rest*

σάββατον, ου n (often in pl.; Jewish sacred day of worship and rest) *the seventh day, Sabbath* (ἡμέρα σαββάτου *the Sabbath day*); *week* (μία or πρώτη σαββάτων *the first day of the week;* κατὰ μίαν σ. *on the first day of every week, every Sunday* 1 Cor 16.2; δὶς τοῦ σ. *twice a week* Lk 18.12); ὁδὸς σ. cf. ὁδός

σαγήνη, ης f *dragnet* (for fishing)

Σαδδουκαῖος, ου m *Sadducee* (member of a Jewish religious party)

Σαδώκ m *Zadok* (Mt 1.14)

σαίνομαι *be disturbed* or *upset*

σάκκος, ου m *sackcloth* (worn especially by persons in mourning)

Σαλά m *Shelah:* (1) father of Boaz (Lk 3.32); (2) father of Eber (Lk 3.35)

Σαλαθιήλ m *Salathiel* (Mt 1.12; Lk 3.27)

Σαλαμίς, ῖνος f *Salamis* (4 G–3)

σαλεύω *shake* (σαλευθῆναι ἀπὸ τοῦ νοός *be unsettled in mind, be confused* 2 Th 2.2); *stir up* (a crowd); pf. pass. ptc. *shaken together* (Lk 6.38)

Σαλήμ f *Salem* (βασιλεὺς Σ. *king of Salem* or *king of peace* He 7.1, 2)

Σαλίμ n *Salim* (2 C–4)

Σαλμών m *Salmon* (Mt 1.4, 5; Lk 3.32)

Σαλμώνη, ης f *Salmone* (4 E–3)

σάλος, ου m *wave* (of a rough sea)

σάλπιγξ, ιγγος f *trumpet; trumpet-blast*

σαλπίζω *sound a trumpet*

σαλπιστής, οῦ m *trumpeter*

Σαλώμη, ης f *Salome* (Mk 15.40; 16.1)

Σαμάρεια, ας f *Samaria:* (1) region (2 C–4); (2) city (1 C–5)

Σαμαρίτης, ου m *Samaritan*

Σαμαρῖτις, ιδος f *Samaritan* (woman)

Σαμοθράκη, ης f *Samothrace* (4 E–2)

Σάμος, ου f *Samos* (4 E–3)

Σαμουήλ m *Samuel*

Σαμψών m *Samson*

σανδάλιον, ου n sandal

σανίς, ίδος f board, plank

Σαούλ m Saul: (1) Hebrew name of the apostle Paul; (2) first Israelite king (Ac 13.21)

σαπρός, ά, όν bad, rotten, worthless; bad or harmful (word)

Σάπφειρα, ης f Sapphira (Ac 5.1)

σάπφιρος, ου f sapphire (a very valuable stone, usually blue in color)

σαργάνη, ης f (rope-)basket

Σάρδεις, εων f Sardis, Sepharad (3 B–2, 4 E–2)

σάρδιον, ου n carnelian or cornelian (a semiprecious stone, usually red in color)

σαρδόνυξ, υχος m sardonyx (a variety of agate, a semiprecious stone of varying colors)

Σάρεπτα, ων n Zarephath (1 C–1, 2 C–1)

σαρκικός, ή, όν belonging to this world, not under the control of God's Spirit; material (Ro 15.27; 1 Cor 9.11)

σάρκινος, η, ον belonging to this world, not under the control of God's Spirit; human

σάρξ, σαρκός f flesh, physical body; human nature, earthly descent (κατὰ σ. by earthly descent; τέκνα τῆς σαρκός physical descendants Ro 9.8;

εἴ πως παραζηλώσω μου τὴν σάρκα perhaps I can make the people of my own race jealous Ro 11.14); one's lower nature, sinful human nature (κατὰ σ. or ἐν σ. under the control of one's sinful nature); human being, person, man (κατὰ σ. by human standards, from a human point of view, as far as externals are concerned); earthly life, human realm of existence (ὁ κατὰ σ. κύριος earthly master Col 3.22; ὁ τῆς σ. πατήρ human father He 12.9; ἐν ταῖς ἡμέραις τῆς σαρκὸς αὐτοῦ during his earthly life He 5.7); sexual impulse (ἐκ θελήματος σαρκός from sexual desire Jn 1.13; ἀπέρχομαι ὀπίσω σ. ἑτέρας commit sexual immorality Jd 7)

σαρόω sweep (a house)

Σάρρα, ας f Sarah

Σαρών, ῶνος m Sharon (1 B–4, 2 B–4)

Σατανᾶς, ᾶ m the Adversary, Satan

σάτον, ου n saton (a dry measure of 21.6 pints)

Σαῦλος, ου m Saul (Hebrew name of the apostle Paul)

σβέννυμι (fut. σβέσω; aor. ἔσβεσα, inf. σβέσαι) extinguish, put out; restrain (the Spirit); pass. go out, be extinguished

σεαυτοῦ, ῆς reflexive pro.

yourself (κατὰ σ. ἔχε ἐνώπιον τοῦ θεοῦ *keep it a matter between yourself and God* Ro 14.22)

σεβάζομαι *worship, reverence*

σέβασμα, τος n *object of worship; place of worship*

σεβαστός, ή, όν *belonging to the emperor, imperial;* ὁ Σ. *the (Roman) emperor*

σέβομαι *worship;* ὁ σ. (τὸν θεόν) *worshiper of God* (Gentile who accepted the one God of Judaism and attended the synagogue but did not follow all the details of the Jewish way of life)

Σειλεᾶς alt. form of **Σιλᾶς**

σεισμός, οῦ m *earthquake; storm* (on the sea)

σείω *shake; excite, stir up* (a city); *tremble, shake with fear* (Mt 28.4)

Σεκοῦνδος, ου m *Secundus* (Ac 20.4)

Σελεύκεια, ας f *Seleucia* (4 G–3)

σελήνη, ης f *moon*

σεληνιάζομαι (lit. *be moonstruck*) *be an epileptic*

Σεμεῖν m *Semein* (Lk 3.26)

σεμίδαλις, εως f *fine wheat flour*

σεμνός, ή, όν *serious; of good character, honorable, worthy, respectable*

σεμνότης, ητος f *seriousness, proper conduct, respectability*

Σέργιος, ου m *Sergius* (Ac 13.7)

Σερούχ m *Serug* (Lk 3.35)

σέσηπα pf. of **σήπω**

σέσωκα pf. of **σώζω**

Σήθ m *Seth* (Lk 3.38)

Σήμ m *Shem* (Lk 3.36)

σημαίνω (aor. ἐσήμανα, inf. σημᾶναι) *indicate, make known; predict* (Ac 11.28)

σημεῖον, ου n *miraculous sign, miracle; sign, that by which something is known or distinguished, indication, mark, signal; portent, warning sign* παρα - ιλομη, with bee ge, εφ

σημειόομαι *take note of*

σήμερον adv. *today;* ἡ σ. or ἡ σ. ἡμέρα *today, this very day* επι- υμοη,οη,αι, αιοπι

σήπω (pf. σέσηπα) *rot, decay*

σής, σητός m *moth*

σητόβρωτος, ον *motheaten*

σθενόω *strengthen*

σιαγών, όνος f *cheek*

σιγάω intrans. *keep silent, be silent; become silent, stop talking;* trans. *keep secret, keep in silence*

σιγή, ῆς f *silence*

σίδηρος, ου m *iron*

σιδηροῦς, ᾶ, οῦν *made of iron*

Σιδών, ῶνος f *Sidon* (**1** C–1, **2** C–1, **3** D–3, **4** G–4)

Σιδώνιος, α, ον *of Sidon*

σικάριος, ου m *terrorist, cutthroat, assassin* (member of a fanatical group of Jewish nationalists) σίκερα n *strong drink*

Σίλας, α m *Silas*

Σιλουανός, οῦ m *Silvanus*
(perhaps the same person as
Σίλας)

Σιλωάμ m *Siloam*

σιμικίνθιον, ου n *apron* (as
worn by a workman)

Σίμων, ωνος m *Simon:* (1)
Simon Peter; (2) Simon ὁ
Καναναῖος (ὁ ζηλωτής), one
of the twelve; (3) brother of
Jesus (Mt 13.55; Mk 6.3);
(4) Simon of Cyrene (Mt
27.32; Mk 15.21; Lk 23.26);
(5) father of Judas Iscariot
(Jn 6.71; 13.2, 26); (6) a
tanner in Joppa (Ac 9.43;
10.6, 17, 32b); (7) a magician of Samaria (Ac 8.9,
13, 18, 24); (8) the leper
(Mt 26.6; Mk 14.3); (9) the
Pharisee (Lk 7.40, 43, 44)

Σινᾶ *Sinai* (3 C–5)

σίναπι, εως n *mustard* (a plant
noted for its small seeds)

σινδών, όνος f *linen cloth*
(used for clothing or burial)

σινιάζω *sift* (of wheat)

σιρά, ᾶς f *chain, rope*

σιρικόν, οῦ n *silk cloth*

σιρός, οῦ m *pit, cave*

σιτευτός, ή, όν *fatted, fattened*

σιτίον, ου n *grain;* pl. *food*

σιτιστός, ή, όν *fattened* (τὰ σ.
fattened calves)

σιτομέτριον, ου n *food allow-
ance, ration*

σῖτος, ου m *grain; wheat*

Σιών f *Mount Zion; Jerusalem*
(θυγάτηρ Σιών *Jerusalem*)

σιωπάω *be silent* or *quiet*
(ἔσῃ σ. *you shall be struck
dumb* Lk 1.20); *stop talking;
calm down* (of the sea)

σκανδαλίζω *cause* (someone)
to sin, cause (someone) *to
give up his faith* (pass. *give
up one's faith, be led into sin,
fall into sin;* pass. with ἐν
*reject, desert, have doubts
about); anger, shock*

σκάνδαλον, ου n *that which
causes sin* or *gives occasion
for sin; that which causes
stumbling* or *trouble, obstacle*

σκάπτω *dig*

Σκαριότα, Σκαριώτης and
Σκαριώθ alt. forms of
Ἰσκαριώτης

σκάφη, ης f *ship's boat*

σκέλος, ους n *leg*

σκέπασμα, τος n *clothing,
shelter*

Σκευᾶς, ᾶ m *Sceva* (Ac 19.14)

σκευή, ῆς f *tackle, gear* (of a
ship)

σκεῦος, ους n *object, thing* (pl.
often *goods, property); vessel,
container, dish; instrument*
(Ac 9.15); *sail* or *sea-anchor*
(Ac 27.17); *one's body* or
one's wife (cf. κτάομαι 1 Th
4.4); ἀσθενέστερον σ. *the
weaker sex* (1 Pe 3.7)

σκηνή, ῆς f *tent, temporary
shelter; tabernacle* (of a wor-

ship place); *house*, *home*, *dwelling-place*

σκηνοπηγία, ας f *Feast of Tabernacles* (a Jewish religious festival commemorating God's provision during the wilderness wanderings)

σκηνοποιός, οῦ m *tent-maker*

σκῆνος, ους n *tent* (of one's body)

σκηνόω *live, dwell*

σκήνωμα, τος n *body; house, dwelling-place*

σκιά, ᾶς f *shadow, shade; foreshadowing, shadow, faint outline*

σκιρτάω *stir, move* (of an unborn child); *leap for joy*

σκληροκαρδία, ας f *stubbornness* (of persons hard to teach)

σκληρός, ά, όν *hard, difficult* (σκληρόν σοι *it is hard for you* Ac 26.14); *strong* (wind); *harsh, terrible* (Jd 15)

σκληρότης, ητος f *hardness, stubbornness*

σκληροτράχηλος, ον *stubborn, hardened*

σκληρύνω *make stubborn;* pass. *be stubborn, be hardened*

σκολιός, ά, όν *crooked, perverse, dishonest* (of people); *crooked* (of roads)

σκόλοψ, οπος m *thorn, splinter*

σκοπέω *pay attention to, keep one's attention on; be con-*

cerned about; watch out (for), *be careful*

σκοπός, οῦ m *goal* (κατὰ σ. *toward the goal* Php 3.14)

σκορπίζω *scatter, disperse; be generous* (2 Cor 9.9)

σκορπίος, ου m *scorpion*

σκοτεινός, ή, όν *dark, in darkness*

σκοτία, ας f *darkness;* λέγω ἐν τῇ σ. *speak in private* (Mt 10.27; Lk 12.3)

σκοτίζομαι *be* or *become darkened*

σκοτόομαι *be* or *become darkened*

σκότος, ους n *darkness; sin, evil*

σκύβαλον, ου n *dung, garbage*

Σκύθης, ου m *Scythian* (regarded by the Roman world as the absolute example of paganism Col 3.11)

σκυθρωπός, ή, όν *sad, gloomy*

σκῦλα, ων n *spoils, plunder*

σκύλλω (midd. impv. **σκύλου**; pf. pass. **ἔσκυλμαι**) *trouble, annoy* (midd. *trouble oneself* Lk 7.6); pf. pass. ptc. *worried, troubled* (Mt 9.36)

σκωληκόβρωτος, ον *eaten by worms*

σκώληξ, ηκος m *worm*

σμαράγδινος, η, ον *made of emerald*

σμάραγδος, ου m *emerald* (a very valuable stone, green in color)

σμῆγμα, τος n *ointment*

σμίγμα alt. form of μίγμα

σμύρνα, ης f *myrrh* (a resinous gum used for aromatic purposes)

Σμύρνα, ης f *Smyrna* (4 E–2)

σμυρνίζω *flavor with myrrh*

Σόδομα, ων n *Sodom* (city located at the southern part of the Dead Sea which God destroyed because of its evil)

Σολομών, ῶνος and Σολομῶν, ῶντος m *Solomon*

σορός, οῦ f *a stand on which a corpse is carried, bier, coffin*

σός, σή, σόν possessive adj. *your, yours*

σουδάριον, ου n *handkerchief; facecloth* (used for the dead)

Σουσάννα, ης f *Susanna* (Lk 8.3)

σοφία, ας f *wisdom, insight, intelligence, knowledge; Wisdom* (of God)

σοφίζω *give wisdom;* pf. pass. ptc. *cleverly made-up* (2 Pe 1.16)

σοφός, ή, όν *wise, experienced, clever, learned; skilled* (builder); comp. σοφώτερος *wiser*

Σπανία, ας f *Spain*

σπάομαι *draw* (of swords)

σπαράσσω *throw into convulsions*

σπαργανόω *wrap in baby clothes*

σπαταλάω *live in self-indulgence, live in luxury*

σπεῖρα, ης f *cohort* (the tenth part of a Roman legion having about 600 men), *band of soldiers*

σπείρω (aor. pass. ptc. σπαρείς; pf. pass. ἔσπαρμαι) *sow*

σπεκουλάτωρ, ορος m *soldier on special duty; executioner*

σπένδομαι *be poured out as a drink-offering* (of one's life), *give one's life in sacrifice*

σπέρμα, τος n *seed; offspring, children, descendants, posterity;* perhaps *nature* (1 Jn 3.9)

σπερμολόγος, ου m *one who picks up scraps of information*

σπεύδω intrans. *hasten, hurry;* trans. *hasten* or *strive for* (2 Pe 3.12)

σπήλαιον, ου n *cave; hideout* (for robbers)

σπιλάς, άδος f *spot, blemish, stain;* or perhaps *danger, threat* (Jd 12)

σπίλος, ου m *spot, blemish, stain*

σπιλόω *spot, stain, pollute*

σπλαγχνίζομαι *be moved with pity* or *compassion, have pity* or *compassion*

σπλάγχνον, ου n *one's inmost self* or *feelings, heart; affection, love* (διὰ σ. ἐλέους θεοῦ *because of God's tender mercy* Lk 1.78); τὰ σ. *entrails* (Ac 1.18)

σπόγγος, ου m *sponge*

σποδός, οῦ f *ashes*

σπορά, ᾶς f *seed; origin, parentage*

σπόριμα, ων n *grainfields*

σπόρος, ου m *seed; supply of seed, resources for sowing* (2 Cor 9.10)

σπουδάζω *do one's best, spare no effort, work hard*

σπουδαῖος, α, ον *earnest, eager;* comp. σπουδαιότερος *very earnest* (2 Cor 8.17), πολὺ σ. *more earnest than ever* (2 Cor 8.22)

σπουδαίως adv. *earnestly, diligently, eagerly* (αὐτοὺς σ. πρόπεμψον *do your best to help them get started on their travels* Tt 3.13); comp. σπουδαιοτέρως *all the more eagerly or with great urgency* (Php 2.28)

σπουδή, ῆς f *earnestness, diligence, eagerness, zeal, effort;* μετὰ σ. *with haste or eagerly* (Mk 6.25; Lk 1.39)

σπυρίς, ίδος f *basket* (larger than the κόφινος)

στάδιοι, ων m *stades, furlongs* (about 607 feet); τὸ στάδιον *arena, stadium* (1 Cor 9.24)

σταθείς aor. pass. ptc. of ἵστημι

σταθῆναι aor. pass. inf. of ἵστημι

σταθήσομαι fut. pass. of ἵστημι

στάμνος, ου f *jar*

στάς 2 aor. ptc. of ἵστημι

στασιαστής, οῦ m *rebel, insurrectionist*

στάσις, εως f *dispute, argu-*

ment, discord; riot; revolt, rebellion; standing, existence (He 9.8)

στατήρ, ῆρος m *stater, four-drachmas* (Greek coin worth two didrachmas or four denarii)

σταυρός, οῦ m *cross*

σταυρόω *crucify*

σταφυλή, ῆς f *(bunch of) grapes*

στάχυς, υος m *head of grain, head of wheat*

Στάχυς, υος m *Stachys* (Ro 16.9)

στέγη, ης f *roof*

στέγω *endure, put up with; perhaps pass over in silence*

στεῖρα, ας f *a woman incapable of having children*

στέλλομαι *try to guard against or avoid;* σ. ἀπό *keep away from, shun*

στέμμα, τος n *garland, wreath*

στεναγμός, οῦ m *groaning; sigh*

στενάζω *sigh, groan; complain, grumble*

στενός, ή, όν *narrow*

στενοχωρέομαι *be held in check, be limited; be crushed* (with difficulties)

στενοχωρία, ας f *distress, difficulty, trouble, calamity*

στερεός, ά, όν *firm; solid* (food)

στερεόω *make strong, strengthen*

στερέωμα, τος n *firmness, steadfastness*

Στεφανᾶς, ᾶ m *Stephanas* (a Christian of Corinth)

Στέφανος, ου m *Stephen*

στέφανος, ου m *wreath, crown; prize, reward, gift; reason for pride* or *boasting* (Php 4.1; 1 Th 2.19)

στεφανόω *crown; reward*

στῆθι 2 aor. impv. of ἵστημι

στῆθος, ους n *chest, breast*

στήκω *stand; stand firm*

στῆναι 2 aor. inf. of ἵστημι

στηριγμός, οῦ m *firm footing, firmness*

στηρίζω *strengthen, make firm, establish; fix, set up* (Lk 16.26); τὸ πρόσωπον σ. *make a firm resolve* (Lk 9.51)

στήσομαι fut. midd. of ἵστημι

στήσω fut. of ἵστημι

στιβάς, άδος f *leafy branch*

στίγμα, τος n *mark; scar; brand indicating ownership*

στιγμή, ῆς f *moment, instant*

στίλβω *glisten, dazzle, shine*

στοά, ᾶς f *porch, portico*

Στοϊκός, ή, όν *Stoic* (Ac 17.18)

στοιχεῖα, ων n *elements* (of which the world is made); *basic principles* (τὰ σ. τῆς ἀρχῆς *the first principles* or *lessons* He 5.12); perhaps *elemental spirits* (of supernatural powers which were believed to exercise control over man's fate)

στοιχέω *walk; conduct oneself, live*

στολή, ῆς f *robe, long robe;* pl. *clothes*

στόμα, τος n *mouth* (σ. πρὸς σ. *face to face* 2 Jn 12; 3 Jn 14); *word(s), utterance; power of speech* (ἀνεῴχθη δὲ τὸ σ. αὐτοῦ παραχρῆμα καὶ ἡ γλῶσσα αὐτοῦ and *immediately his power of speech was restored* Lk 1.64); *eloquence, ability to speak with persuasion* (Lk 21.15); *evidence, testimony* (Mt 18.16); *edge* (of a sword)

στόμαχος, ου m *stomach*

στρατεία, ας f *warfare, fight*

στράτευμα, τος n *troops, soldiers; army*

στρατεύομαι *serve as a soldier; wage war, battle*

στρατηγός, οῦ m *chief magistrate* (the highest civil official in Philippi); σ. τοῦ ἱεροῦ *captain of the temple guard*

στρατιά, ᾶς f *army* (σ. τοῦ οὐρανοῦ *the stars of heaven* Ac 7.42)

στρατιώτης, ου m *soldier*

στρατολογέω *enlist soldiers*

στρατοπεδάρχης or στρατοπέδαρχος, ου m *military officer, commander of a military camp*

στρατόπεδον, ου n *army*

στρεβλόω *distort, twist*

στρέφω (aor. pass. ἐστρά-

φην, ptc. **στραφείς**) intrans. (mostly in pass.) *turn, turn around* (*ἐστράφη εἰς τὰ ὀπίσω she turned around* Jn 20.14); *change inwardly* (Mt 18.3); *turn away* (Ac 7.42); trans. *turn, offer* (Mt 5.39); *turn, change* (Re 11.6); *return, give back* (Mt 27.3)

στρηνιάω *live in sensuality* or *luxury*

στρῆνος, ους n *sensuality, luxury*

Στρογγύλιον alt. form of **Τρωγύλλιον**

στρουθίον, ου n *sparrow*

στρώννυμι and **στρωννύω** (aor. **ἔστρωσα**, impv. **στρῶσον**; pf. pass. ptc. **ἐστρωμένος**) *spread; make one's bed* (Ac 9.34); *ἀνάγαιον ἐστρωμένον furnished* or *floored upstairs room* (Mk 14.15; Lk 22.12)

στυγητός, ή, όν *hated, hateful*

στυγνάζω *be shocked* or *sad* (Mk 10.22); *be dark* (of the sky)

στῦλος, ου m *pillar, column*

σύ 2 pers. pro. **σοῦ** (**σου**), **σοί** (**σοι**), **σέ** (**σε**); pl. **ὑμεῖς, ὑμῶν, ὑμῖν, ὑμᾶς** *you*

συγγένεια, ας f *kindred, relatives*

συγγενής, οῦς dat. pl. **συγγενεῦσιν** m *relative, kinsman; fellow-countryman*

συγγενίς, ίδος f *kinswoman, female relative*

συγγνώμη, ης f *concession*

συγκάθημαι *sit with*

συγκαθίζω intrans. *sit together with;* trans. *seat with*

συγκακοπαθέω *undergo one's share of suffering* or *share in hardship with someone*

συγκακουχέομαι *share hardship with, suffer with*

συγκαλέω *call together, summon;* midd. *call to oneself, summon*

συγκαλύπτω *cover up, conceal*

συγκάμπτω *bend*

συγκαταβαίνω (aor. ptc. **συγκαταβάς**) *go* or *come down with*

συγκατάθεσις, εως f *agreement*

συγκατατίθεμαι (pf. ptc. **συγκατατεθειμένος**) *agree with, consent to*

συγκαταψηφίζομαι *be enrolled* (**μετά**) *with* or *included* (**μετά**) *among*

συγκεράννυμι (aor. **συνεκέρασα**; pf. pass. **συγκεκέρασμαι** and **συγκέκραμαι**) *unite; put together, arrange* (the body)

συγκέχυμαι pf. pass. of **συγχέω**

συγκινέω *stir up, arouse*

συγκλείω *make* or *keep* (someone) *a prisoner; declare* (someone) *to be a prisoner* (Ga 3.23); *catch* (fish)

συγκληρονόμος, ον *sharing together; sharing together God's blessings*

συγκοινωνέω *take part in; help*

συγκοινωνός, οῦ m *sharer, participant*

συγκομίζω *bury*

συγκρίνω *compare; interpret, explain* or *combine* (1 Cor 2.13)

συγκύπτω *bend double*

συγκυρία, ας f *chance, coincidence* (κατὰ σ. *by chance* Lk 10.31)

συγχαίρω (aor. impv. 2 pl. **συγχάρητε**) *rejoice with* or *together; congratulate*

συγχέω and **συγχύννω** (impf. **συνέχεον** and **συνέχυννον**; aor. pass. **συνεχύθην**; pf. pass. **συγκέχυμαι**) *confound* or *bewilder* (by argument); *stir up* (Ac 21.27); pass. *be confused* or *bewildered*

συγχράομαι *associate on friendly terms; use dishes in common* (with someone else)

σύγχυσις, εως f *confusion*

συζάω *live with* or *together*

συζεύγνυμι (aor. **συνέζευξα**) *join together* (of the marriage relationship)

συζητέω *argue; discuss; question*

συζήτησις, εως f *argument, discussion*

συζητητής, οῦ m *skillful debater, reasoner*

σύζυγος, ου m *fellow-worker, partner* or perhaps a proper name (Php 4.3)

συζωοποιέω *make alive together with; make alive together*

συκάμινος, ου f *mulberry tree*

συκῆ, ῆς f *fig tree*

συκομορέα, ας f *sycamore tree* or *fig mulberry tree*

σῦκον, ου n *fig*

συκοφαντέω *take money* (from someone) *by false charges; cheat*

συλαγωγέω *make a captive of*

συλάω *rob*

συλλαλέω *talk* or *speak with; confer with*

συλλαμβάνω (fut. **συλλήμψομαι**; aor. **συνέλαβον**, inf. **συλλαβεῖν**; pf. **συνείληφα**; aor. pass. inf. **συλλημφθῆναι**) *seize, arrest; become pregnant; catch* (fish): midd. *help, assist* (Lk 5.7; Php 4.3); *seize, arrest* (Ac 26.21)

συλλέγω *gather* (of crops)

συλλογίζομαι (aor. **συνελογισάμην**) *discuss*

συλλυπέομαι *be deeply grieved, feel sorry for*

συμβαίνω (aor. **συνέβην**, ptc. **συμβάς**; pf. **συμβέβηκα**) *happen, come about* συμβάλλω (aor. inf. συμ-βαλεῖν; aor. midd. συνε-βαλόμην) intrans. *meet, en-counter; discuss, confer; de-bate;* midd. *help, assist* (Ac 18.27); trans. *think about, consider* (Lk 2.19)

συμβασιλεύω *live together as kings; reign with*

συμβιβάζω *bring together, unite; hold together; advise, instruct, inform; conclude, de-cide* (Ac 16.10; perhaps Ac 19.33); *prove, offer proof* (Ac 9.22)

συμβουλεύω *advise, counsel;* midd. *confer, consult, plot*

συμβούλιον, ου n *plan, plot* (σ. λαμβάνω *plan, plot, hold counsel); council, advisers* (Ac 25.12)

σύμβουλος, ου m *counselor, adviser*

Συμεών m *Simeon:* (1) one form of the apostle Peter's Aramaic name (Ac 15.14; 2 Pe 1.1); (2) son of Jacob (Re 7.7); (3) an elderly man of Jerusalem (Lk 2.25, 34); (4) surnamed Niger, a Chris-tian at Antioch (Ac 13.1); (5) person in the genealogy of Jesus (Lk 3.30)

συμμαθητής, οῦ m *fellow disciple*

συμμαρτυρέω *show to be true, give evidence in sup-port of*

συμμερίζομαι *share with*

συμμέτοχος, ου m *sharer, participant*

συμμιμητής, οῦ m *one who joins in following the example of another*

συμμορφίζομαι *take on the same form as, share the like-ness of*

σύμμορφος, ον *having the same form, sharing the like-ness*

συμπαθέω *feel sympathy with;* perhaps *share sufferings with* (He 10.34)

συμπαθής, ές *sharing the same feeling*

συμπαραγίνομαι (aor. ptc. συμπαραγενόμενος) *as-semble, come together*

συμπαρακαλέομαι (aor. inf. συμπαρακληθῆναι) *be en-couraged together*

συμπαραλαμβάνω (aor. inf. συμπαραλαβεῖν) *take* or *bring along with*

συμπάρειμι *be present with*

συμπάσχω *suffer together, share the same suffering*

συμπέμπω *send along with*

συμπεριλαμβάνω (aor. ptc. συμπεριλαβών) *take in one's arms, embrace, hug*

συμπίνω (aor. συνέπιον) *drink with*

συμπίπτω (aor. συνέπεσον) *collapse, fall*

συμπληρόω *draw near, come* (of time); *swamp* (of per-sons in a boat) συμπνίγω   *choke; crowd around, crush*

συμπολίτης, ου   m *fellow-citizen*

συμπορεύομαι   *go or walk along with;* σ. πρός *flock to or gather around* (Mk 10.1)

συμπόσιον, ου   n *group sharing a meal* (συμπόσια συμπόσια *in groups* Mk 6.39)

συμπρεσβύτερος, ου   m *fellow-elder*

συμφέρω   (aor. ptc. συνενέγκας) *most often impers. it is better, it is to one's advantage, it is helpful, good or useful* (ἐπὶ τὸ συμφέρον *for our good* He 12.10; οὐ συμφέρον *it does no good* 2 Cor 12.1); *bring together, collect* (Ac 19.19)

σύμφημι *agree with*

σύμφορον, ου   n *good, advantage, benefit*

συμφυλέτης, ου   m *fellow-countryman*

συμφύομαι   (aor. ptc. fem. nom. pl. συμφυεῖσαι) *grow up with*

σύμφυτος, ον   *sharing in, united with, at one with*

συμφωνέω *agree with, be in agreement, agree* (συνεφωνήθη ὑμῖν *you agreed* Ac 5.9); *match, fit together* (of cloth)

συμφώνησις, εως   f *agreement, common ground*

συμφωνία, ας   f *music*

σύμφωνον, ου   n *mutual consent*

συμψηφίζω *count up, add up*

σύμψυχος, ον *united in spirit, as one*

σύν   prep. with dat. *with, in company with, along with, together with; by, through* (Ac 7.35); σὺν πᾶσιν τούτοις *besides all this* (Lk 24.21)

συνάγω   (aor. συνήγαγον, inf. συναγαγεῖν; pf. pass. ptc. συνηγμένος; aor. pass. συνήχθην; fut. pass. συναχθήσομαι) *gather; gather together, assemble, call together; welcome, receive as a guest* (of strangers); *catch* (fish); *store* (Lk 12.17, 18); pass. often equivalent to intrans. *gather, assemble, come together; meet*

συναγωγή, ῆς   f *synagogue, Jewish place of worship* (the same building was also used for judicial proceedings, e.g. Mt 10.17); *congregation of a synagogue; assembly, meeting* (for worship)

συναγωνίζομαι *help, join with*

συναθλέω *fight together with, work together with*

συναθροίζω *gather, gather together*

συναίρω   (aor. inf. συνᾶραι) *settle* (σ. λόγον *settle accounts*)

συναιχμάλωτος, ου   m *fellow-prisoner*

συνακολουθέω *follow, accompany; follow as a disciple*

συναλίζομαι *eat with; assemble;* perhaps an alternative spelling of *συναυλίζομαι stay with*

συναλλάσσω *reconcile* (σ. αὐτοὺς εἰς εἰρήνην *he tried to make peace between them* Ac 7.26)

συναναβαίνω (aor. ptc. συναναβάς) *come up together with, travel with*

συνανάκειμαι *sit at table with, eat with* (ὁ σ. *guest*)

συναναμίγνυμι *associate with, have dealings with*

συναναπαύομαι *have a time of rest with, enjoy a refreshing visit with*

συναντάω *meet; happen* (Ac 20.22)

συναντιλαμβάνομαι (aor. subj. συναντιλάβωμαι) *help, come to help*

συναπάγομαι (aor. pass. συναπήχθην, ptc. συναπαχθείς) *be carried away or led astray;* τοῖς ταπεινοῖς σ. *associate with humble people or be engaged in humble tasks* (Ro 12.16)

συναποθνήσκω (aor. συναπέθανον, inf. συναποθανεῖν) *die together or with*

συναπόλλυμαι (aor. 3 sg. συναπώλετο) *perish with, be put to death with*

συναποστέλλω (aor. συναπέστειλα) *send along with*

συνᾶραι aor. inf. of συναίρω

συναρμολογέομαι *be joined together, fit together*

συναρπάζω (aor. συνήρπασα; plpf. συνηρπάκειν) *seize, grab; drag;* pass. *be caught or dragged off course* (by the wind)

συναυξάνομαι *grow together*

συναχθήσομαι fut. pass. of συνάγω

συνβ- see συμβ-

συνγ- see συγγ-

συνδέομαι *be in prison with* (ὁ συνδεδεμένος *fellow-prisoner* He 13.3)

σύνδεσμος, ου m *that which binds together, bond; chain or bundle* (σ. ἀδικίας *bound by sin or a bundle of sin* Ac 8.23); *ligament* (Col 2.19)

συνδοξάζομαι *share in another's glory*

σύνδουλος, ου m *fellow-slave, fellow-servant*

συνδρομή, ῆς f *rushing together*

συνεβαλόμην aor. midd. of συμβάλλω

συνέβην aor. of συμβαίνω

συνεγείρω (aor. pass. συνηγέρθην) *raise together with*

συνέδραμον aor. of συντρέχω

συνέδριον, ου n *Sanhedrin* (the highest Jewish council in religious and civil matters); pl. *local city councils* (Mt 10.17; Mk 13.9)

συνέζευξα aor. of **συζεύγνυμι**

συνέθεντο aor. 3 pl. of **συντίθεμαι**

συνείδησις, εως f *conscience* (ἔχω σ. ἁμαρτιῶν *feel guilty of sin* He 10.2); *awareness, consciousness* (1 Pe 2.19)

συνειδυῖα fem. ptc. of **σύνοιδα**

συνείληφα pf. of **συλλαμβάνω**

σύνειμι (from εἶμι; ptc. **συνιών**) *gather, collect* (of crowds)

σύνειμι (from εἰμί; ptc. **συνών**; impf. 3 pl. **συνῆσαν**) *be present, be with*

συνείπετο impf. 3 sg. of **συνέπομαι**

συνεισέρχομαι (aor. **συνεισῆλθον**) *go in with, enter with*

συνέκδημος, ου m *traveling companion*

συνεκέρασα aor. of **συγκεράννυμι**

συνεκλεκτή, ῆς f *one who is also chosen*

συνέλαβον aor. of **συλλαμβάνω**

συνελήλυθα pf. of **συνέρχομαι**

συνελθεῖν aor. inf. of **συνέρχομαι**

συνελογισάμην aor. of **συλλογίζομαι**

συνενέγκας aor. ptc. of **συμφέρω**

συνέπεσον aor. of **συμπίπτω**

συνεπέστην aor. of **συνεφίστημι**

συνεπιμαρτυρέω *add further testimony, testify at the same time*

συνέπιον aor. of **συμπίνω**

συνεπιτίθεμαι (aor. 3 pl. **συνεπέθεντο**) *join in the attack*

συνέπομαι (impf. 3 sg. **συνείπετο**) *accompany, go with*

συνεργέω *work with, work together with, cooperate with, help*

συνεργός, οῦ m *fellow-worker*

συνέρχομαι (aor. **συνῆλθον**, inf. **συνελθεῖν**; pf. **συνελήλυθα**) *come together, gather; assemble, meet; come or go with, accompany, be with; be married, have marital relationships* (Mt 1.18)

συνεσθίω (aor. **συνέφαγον**) *eat with*

σύνεσις, εως f *understanding, power of comprehension, insight, intelligence*

συνεσπάραξα aor. of **συσπαράσσω**

συνέσταλμαι pf. pass. of **συστέλλω**

συνέστειλα aor. of **συστέλλω**

συνέστηκα pf. of **συνίστημι**

συνέστησα aor. of **συνίστημι**

συνεστώς pf. ptc. of **συνίστημι**

συνέσχον aor. of **συνέχω**

συνετάφην aor. of **συνθάπτομαι**

σύνετε aor. impv. 2 pl. of **συνίημι**

συνετέθειντο plpf. 3 pl. of **συντίθεμαι**

συνετός, ή, όν intelligent, possessing understanding

συνευδοκέω approve of; be willing, agree to (1 Cor 7.12, 13)

συνευωχέομαι eat together; perhaps carouse together

συνέφαγον aor. of **συνεσθίω**

συνεφίστημι (aor. **συνεπέστην**) join in an attack

συνέχεον impf. of **συγχέω**

συνεχύθην aor. pass. of **συγχέω**

συνέχυννον impf. of **συγχέω**

συνέχω (aor. **συνέσχον**) surround, hem in, encircle; stop (of ears); control, rule (2 Cor 5.14); hold prisoner, guard (Lk 22.63); pass. be sick or suffer with; be distressed, be under tension (Lk 12.50; Php 1.23); be occupied with or absorbed in (Ac 18.5); be seized (with terror)

συνζ- see **συζ-**

συνήγαγον aor. of **συνάγω**

συνηγέρθην aor. pass. of **συνεγείρω**

συνηγμένος pf. pass. ptc. of **συνάγω**

συνήδομαι delight in

συνήθεια, ας f custom, prac-

tice; τῇ σ. τοῦ εἰδώλου by being used to idols (1 Cor 8.7)

συνῆκα aor. of **συνίημι**

συνῆλθον aor. of **συνέρχομαι**

συνηλικιώτης, ου m contemporary, person of one's own age

συνηρπάκειν plpf. of **συναρπάζω**

συνήρπασα aor. of **συναρπάζω**

συνῆσαν impf. 3 pl. of **σύνειμι** (**εἰμί**)

συνήσω fut. of **συνίημι**

συνῆτε aor. subj. 2 pl. of **συνίημι**

συνήχθην aor. pass. of **συνάγω**

συνθάπτομαι (aor. **συνετάφην**, ptc. **συνταφείς**) be buried together with

συνθλάομαι be broken to pieces

συνθλίβω crowd, press upon

συνθρύπτω break (of one's heart)

συνιδών aor. ptc. of **συνοράω**

συνίημι and **συνίω** (3 pl. **συνιᾶσιν** and **συνίουσιν**, inf. **συνιέναι**, ptc. **συνιείς** and **συνίων**, subj. 3 pl. **συνιῶσιν**; fut. **συνήσω**; aor. **συνῆκα**, subj. 2 pl. **συνῆτε**, 3 pl. **συνῶσιν**, impv. 2 pl. **σύνετε**) understand, comprehend, perceive, have insight into

συνίστημι and **συνιστάνω**

(aor. **συνέστησα**; pf. **συν-**
έστηκα, ptc. **συνεστώς**)
trans. *recommend, commend,*
give approval to; show, prove,
demonstrate; intrans. *hold to-*
gether, have one's proper
place (Col 1.17); *be formed,*
consist (2 Pe 3.5); *stand*
with or *beside* (Lk 9.32)

συνιών ptc. of **σύνειμι (εἶμι)**

συνίων ptc. of **συνίημι**

συνιῶσιν pres. subj. 3 pl. of
συνίημι

συνκεκέραμμαι, συνκεκέρα-
σμαι and **συνκέκραμαι** alt.
forms of **συγκεκέρασμαι**

συνοδεύω *travel with*

συνοδία, ας f *group of trav-*
elers

σύνοιδα (pf. with pres. mng;
ptc. fem. **συνειδυῖα**) *share*
knowledge with; οὐδὲν ἐμαυτῷ σ. *I am aware of*
nothing against myself, i. e.
my conscience is clear (1 Cor
4.4)

συνοικέω *live with*

συνοικοδομέω *build together*

συνομιλέω *talk with*

συνομορέω *be next door*

συνοράω (aor. ptc. **συνιδών**)
realize, learn of, become aware
of

συνοχή, ῆς f *distress, anxi-*
ety

συνπ- see **συμπ-**

συνσ- see **συσσ-**

συνσπ- see **συσπ-**

συνστ- see **συστ-**

συντάσσω *direct, instruct, or-*
der

συνταφείς aor. ptc. of **συν-**
θάπτομαι

συντέλεια, ας f *end, comple-*
tion

συντελέω *end, complete, fin-*
ish; establish, make (a covenant); *carry out, bring about*
(Ro 9.28)

συντέμνω (pf. ptc. **συντετ-**
μημένος) *cut short, bring*
about swiftly

συντηρέω *protect, keep safe;*
preserve; keep in good condi-
tion; remember, treasure up
(Lk 2.19)

συντίθεμαι (aor. 3 pl. **συν-**
έθεντο; plpf. 3 pl. **συν-**
ετέθειντο) *agree, arrange*

συντόμως adv. *briefly*

συντρέχω (aor. **συνέδρα-**
μον) *run together; join with,*
plunge with (1 Pe 4.4)

συντρίβω (pf. pass. inf. **συν-**
τετρίφθαι, ptc. **συντετριμ-**
μένος) *break in pieces,*
crush, shatter; break (of
bones); *break open* (of
bottles); pf. pass. ptc.
bruised, bent (Mt 12.20)

σύντριμμα, τος n *ruin, de-*
struction

σύντροφος, ου m *foster-*
brother; close friend (from
childhood)

συντυγχάνω (aor. inf. **συν-**
τυχεῖν) *reach, get near to,*
join

Συντύχη, ης f *Syntyche* (Php 4.2)

συνυποκρίνομαι *join in acting with insincerity* or *cowardice*

συνυπουργέω *join in and help, help*

συνφ- see συμφ-

συνχ- see συγχ-

συνψ- see συμψ-

συνωδίνω *suffer great pain together* (as of a woman in childbirth)

συνωμοσία, ας f *conspiracy, plot*

συνών ptc. of σύνειμι (εἰμί)

συνῶσιν aor. subj. 3 pl. of συνίημι

Συράκουσαι, ῶν f *Syracuse* (4 A-3)

Συρία, ας f *Syria* (4 H-3), *Aram* (3 D-3)

Σύρος, ου m *Syrian*

Συροφοινίκισσα, ης f *Syrophoenician woman* (*Syro-Phoenicia* 2 C-2)

Σύρτις, εως f *the Syrtis* (name of two shallow and treacherous Mediterranean gulfs along the African coastline) (4 B-5)

σύρω *drag; drag away* (by force); *sweep down, drag down* (Re 12.4)

συσπαράσσω (aor. συνεσπάραξα) *throw into convulsions, throw into a fit*

σύσσημον, ου n *sign, signal*

σύσσωμος, ον *member of the same body*

συστατικός, ή, όν *commendatory* (σ. ἐπιστολή *letter of recommendation* 2 Cor 3.1)

συσταυρόομαι *be crucified together* (with someone else)

συστέλλω (aor. συνέστειλα; pf. pass. συνέσταλμαι) *carry out* or *wrap up* (of the dead); pass. *grow short* (of time)

συστενάζω *groan together*

συστοιχέω *correspond to, be a figure of*

συστρατιώτης, ου m *fellow-soldier*

συστρέφω *gather up* (wood); *gather, come together*

συστροφή, ῆς f *uproar, unruly gathering; plot, conspiracy, plan*

συσχηματίζομαι *be conformed to, be shaped by, live after the pattern of*

Συχάρ f *Sychar* (2 C-5)

Συχέμ *Shechem:* (1) f *city* (1 C-5, 2 C-5); (2) m *son of Hamor* (Ac 7.16)

σφαγή, ῆς f *slaughter*

σφάγιον, ου n *sacrificial victim, offering*

σφάζω *slaughter, put to death, murder;* ἐσφαγμένην εἰς θάνατον *fatally wounded* (Re 13.3)

σφόδρα adv. *very much, very, greatly*

σφοδρῶς adv. *violently, greatly*

σφραγίζω *seal, secure with a seal; mark with a seal, set apart by a seal; affirm to be true, acknowledge, prove* (Jn 3.33); σ. αὐτοῖς τὸν καρπὸν τοῦτον *when I have safely delivered to them the sum that has been raised* (Ro 15.28)

σφραγίς, ῖδος f *seal; mark, imprint* (Re 9.4); *inscription* (2 Tm 2.19); *instrument used to seal* or *mark* (Re 7.2); *evidence, proof* (Ro 4.11; 1 Cor 9.2)

σφυδρόν, οῦ n *ankle*

σχεδόν adv. *almost, nearly*

σχῆμα, τος n *outward form, present form* (of this world); *form, likeness, nature* (σ. εὑρεθεὶς ὡς ἄνθρωπος *assuming human form, appearing in human likeness* Php 2.7)

σχίζω *split, tear, separate; divide, disunite* (Ac 14.4; 23.7)

σχίσμα, τος n *division, split; opposing group; tear* (of cloth)

σχοινίον, ου n *rope*

σχολάζω *be empty* or *unoccupied; spend time in, devote oneself to* (prayer)

σχολή, ῆς f *lecture hall*

σχῶ aor. subj. of **ἔχω**

σώζω *save* (of Christian salvation); *save, rescue, deliver;*

keep safe, preserve; cure, make well

σῶμα, τος n *body, living body, physical body; the body* (of Christ), *the church; dead body, corpse; the reality* or *substance* (as opposed to a shadow); pl. *slaves* (Re 18.13)

σωματικός, ή, όν *bodily, physical*

σωματικῶς adv. *in bodily form, in human form;* perhaps *in reality, truly*

Σώπατρος, ου m *Sopater* (Ac 20.4) ·

σωρεύω *heap* (of coals); pf. pass. ptc. *weighed down, overwhelmed* (2 Tm 3.6)

Σωσθένης, ους m *Sosthenes:* (1) leader of a synagogue in Corinth (Ac 18.17); (2) Christian of Corinth (1 Cor 1.1). Perhaps (1) and (2) are the same man.

Σωσίπατρος, ου m *Sosipater* (Ro 16.21)

σωτήρ, ῆρος m *Savior, Redeemer, Deliverer*

σωτηρία, ας f *salvation* (in the Christian sense); *deliverance, preservation, release*

σωτήριον, ου n *salvation, saving power*

σωτήριος, ον *bringing salvation*

σωφρονέω *be in one's right mind; think sensibly, be sensible* or *serious*

σωφρονίζω *train, teach, advise*
σωφρονισμός, οῦ m *sound judgment; self-control*
σωφρόνως adv. *according to good sense, showing self-control*

σωφροσύνη, ης f *good sense, sound judgment; modesty, decency* (1 Tm 2.9, 15)
σώφρων, ον gen. ονος *sensible, self-controlled; chaste, modest* (of women)

T

ταβέρνη, ης f *rest-house, inn, tavern* (Τρεῖς Τ. *Three Taverns* Ac 28.15) (4 A-1)
Ταβιθά f *Tabitha* (Ac 9.36, 40)
τάγμα, τος n *proper order or turn*
τακτός, ή, όν *appointed, fixed*
ταλαιπωρέω *be sorrowful, lament*
ταλαιπωρία, ας f *misery, trouble*
ταλαίπωρος, ον *miserable, wretched*
ταλαντιαῖος, α, ον *weighing a talent* (perhaps about 90 pounds)
τάλαντον, ου n *talent* (Greek coin with value of 5000–6000 denarii)
ταλιθα (Aramaic word) *girl, little girl*
ταμεῖον, ου n *inner or private room; storeroom* (Lk 12.24)
τάξις, εως f *order, division, succession* (of priests); *good order, orderliness* (κατὰ τ.

in an orderly way 1 Cor 14.40); *rank* or perhaps *nature, quality* (κατὰ τ. Μελχισέδεκ *just like Melchizedek*)
ταπεινός, ή, όν *humble, lowly; poor, of humble circumstances; downcast, downhearted* (2 Cor 7.6); *lacking confidence, meek and mild* (2 Cor 10.1)
ταπεινοφροσύνη, ης f *humility; false humility* (Col 2.18, 23)
ταπεινόφρων, ον gen. ονος *humble-minded, humble*
ταπεινόω *humble; make ashamed, humiliate* (2 Cor 12.21); *level* (a mountain); midd. *live in humble circumstances* (Php 4.12)
ταπείνωσις, εως f *humble state; humiliation*
ταράσσω (pf. pass. τετάραγμαι, 3 sg. τετάρακται; aor. pass. ἐταράχθην, subj.

ταραχθῶ) *trouble, disturb, upset; terrify, frighten; stir up* (of water)

ταραχή, ῆς f *stirring up; disturbance, trouble, disorder*

τάραχος, ου m *confusion, commotion, disturbance*

Ταρσεύς, έως m *man of Tarsus*

Ταρσός, οῦ f *Tarsus* (4 G–3)

ταρταρόω *put in hell*

τάσσω (pf. inf. τεταχέναι; pf. pass. τέταγμαι, 3 sg. τέτακται) *appoint, designate, set aside; command, order, direct* (ὑπὸ ἐξουσίαν τασσόμενος *under the authority of superior officers* Lk 7.8); *institute* (of governmental authority); *devote* (to service); midd. equivalent to act. *fix, set* (Ac 28.23); *tell, direct* (Mt 28.16)

ταῦρος, ου m *bull, ox*

ταφή, ῆς f *burial-place*

τάφος, ου m *grave, tomb*

τάχα adv. *perhaps, possibly*

ταχέως adv. *quickly, at once, soon* (οὕτως τ. *so quickly* Ga 1.6); *too hastily, too quickly*

ταχινός, ή, όν *soon, in the near future; swift, speedy*

τάχιον adv. (comp. of ταχέως) *quickly, at once, soon; the sooner, more quickly* (προτρέχω τ. *outrun* Jn 20.4)

τάχιστα adv. (superl. of τα-χέως) ὡς τ. *as soon as possible* (Ac 17.15)

τάχος, ους n *speed, quickness* (ἐν τ. *speedily, quickly, without delay; soon, shortly, before long*)

ταχύ adv. *quickly, without delay; soon, soon afterward* (Mk 9.39)

ταχύς, εῖα, ύ *quick, swift*

τέ enclitic particle *and; and so, so;* τέ... τέ or τέ... δέ *both ... and, not only ... but also*

τεθῆναι aor. pass. inf. of τίθημι

τεθλιμμένος pf. pass. ptc. of θλίβω

τέθνηκα pf. of θνήσκω

τέθραμμαι pf. pass. of τρέφω

τεθῶ aor. pass. subj. of τίθημι

τεῖχος, ους n *wall*

τεκεῖν aor. inf. of τίκτω

τεκμήριον, ου n *(decisive) proof*

τεκνίον, ου n *little child, child*

τεκνογονέω *have (bear) children*

τεκνογονία, ας f *childbirth; bearing of children*

τέκνον, ου n *child* (*my child* in the vocative for familiar address); pl. *descendants; posterity; people, inhabitants*

τεκνοτροφέω *bring up children*

τέκτων, ονος m *wood-craftsman, carpenter*

τέλειος, α, ον complete, perfect, whole (ἔργον τ. full effect, successful results Jas 1.4); full-grown, mature (of persons); τελειότερος more perfect (He 9.11)

τελειότης, ητος f completeness (σίνδεσμος τῆς τ. bond which unites everything in complete harmony Col 3.14); maturity

τελειόω make perfect, perfect, make complete (pass. often attain perfection; τετελειωμένοι εἰς ἕν become completely one Jn 17.23); complete, finish, accomplish, end (midd. reach one's goal or finish one's work Lk 13.32); make mature; fulfill, make come true (of Scripture)

τελείως adv. fully, completely

τελείωσις, εως f fulfillment, coming true; perfection

τελειωτής, οῦ m perfecter

τελεσφορέω produce mature fruit

τελευτάω die (θανάτῳ τελευτάτω let him be put to death Mt 15.4; Mk 7.10); be at the point of death (He 11.22)

τελευτή, ῆς f death

τελέω finish, complete, end (τ. τὰς πόλεις finish going through the towns or finish your work in the towns Mt 10.23); fulfill, carry out, accomplish; come to an end, be

over; pay (taxes); keep, obey (of law); find full strength, be at one's strongest (2 Cor 12.9)

τέλος, ους n end, termination, conclusion (ἄχρι τ. until the end; εἰς τ. to the end, forever, continually, at last; ἕως τ. to the end, fully; μέχρι τ. to the end; ἔχω τ. be at an end; τὸ δὲ τ. finally, to sum up 1 Pe 3.8); outcome, result, goal, aim, fulfilment (τὸ περὶ ἐμοῦ τ. ἔχει that which was written about me is coming true or my life's work is completed Lk 22.37); tax, revenue (Mt 17.25; Ro 13.7)

τελώνης, ου m tax-collector, collector of revenue

τελώνιον, ου n tax or revenue office

τέξομαι fut. of τίκτω

τέρας, ατος n a wonder, object of wonder; omen, something indicating a coming event

Τέρτιος, ου m Tertius (Ro 16.22)

Τέρτυλλος, ου m Tertullus (Ac 24.1, 2)

τεσσαράκοντα forty

τεσσαρακονταετής, ές forty years (ὡς δὲ ἐπληροῦτο αὐτῷ τ. χρόνος when he was about forty years old Ac 7.23; ὡς τ. χρόνον for about forty years Ac 13.18)

τέσσαρες neut. τέσσαρα gen. τεσσάρων four

τεσσαρεσκαιδέκατος, η, ον
fourteenth

τέταγμαι (3 sg. τέτακται) pf.
pass. of τάσσω

τετάραγμαι (3 sg. τετάρακται) pf. pass. of ταράσσω

τεταρταῖος, α, ον happening
on the fourth day (τ. ἐστιν
he has been dead four days
Jn 11.39)

τέταρτος, η, ον fourth (ἀπὸ
τ. ἡμέρας three days ago or
perhaps four days ago Ac
10.30); τὸ τ. a fourth part,
a quarter (of the earth)

τετρααρχέω be tetrarch, be
ruler (cf. τετραάρχης)

τετραάρχης, ου m tetrarch
(title of a petty ruler
with less authority than a
king)

τετράγωνος, ον in a square

τετράδιον, ου n squad, de-
tachment (of four men)

τετρακισχίλιοι, αι, α four
thousand

τετρακόσιοι, αι, α four hundred

τετράμηνος, ου f period of
four months

τετραπλοῦς, ῆ, οῦν (from
-όος, -όη, -όον) four times
as much

τετράπουν, ποδος n four-
footed animal, animal

τέτυχα pf. of τυγχάνω

τεφρόω reduce to ashes

τεχθείς aor. pass. ptc. of
τίκτω

τέχνη, ης f craft, trade; ar-
tistic ability, craftsmanship

τεχνίτης, ου m craftsman,
workman; designer

τήκομαι dissolve, be melted

τηλαυγῶς adv. clearly, plainly

τηλικοῦτος, αύτη, οῦτο demon. pro. so great, so large;
τ. μέγας so terrible (Re
16.18); ἐκ τ. θανάτου from
so terrible dangers of death
(2 Cor 1.10)

τηρέω keep, observe, obey, pay
attention to; keep under
guard, keep in custody; keep
back, hold, reserve; maintain,
keep firm; τ. τὴν ἑαυτοῦ
παρθένον (if of an engaged
couple) not to marry the
girl to whom he is engaged
or (if of one's daughter) to
keep his daughter from mar-
rying (1 Cor 7.37)

τήρησις, εως f custody; prison; keeping, obeying

Τιβεριάς, άδος f Tiberias:
(1) city (2 C-3); (2) Sea of
Tiberias (cf. Chinnereth or
Galilee, Sea of)

Τιβέριος, ου m Tiberius (Lk
3.1)

τίθημι (3 pl. τιθέασιν, ptc.
τιθείς; impf. 3 sg. ἐτίθει,
3 pl. ἐτίθουν and ἐτίθεσαν;
fut. θήσω; aor. ἔθηκα, subj.
θῶ, impv. 2 pl. θέτε, inf.
θεῖναι, ptc. θείς; pf. τέ-
θεικα, ptc. τεθεικώς; aor.
midd. 2 sg. ἔθου, 3 pl.

ἔθεντο, impv. 2 pl. θέσθε; pf. pass. 3 sg. τέθειται; aor. pass. ἐτέθην, subj. τεθῶ, inf. τεθῆναι) *put, place, lay, set* (τ. τὰ γόνατα *kneel;* τ. ἐν καρδίᾳ *make up one's mind* Lk 21.14); *lay down, give up* (one's life); *lay aside, store up* (τ. παρ᾽ ἐμαυτῷ *lay aside* 1 Cor 16.2); *make* (someone something), *appoint, destine* (τ. τὸ μέρος τινός *assign one a place* Mt 24.51; Lk 12.46); *present, describe* (by a parable); *lay aside, remove* (clothes); *serve* (wine); midd. *put, place, lay, set* (τ. εἰς ὦτα *keep in mind* Lk 9.44; τ. ἐν καρδίᾳ *keep in mind* Lk 1.66; *think of, decide* Ac 5.4; τ. βουλήν *advise, be in favor of* Ac 27.12); *make* (someone something), *appoint, destine; arrange* (parts of the body); τ. ἐν τῷ πνεύματι *resolve, make up one's mind* (Ac 19.21)

τίκτω (fut. τέξομαι; aor. ἔτεκον, inf. τεκεῖν; aor. pass. ἐτέχθην, ptc. τεχθείς) *bear, give birth to* (pass. *be born*); *yield, produce* (of crops)

τίλλω *pluck, pick*

Τιμαῖος, ου m *Timaeus* (Mk 10.46)

τιμάω *honor, regard, reverence; set a price on* (Mt 27.9a; midd. Mt 27.9b); *acknowl-*

edge the status of or *give financial aid to* (1 Tm 5.3)

τιμή, ῆς f *honor, respect, recognition; price, value* (τ. αἵματος *blood money* Mt 27.6); *sum* (of money); *proceeds* (of a sale); *place of honor, honor* (He 5.4); perhaps *pay, compensation* (1 Tm 5.17)

τίμιος, α, ον *precious, valuable, of great worth; held in honor, highly respected;* τιμιώτατος *priceless, rare* (Re 21.11)

τιμιότης, ητος f *wealth, abundance*

Τιμόθεος, ου m *Timothy*

Τίμων, ωνος m *Timon* (Ac 6.5)

τιμωρέω *punish, have* (someone) *punished*

τιμωρία, ας f *punishment, penalty*

τίνω (fut. τίσω) *undergo, suffer*

τίς, τί gen. τίνος dat. τίνι acc. τίνα, τί interrog. pro. and adj. *who? which? what? what sort of?* τί, διὰ τί, εἰς τί, τί ὅτι *why? for what reason* or *purpose?* τί γάρ, τί οὖν *why then?* (τί γάρ *how?* 1 Cor 7.16); τί ἡμῖν (ἐμοί) καὶ σοί *what have you to do with us* (me)? κατὰ τί *how?* (Lk 1.18); τί θέλω εἰ *would that, how I wish that* (Lk 12.49)

τὶς, τὶ gen. τινός dat. τινί

acc. **τινά, τὶ** enclitic pro. and adj. *anyone, anything; someone, something; any, some, a certain, several;* ἐάν τις (τι), εἴ τις (τι) *whoever (whatever);* εἶναί τις (τι) *be someone (something) of importance*

Τίτιος, ου m *Titius* (Ac 18.7)

τίτλος, ου m *notice, inscription* (indicating the cause for crucifixion)

Τίτος, ου m *Titus:* (1) companion of Paul; (2) surnamed Justus (Ac 18.7)

τοιγαροῦν inferential particle *therefore, then, for that very reason then*

τοίνυν inferential particle *therefore, then, for that very reason then*

τοιόσδε, άδε, όνδε gen. **οὖδε, ᾶσδε, οὖδε** *of such quality, of such kind*

τοιοῦτος, αύτη, οὖτον correlative pro. and adj. *such, of such kind; similar, like* (ὁ περὶ τὰ τ. ἐργάτης *person of a similar trade* Ac 19.25)

τοῖχος, ου m *wall*

τόκος, ου m *interest* (on money)

τολμάω *dare, be brave* or *bold enough; take upon oneself* (to do something)

τολμηροτέρως adv. *somewhat freely, rather boldly*

τολμητής, οῦ m *daring* or *reckless man*

τομός, ή, όν *sharp, cutting;* τομώτερος *sharper* (He 4.12)

τόξον, ου n *bow* (of an archer)

τοπάζιον, ου n *topaz* (a semiprecious stone, usually yellow in color)

τόπος, ου m *place, location, region, vicinity, spot* (κατὰ τόπους *in various places;* κατὰ τὸν τ. *to that place* Lk 10.32); *station, position, office; chance, opportunity;* (Jerusalem) *temple; passage* (of Scripture); *seaport* (Ac 27.2)

τοσοῦτος, αύτη, οὖτον correlative adj. *so much, so great, so large,* etc., pl. *so many, many* (τ. ἔτη *all these years* Lk 15.29; τ. χρόνῳ *all this time, for a long time* Jn 14.9; μετὰ τ. χρόνον *many years later* He 4.7; τοσούτου *for such and such a price, the full amount* Ac 5.8); *enough* (bread); καθ' ὅσον . . . κατὰ τ. or ὅσα . . . τοσοῦτον *to the degree that* . . . *to that same degree;* τοσούτῳ . . . ὅσῳ *(by) as much* . . . *as* (He 1.4)

τότε adv. *then, at that time* (ἀπὸ τότε *from that time on, after that;* ὁ τ. κόσμος *the then-existing world* 2 Pe 3.6); *thereupon, next, after that*

τοὐναντίον (τὸ ἐναντίον) *on the contrary, rather*

τοὔνομα (τὸ ὄνομα) named,
by name

τράγος, ου m he-goat

τράπεζα, ης f table; food,
meal; bank (Lk 19.23)

τραπεζίτης, ου m banker

τραῦμα, τος n wound

τραυματίζω injure, wound

τραχηλίζομαι be laid bare, be
exposed

τράχηλος, ου m neck

τραχύς, εῖα, ύ rough; κατὰ
τ. τόπους on a rocky coast
(Ac 27.29)

Τραχωνῖτις, ιδος f Tracho-
nitis (ἡ Τ. χώρα the Tracho-
nitis region) (2 E–2)

τρεῖς, τρία gen. τριῶν dat.
τρισίν three (διὰ τ. ἡμερῶν
in three days)

τρέμω tremble; be afraid, fear

τρέφω (aor. ἔθρεψα; pf. pass.
τέθραμμαι) feed, provide
with food; nourish, sustain,
support; nurse (at the
breast); bring up (children)

τρέχω (aor. ἔδραμον, ptc.
δραμών) run; exert oneself,
make an effort; speed on,
make progress (τ. καλῶς
make good progress, do well
Ga 5.7); rush (into bat-
tle)

τρῆμα, τος n eye (of a needle)

τριάκοντα thirty

τριακόσιοι, αι, α three hundred

τρίβολος, ου m briar, thistle

τρίβος, ου f path, pathway

τριετία, ας f period of three
years

τρίζω grind (of teeth)

τρίμηνον, ου n (a period of)
three months

τρίς adv. three times (ἐπὶ τρίς
three times or a third time
Ac 10.16; 11.10)

τρίστεγον, ου n third floor

τρισχίλιοι, αι, α three thousand

τρίτον (or τὸ τ.) adv. the
third time; for the third time;
in the third place, third
(1 Cor 12.28)

τρίτος, η, ον adj. third (ἐκ τ.
for the third time Mt 26.44);
τὸ τ. one-third, a third

τρίχινος, η, ον of hair (σάκκος
τ. sackcloth Re 6.12)

τριχός gen. of θρίξ

τρόμος, ου m trembling

τροπή, ῆς f turning, change,
variation

τρόπος, ου m way, manner
(ὃν τ. in the same way as,
as, like; καθ' ὃν τ. as, just as;
κατὰ πάντα τ. in every way;
κατὰ μηδένα τ. in no way);
life, way of life (He 13.5)

τροποφορέω put up with
(someone's conduct)

τροφή, ῆς f food, nourish-
ment; keep, living, rations

Τρόφιμος, ου m Trophimus
(a Christian of Ephesus and
a companion of Paul)

τροφός, οῦ f nurse: perhaps
nursing mother (1 Th 2.7)

τροφοφορέω *care for*

τροχιά, ᾶς f *path, way*

τροχός, οῦ m *wheel, cycle* (τ. τῆς γενέσεως *course of existence* Jas 3.6)

τρύβλιον, ου n *dish, bowl* (of food)

τρυγάω *gather, pick*

τρυγών, όνος f *dove*

τρυμαλιά, ᾶς f *eye* (of a needle)

τρύπημα, ατος n *eye* (of a needle)

Τρύφαινα, ης f *Tryphaena* (Ro 16.12)

τρυφάω *live in luxury or self-indulgence*

τρυφή, ῆς f *luxury; self-indulgence*

Τρυφῶσα, ης f *Tryphosa* (Ro 16.12)

Τρῳάς, άδος f *Troas* (4 D–2)

Τρωγύλλιον, ου n *Trogyllium* (4 E–3)

τρώγω *eat, chew*

τυγχάνω (aor. opt. 3 sg. τύχοι, inf. τυχεῖν, ptc. neut. τυχόν; pf. τέτυχα) *obtain, receive, attain, experience; τυχόν or εἰ τυχόν if it should turn out that way, perhaps, if possible, for example; οὐχ ὁ τυχών unusual, extraordinary* (Ac 19.11; 28.2)

τυμπανίζω *torture*

τυπικῶς adv. *by way of example, as a warning*

τύπος, ου m *pattern, example, model, standard* (γράψας ἐπιστολὴν ἔχουσαν τὸν τ. τοῦτον *he wrote a letter that went like this* Ac 23.25); *type, figure* (of someone to come in the future Ro 5.14); *scar, mark* (Jn 20.25); *image, statue* (Ac 7.43); *warning* (1 Cor 10.6)

τύπτω *beat, hit, strike; wound, injure* (of conscience)

Τύραννος, ου m *Tyrannus* (Ac 19.9)

τυρβάζομαι *b e t r o u b l e d; trouble oneself*

Τύριος, ου m *Tyrian*

Τύρος, ου f *Tyre* (1 C–2, 2 C–2, 3 C–3, 4 G–4)

τυφλός, ή, όν *blind*

τυφλόω *blind*

τύφομαι *smolder, smoke*

τυφόομαι *be swollen with pride*

τυφωνικός, ή, όν *whirlwind-like* (τ. ἄνεμος *a very strong wind* Ac 27.14)

τυχεῖν aor. inf. of τυγχάνω

Τυχικός, οῦ m *Tychicus* (a traveling companion of Paul)

τύχοι aor. opt. 3 sg. of τυγχάνω

τυχόν aor. ptc. neut. of τυγχάνω

Υ

ὑακίνθινος, η, ον *hyacinth-colored* (either dark blue or dark red)

ὑάκινθος, ου m *jacinth, hyacinth* (a precious stone, perhaps blue in color)

ὑάλινος, η, ον *of glass, clear as glass*

ὕαλος, ου f *glass, crystal*

ὑβρίζω *treat disgracefully, insult, mistreat*

ὕβρις, εως f *insult, mistreatment; damage* (of ships)

ὑβριστής, οῦ m *insolent person, person of insulting behavior*

ὑγιαίνω *be sound, correct* or *well-grounded* (of Christian teachings and teachers); *be in good health*

ὑγιής, ές acc. **ὑγιῆ** *whole, sound, healthy; well, cured; sound* (teaching)

ὑγρός, ά, όν *green* (of wood)

ὑδρία, ας f *water jar*

ὑδροποτέω *drink water*

ὑδρωπικός, ή, όν *suffering from dropsy, having swollen arms and legs*

ὕδωρ, ὕδατος n *water*

ὑετός, οῦ m *rain*

υἱοθεσία, ας f *adoption, sonship*

υἱός, οῦ m *son; descendant,* *offspring, heir;* (with gen.) often *one who shares a special relationship with* or *a likeness to someone* or *something; disciple, follower*

ὕλη, ης f *forest; amount of wood*

ὑμεῖν alt. form of **ὑμῖν**; cf. **σύ**

Ὑμέναιος, ου m *Hymenaeus* (1 Tm 1.20; 2 Tm 2.17)

ὑμέτερος, α, ον possessive adj. of 2 pl. *your* (νὴ τὴν ὑ. καύχησιν ἣν ἔχω *by my pride in you* 1 Cor 15.31; τῷ ὑ. ἐλέει *by the mercy shown to you* Ro 11.31)

ὑμνέω intrans. *sing a hymn;* trans. *sing praises to*

ὕμνος, ου m *hymn*

ὑπάγω *go, go one's way; go away, depart* (ὕπαγε ὀπίσω μου *get away from me* Mt 16.23; Mk 8.33); *go home; go back, return*

ὑπακοή, ῆς f *obedience*

ὑπακούω *obey, be subject to; respond to, accept, adhere to; answer* (the door)

ὕπανδρος, ον *married* (of a woman)

ὑπαντάω *meet; fight, oppose* (in battle)

ὑπάντησις, εως f *meeting* (εἰς ὑ. *to meet*)

ὕπαρξις, εως f possession, property

ὑπάρχω be (= εἰμί); be at one's disposal (τὰ ὑ. possessions, property; means, resources)

ὑπέβαλον aor. of ὑποβάλλω

ὑπέδειξα aor. of ὑποδείκνυμι

ὑπέθηκα aor. of ὑποτίθημι

ὑπείκω accept (someone's) authority, submit to, be subject to

ὑπέλαβον aor. of ὑπολαμβάνω

ὑπελείφθην aor. pass. of ὑπολείπω

ὑπέμεινα aor. of ὑπομένω

ὑπεμνήσθην aor. pass. of ὑπομιμνήσκω

ὑπεναντίος, α, ον against, opposed to; ὁ ὑ. foe, enemy (He 10.27)

ὑπενεγκεῖν aor. inf. of ὑποφέρω

ὑπέπλευσα aor. of ὑποπλέω

ὑπέρ prep. with: (1) gen. for, in behalf of, for the sake of (εἶναι ὑπέρ τινος be on someone's side, be in favor of someone); of, about, concerning; (2) acc. over and above, beyond; more than, than; (3) adv. ὑπέρ ἐγώ I am even more (2 Cor 11.23)

ὑπεραίρομαι be puffed up with pride; rise in pride (ἐπί) against

ὑπέρακμος, ον past the best age for marriage, past one's

prime (of women); having strong passions (of men)

ὑπεράνω prep. with gen. far above; above, over

ὑπερασπίζω protect (Jas 1.27)

ὑπεραυξάνω grow abundantly

ὑπερβαίνω do wrong to, sin against

ὑπερβαλλόντως adv. much more or more severely

ὑπερβάλλω surpass (ptc. immeasurable, tremendous; ὑπερβάλλουσα τῆς γνώσεως ἀγάπη love that surpasses knowledge Eph 3.19)

ὑπερβολή, ῆς f surpassing or outstanding quality; καθ' ὑ. beyond measure, utterly, to the extreme; καθ' ὑ. ὁδός a way which surpasses all others (1 Cor 12.31); καθ' ὑ. εἰς ὑ. beyond all comparison (2 Cor 4.17); καθ' ὑ. ὑπέρ δύναμιν far beyond one's ability to endure (2 Cor 1.8)

ὑπερέκεινα prep. with gen. beyond (τὰ ὑ. ὑμῶν lands beyond you 2 Cor 10.16)

ὑπερεκπερισσοῦ: (1) adv. with all earnestness, more than ever; very highly indeed; (2) prep. with gen. far beyond, so much more than (Eph 3.20)

ὑπερεκτείνω go beyond (ὑ. ἐμαυτόν go beyond one's limits or authority 2 Cor 10.14) ὑπερεκχύννομαι *run over, overflow*

ὑπερεντυγχάνω *intercede, plead* (for someone)

ὑπερέχω *be of more value than, be better than, surpass* (τὸ ὑ. *something of much more value* Php 3.8); *govern, rule, have power over*

ὑπερηφανία, ας f *arrogance, pride*

ὑπερήφανος, ον *arrogant, proud*

ὑπεριδών aor. ptc. of ὑπερ-οράω

ὑπερλίαν (adv. used as adj.) *outstanding, special, extra-special*

ὑπερνικάω *be completely victorious*

ὑπέρογκος, ον *boastful, high-sounding*

ὑπεροράω (aor. ptc. ὑπερι-δών) *overlook, disregard, pass over*

ὑπεροχή, ῆς f *position of authority;* καθ᾽ ὑ. λόγου *with high-sounding words* (1 Cor 2.1)

ὑπερπερισσεύω *be present in far greater measure, increase much more;* pass. *overflow, run over* (2 Cor 7.4)

ὑπερπερισσῶς adv. *completely*

ὑπερπλεονάζω *overflow, be present beyond measure*

ὑπερυψόω *raise to the highest position*

ὑπερφρονέω *hold too high an opinion of oneself*

ὑπερῷον, ου n *upstairs room*

ὑπεστειλάμην aor. midd. of ὑποστέλλω

ὑπετάγην aor. pass. of ὑπο-τάσσω

ὑπέταξα aor. of ὑποτάσσω

ὑπέχω *undergo, suffer* (punishment)

ὑπήκοος, ον *obedient*

ὑπήνεγκα aor. of ὑποφέρω

ὑπηρετέω *serve, render service; provide for, look after* (one's needs)

ὑπηρέτης, ου m *attendant, assistant, helper, servant*

ὕπνος, ου m *sleep*

ὑπό prep. with: (1) gen. *by, by means of; at the hands of;* (2) acc. *under, below; under the authority of;* ὑπὸ τὸν ὄρθρον *at daybreak* (Ac 5.21)

ὑποβάλλω (aor. ὑπέβαλον) (secretly) *put* (someone) *up to* (something); perhaps *pay* (secretly) *or bribe*

ὑπογραμμός, οῦ m *example*

ὑπόδειγμα, τος n *example, pattern; copy, imitation* (He 8.5; 9.23)

ὑποδείκνυμι (fut. ὑποδεί-ξω; aor. ὑπέδειξα) *show, make known; warn*

ὑποδέομαι (aor. impv. ὑπό-δησαι) *put on* (ὑ. τοὺς πόδας *put on one's shoes* Eph 6.15) ὑποδέχομαι *receive* or *welcome as a guest*

ὑπόδημα, τος n *sandal, shoe*

ὑπόδικος, ον *answerable to, exposed to the judgment of*

ὑποδραμών aor. ptc. of ὑποτρέχω

ὑποζύγιον, ου n *donkey*

ὑποζώννυμι *brace* or *strengthen* (a ship with cables during a storm)

ὑποκάτω prep. with gen. *under, beneath*

ὑποκάτωθεν adv. *from below*

ὑποκρίνομαι *pretend*

ὑπόκρισις, εως f *hypocrisy, insincerity, pretense*

ὑποκριτής, οῦ m *hypocrite, one who pretends to be other than what he is*

ὑπολαμβάνω (aor. ὑπέλαβον, ptc. ὑπολαβών) *suppose, imagine, think; answer* (Lk 10.30); *take away, remove* (Ac 1.9); *support, help* (3 Jn 8)

ὑπόλειμμα, τος n *remnant*

ὑπολείπω (aor. pass. ὑπελείφθην) *leave, leave remaining*

ὑπολήνιον, ου n *trough placed under a wine press*

ὑπολιμπάνω *leave (behind)*

ὑπομένω (aor. ὑπέμεινα, ptc. ὑπομείνας; pf. ptc. ὑπομεμενηκώς) *endure, hold out, stand firm; bear, put up with, undergo; remain,*

stay behind (Lk 2.43; Ac 17.14)

ὑπομιμνῄσκω (fut. ὑπομνήσω; aor. inf. ὑπομνῆσαι; aor. pass. ὑπεμνήσθην) *remind, call to mind* (pass. *remember); recall to the attention* (3 Jn 10)

ὑπόμνησις, εως f *remembering, remembrance* (ἐν ὑ. by *way of reminder* 2 Pe 1.13; 3.1; ὑ. λαμβάνω *remember* 2 Tm 1.5)

ὑπομονή, ῆς f *patient endurance, steadfastness, perseverance*

ὑπονοέω *suppose, think, suspect*

ὑπόνοια, ας f *suspicion*

ὑποπλέω (aor. ὑπέπλευσα) *sail under the shelter of* (for protection from the wind)

ὑποπνέω (aor. ptc. ὑποπνεύσας) *blow gently*

ὑποπόδιον, ου n *footstool* (ὑπὸ τὸ ὑ. μου *at my feet* Jas 2.3)

ὑπόστασις, εως f *confidence, assurance, conviction* (ἀρχὴ τῆς ὑ. *original conviction* or *confidence* He 3.14); perhaps *realization, confidence* (He 11.1); *nature, being* (He 1.3)

ὑποστέλλω (aor. midd. ὑπεστειλάμην, subj. 3 sg. ὑποστείληται) *draw back;* midd. *turn back, shrink back* (He 10.38); *keep back, hold back, keep silent about* (Ac 20.20, 27)

ὑποστολή, ῆς f *shrinking back, turning back*

ὑποστρέφω *return, turn back; go home;* ὑ. ἐκ *turn from, abandon* (2 Pe 2.21)

ὑποστρωννύω *spread out* (as a carpet)

ὑποταγή, ῆς f *obedience, submission, subordination*

ὑποτάσσω (aor. **ὑπέταξα**; pf. pass. **ὑποτέταγμαι**; aor. pass. **ὑπετάγην**; fut. pass. **ὑποταγήσομαι**) *put in subjection, subject, subordinate;* pass. *be subject, submit to, obey, be under the authority of; take a subordinate place* (1 Cor 14.34)

ὑποτίθημι (aor. **ὑπέθηκα**) *risk* (Ro 16.4); midd. *place before, point out, teach*

ὑποτρέχω (aor. ptc. **ὑποδραμών**) *run under the shelter of* (for protection from the wind)

ὑποτύπωσις, εως f *example, pattern*

ὑποφέρω (aor. **ὑπήνεγκα**, inf. **ὑπενεγκεῖν**) *endure, bear up under*

ὑποχωρέω *withdraw, go away*

ὑπωπιάζω *wear out* (somebody); *treat with severity* or *keep under control* (1 Cor 9.27)

ὗς, ὑός f *sow*

ὑσσός, οῦ m *javelin*

ὕσσωπος, ου m and f and **ὕσσωπον, ου** n *hyssop* (a small bush with aromatic leaves used for ritual purification)

ὑστερέω *lack, have need of, fall short of; be inferior to* or *less than* (pass. ptc. *inferior, lacking apparent importance* 1 Cor 12.24); *give out* (Jn 2.3); midd. *be in want* or *need, lack, fall short of; be worse off* (1 Cor 8.8)

ὑστέρημα, τος n *what is lacking, need, want; absence* (of a person); *poverty* (Lk 21.4)

ὑστέρησις, εως f *need, want* (καθ᾽ ὑ. *because of need* or *want*); *poverty*

ὕστερον adv. *afterwards, then, later; finally, at last* (ὕ. πάντων *last of all, finally* Mt 22.27)

ὕστερος, α, ον *last, later, future* (1 Tm 4.1); *latter, second* (Mt 21.31)

ὑφαίνω *weave*

ὑφαντός, ή, όν *woven* (ἐκ τῶν ἄνωθεν ὑ. δι᾽ ὅλου *woven in one piece throughout* Jn 19.23)

ὑψηλός, ή, όν *high* (ἐν ὑ. *in heaven* He 1.3); *proud, exalted* (φρονῶ ὑ. *be proud* or *arrogant;* τὸ ὑ. *object of pride* or *value* Lk 16.15); *uplifted* (arm); ὑψηλότερος higher, above (He 7.26)

ὑψηλοφρονέω be proud or arrogant

ὕψιστος, η, ον highest; ὁ ὕ. the Most High (of God); ἐν ὕ. in the highest heaven, on high

ὕψος, ους n height; heaven; high position (Jas 1.9)

ὑψόω exalt (someone); lift up, raise

ὕψωμα, τος n height; stronghold or proud obstacle (2 Cor 10.5)

Φ

φαγεῖν aor. inf. of ἐσθίω

φάγομαι fut. of ἐσθίω

φάγος, ου m glutton

φαιλόνης, ου m cloak

φαίνω (aor. subj. 3 sg. φάνῃ; fut. midd. 3 sg. φανεῖται; aor. pass. ἐφάνην, subj. φανῶ; fut. pass. φανήσομαι) shine, give light (midd. Php 2.15); midd. and pass. appear, be seen, be or become visible, be revealed (be revealed as Ro 7.13; ἁμαρτωλὸς ποῦ φανεῖται what will become of the sinner? 1 Pe 4.18); appear to be something, put on an appearance; seem, appear (τί ὑμῖν φαίνεται what is your decision? Mk 14.64)

Φάλεκ m Peleg (Lk 3.35)

φανερός, ά, όν known, evident, plain, visible (ἐλθεῖν εἰς φ. be brought out into the

open Mk 4.22; Lk 8.17; ὁ ἐν τῷ φ. Ἰουδαῖος one who is a Jew outwardly Ro 2.28)

φανερόω make known, reveal, show; make evident or plain; pass. be revealed or made known; be evident or plain; appear, reveal oneself

φανερῶς adv. openly, publicly; clearly

φανέρωσις, εως f bringing to light, disclosure (τῇ φ. τῆς ἀληθείας in the full light of truth 2 Cor 4.2)

φανός, οῦ m lantern, torch

Φανουήλ m Phanuel (Lk 2.36)

φαντάζομαι appear (τὸ φανταζόμενον the sight or spectacle He 12.21)

φαντασία, ας f pomp, outward display

φάντασμα, τος n *ghost, apparition*

φανῶ aor. pass. subj. of φαίνω

φάραγξ, αγγος f *valley, ravine*

Φαραώ m *Pharaoh* (both as a title and a proper name of the Egyptian king)

Φάρες m *Perez* (Mt 1.3; Lk 3.33)

Φαρισαῖος, ου m *Pharisee* (member of a Jewish religious sect)

φαρμακεία, ας f *sorcery, witchcraft*

φαρμακία alt. form of φαρμακεία

φάρμακον, ου n *witchcraft, magic; magic potion*

φάρμακος, ου m *sorcerer, one who practices magic or witchcraft*

φασίν pres. 3 pl. of φημί

φάσις, εως f *news, report*

φάσκω *allege, claim, assert*

φάτνη, ης f *manger, feeding-trough; stable*

φαῦλος, η, ον *evil, wrong, bad, vile*

φέγγος, ους n *light*

φείδομαι *spare; refrain from, keep oneself from doing* (something)

φειδομένως adv. *sparingly*

φέρω (fut. οἴσω; aor. ἤνεγκα, inf. ἐνεγκεῖν and ἐνέγκαι, ptc. ἐνέγκας; aor. pass. ἠνέχθην, ptc. ἐνεχθείς) *bring, bring along, carry;*

endure, bear, put up with; yield, produce (fruit); *drive* (of wind; midd. *rush* Ac 2.2); *bring against* (of charges); *move, guide* (by the Holy Spirit); *lead* (of a gate); *sustain, support* (He 1.3); *establish, validate, prove* (θάνατον ἀνάγκη φ. τοῦ διαθεμένου *the death of the one who made the will must be established* He 9.16); *put, reach out* (Jn 20.27)

φεύγω (aor. ἔφυγον, inf. φυγεῖν) *flee, run away; escape; shun, avoid, turn from; disappear, vanish* (Re 16.20)

Φῆλιξ, ικος m *Felix* (procurator of Palestine, i. e. of Judea and other parts of the Holy Land)

φήμη, ης f *report, news*

φημί (3 sg. φησίν, 3 pl. φασίν; impf. 3 sg. ἔφη) *say* (impers. *it is said* 2 Cor 10.10); *mean, imply*

Φῆστος, ου m *Festus* (successor to Felix as procurator of Palestine)

φθάνω *come upon; attain, achieve; reach, come to; precede* (1 Th 4.15)

φθαρτός, ή, όν *subject to decay, perishable, mortal*

φθέγγομαι *speak*

φθείρω (fut. φθερῶ, 3 sg. φθειρεῖ, φθερεῖ and φθηρεῖ; aor. pass. subj. φθαρῶ; fut. pass. φθαρήσομαι) *cor-*

rupt, ruin, destroy; lead astray, seduce

φθινοπωρινός, ή, όν of late autumn, i. e. in harvest season

φθόγγος, ου m voice; sound, tone

φθονέω envy, be jealous of

φθόνος, ου m envy, jealousy, spite

φθορά, ᾶς f decay, corruption, ruin (εἰς ἅλωσιν καὶ φ. to be caught and killed 2 Pe 2.12); moral ruin, depravity; that which is perishable

φιάλη, ης f bowl

φιλάγαθος, ον loving what is good

Φιλαδέλφεια, ας f Philadelphia (4 E-2)

φιλαδελφία, ας f brotherly love (of one Christian for another)

φιλάδελφος, ον loving one's fellow-Christian or fellow-man

φίλανδρος loving one's husband

φιλανθρωπία, ας f kindness, hospitality; (God's) love of mankind

φιλανθρώπως adv. considerately, kindly

φιλαργυρία, ας f love of money

φιλάργυρος, ον fond of money

φίλαυτος, ον selfish, self-centered

φιλέω love, have deep feeling for; love, like (to do or be something); kiss

φίλη see **φίλος**

φιλήδονος, ον given over to pleasure

φίλημα, τος n kiss

Φιλήμων, ονος m Philemon (Phm 1)

Φίλητος, ου m Philetus (2 Tm 2.17)

φιλία, ας f love, friendship

Φιλιππήσιος, ου m Philippian

Φίλιπποι, ων m Philippi: (1) Caesarea Philippi (2 D-2); (2) in Macedonia (4 D-1)

Φίλιππος, ου m Philip: (1) one of the twelve apostles; (2) son of Herod the Great and tetrarch of territories in northeast Palestine; (3) one of the seven "deacons" of the Jerusalem church; (4) first husband of Herodias (Mt 14.3; Mk 6.17)

φιλόθεος, ον loving God

Φιλόλογος, ου m Philologus (Ro 16.15)

φιλονεικία, ας f dispute, argument

φιλόνεικος, ον argumentative

φιλοξενία, ας f hospitality

φιλόξενος, ον hospitable

φιλοπρωτεύω desire to lead or be first

φίλος, ου m and **φίλη, ης** f friend; friendly (Ac 19.31)

φιλοσοφία, ας f *philosophy* (in a bad sense), *human wisdom*

φιλόσοφος, ου m *philosopher, teacher* (of a philosophy or way of thought)

φιλόστοργος, ον *loving, devoted*

φιλότεκνος, ον *loving one's children*

φιλοτιμέομαι *make it one's ambition* or *aim, endeavor, aspire*

φιλοφρόνως adv. *hospitably, kindly*

φιμόω *silence, put to silence* (pass. *be silenced* or *silent; be speechless* Mt 22.12); *muzzle* (oxen)

Φλέγων, οντος m *Phlegon* (Ro 16.14)

φλογίζω *set on fire*

φλόξ, φλογός f *flame*

φλυαρέω *slander, accuse*

φλύαρος, ον *gossipy*

φοβέομαι trans. *fear, be afraid of; fear, be afraid* (to do something); *fear, worship, reverence* (God); *respect* (Eph 5.33); intrans. *be afraid, be frightened*

φοβερός, ά, όν *fearful, terrifying*

φόβητρον, ου n *dreadful sight* or *event*

φόβος, ου m *fear, terror; fear, reverence* (for God); *respect* (for persons)

Φοίβη, ης f *Phoebe* (Ro 16.1)

Φοινίκη, ης f *Phoenicia* (4 G–4)

φοῖνιξ or **φοίνιξ, ικος** m *palm-tree; palm branch*

Φοῖνιξ, ικος m *Phoenix* (4 D–4)

φονεύς, έως m *murderer*

φονεύω *murder, put to death*

φόνος, ου m *murder, killing*

φορέω *wear* (φ. εἰκόνα *wear the likeness of* 1 Cor 15.49); *hold the power of* (Ro 13.4)

Φόρον, ου n see Ἀππίου Φόρον

φόρος, ου m *tax, tribute*

φορτίζω *burden, load with burdens*

φορτίον, ου n *burden, load; cargo*

Φορτουνᾶτος, ου m *Fortunatus* (1 Cor 16.17)

φραγέλλιον, ου n *whip*

φραγελλόω *beat with a whip*

φραγμός, οῦ m *fence, wall, hedge;* perhaps *lane, path* (Lk 14.23)

φράζω *explain, interpret*

φράσσω (aor. pass. subj. **φραγῶ**; fut. pass. **φραγήσομαι**) *silence, put to silence; muzzle, stop, shut*

φρέαρ, ατος n *well; pit, shaft*

φρεναπατάω *deceive, fool*

φρεναπάτης, ου m *deceiver*

φρήν, φρενός f *thinking, understanding*

φρίσσω *tremble with fear*

φρονέω *think, have in mind* (φ. τά with gen. *think the* *thoughts of, have one's mind controlled by;* τὸ αὐτὸ φ. or ἕν φ. *live in harmony of mind, agree with one another;* ὑψηλὰ φ. *be proud, have proud thoughts); care for, be concerned about (*τὸ φρονεῖν *concern, care* Php 4.10); *think highly of* (Ro 14.6a)

φρόνημα, τος n *way of thinking, mind*

φρόνησις, εως f *insight, wisdom; way of thinking*

φρόνιμος, ον *wise, sensible, thoughtful;* comp. *shrewder* (Lk 16.8)

φρονίμως adv. *wisely, shrewdly*

φροντίζω *concentrate upon, be concerned about* (doing something)

φρουρέω *guard; keep watch over, protect; hold prisoner, keep* (someone) *locked up as a prisoner*

φρυάσσω *rage, be furious*

φρύγανον, ου n *dry wood, stick*

Φρυγία, ας f *Phrygia* (4 E–2)

φυγεῖν aor. inf. of **φεύγω**

Φύγελος, ου m *Phygelus* (2 Tm 1.15)

φυγή, ῆς f *flight*

φυέν aor. pass. ptc. neut. of **φύω**

φυλακή, ῆς f *prison, jail, place of imprisonment; watch* (one of the three or four periods of time into which the night was divided from 6 p.m. – 6 a.m., cf. Mk 13.35); *guard* or *guard post* (Ac 12.10); *haunt, lair* (of evil spirits); φυλάσσω φ. *take turns keeping watch* (Lk 2.8)

φυλακίζω *imprison*

φυλακτήριον, ου n *phylactery* (small case containing scripture verses, worn on the arm and forehead by the Jew while praying, as commanded in Dt 6.8)

φύλαξ, ακος m *guard, sentry*

φυλάσσω *guard, keep under guard; keep, obey, follow; keep safe, protect, defend;* midd. *guard against, avoid; abstain from* (food offered in sacrifice to idols); *keep, obey* (Mk 10.20)

φυλή, ῆς f *tribe; nation, people*

φύλλον, ου n *leaf*

φύραμα, τος n *lump* (of clay or dough)

φυσικός, ή, όν *natural, in accord with nature;* ζῷα γεγεννημένα φ. *mere brute beasts, mere wild animals* (2 Pe 2.12)

φυσικῶς adv. *naturally, by nature*

φυσιόω *cause conceit* or *arrogance;* pass. *be conceited* or *arrogant*

φύσις, εως f *nature, natural condition* (ὁ κατὰ φ. κλάδος *natural branch* Ro 11.21, cf. Ro 11.24; ἡ ἐκ φ. ἀκροβυστία *one who is physically uncircumcised* Ro 2.27; παρὰ φ. *contrary to nature* Ro 11.24);· *nature, the natural order* (ἡ παρὰ φ. χρῆσιν *unnatural intercourse* Ro 1.26); *nature, being, essence* (φ. ἀνθρωπίνη m a n k i n d Jas 3.7b); *kind, species* (Jas 3.7a)

φυσίωσις, εως f *conceit, arrogance, pride*

φυτεία, ας f *plant*

φυτεύω *plant*

φύω (aor. pass. ptc. neut. **φυέν**) *grow, come up*

φωλεός, οῦ m *hole, den*

φωνέω *call, call to; call out, speak loudly; call for, summon; crow* (of roosters); *invite* (Lk 14.12); *address, call, name* (Jn 13.13)

φωνή, ῆς f *voice; sound, note; noise, roar; outcry, cry; language, utterance*

φῶς, φωτός n *light* (often with theological connotations); *fire* (Mk 14.54; Lk 22.56); ἐν τῷ φ. *openly, publicly* (Mt 10.27; Lk 12.3)

φωστήρ, ῆρος m *light, star; radiance, brilliance* (of precious stones)

φωσφόρος, ου m *morning star*

φωτεινός, ή, όν *full of light; bright* (of clouds)

φωτίζω *give light to, light, shine on; bring to light, reveal, make known; enlighten, illumine* (inwardly)

φωτισμός, οῦ m *light, illumination; revelation, bringing to light*

X

χαίρω (fut. **χαρήσομαι**; aor. pass. **ἐχάρην**, inf. **χαρῆναι**) *rejoice, be glad;* χαῖρε, χαίρετε, χαίρειν *greetings, etc.* (of salutations)

χάλαζα, ης f *hail*

χαλάω *lower, let down*

Χαλδαῖος, ου m *Chaldean* (*Chaldea* 3 F–4)

χαλεπός, ή, όν *hard, difficult, full of trouble; violent, fierce* (of men)

χαλιναγωγέω *control, hold in check*

χαλινός, οῦ m *bit, bridle* (of a horse)

χαλκεῖον alt. form of **χαλκίον**

χαλκεύς, έως m *coppersmith, metal worker*

χαλκηδών, όνος m *chalcedony, agate* (a semiprecious stone, usually milky or gray in color)

χαλκίον, ου n *(copper) vessel, bowl*

χαλκολίβανον, ου n and χαλκολίβανος, ου m *brass* (or *copper*) *melted in a furnace and then polished*

χαλκός, οῦ m *copper, brass, bronze; copper coin, small change; gong* (1 Cor 13.1)

χαλκοῦς, ῆ, οῦν (from εος, εα, εον) *made of copper, brass or bronze*

χαμαί adv. *on* or *to the ground*

Χανάαν f *Canaan* (3 C–3)

Χαναναῖος, α, ον *Canaanite*

χαρά, ᾶς f *joy, gladness, happiness; cause* or *object of joy*

χάραγμα, τος n *mark, stamp; image, representation* (Ac 17.29)

χαρακτήρ, ῆρος m *exact likeness, full expression*

χάραξ, ακος m *barricade*

χαρῆναι aor. pass. inf. of χαίρω

χαρήσομαι fut. of χαίρω

χαρίζομαι *grant, give, bestow on; deal generously* or *graciously with, forgive, pardon; hand over* or *release* (of a prisoner); *cancel a debt* (Lk 7.42, 43); *be returned* (Phm 22)

χάριν prep. with gen. gener-

ally occurring after a noun or pronoun *for the sake of, because of, by reason of* (τούτου χ. *for this reason;* οὗ χ. *therefore, for this reason* Lk 7.47; χ. τίνος *why? for what reason?* 1 Jn 3.12)

χάρις, ιτος f *grace, kindness, mercy, goodwill* (ἔχω χ. πρός *have the goodwill of* Ac 2.47); *a special manifestation of the divine presence, activity, power* or *glory; a favor, expression of kindness, gift, blessing* (κατὰ χ. *as a gift* Ro 4.4, 16; ἵνα δευτέραν χ. σχῆτε *in order that you might be blessed twice* 2 Cor 1.15); *thanks, gratitude; graciousness* (ὁ λόγος ὑμῶν πάντοτε ἐν χ. *your speech should always be pleasant* Col 4.6)

χάρισμα, τος n *gift* (as an expression of divine grace)

χαριτόω *bestow on freely;* pf. pass. ptc. *favored* (Lk 1.28)

Χαρράν f *Haran* (3 D–2)

χάρτης, ου m *paper*

χάσμα, τος n *chasm, pit*

χεῖλος, ους n *lip; shore* (of a sea)

χειμάζομαι *be storm-tossed, undergo bad weather*

χείμαρρος or χείμαρρους, ου m *brook which flows only in the winter; valley*

χειμών, ῶνος m *winter; storm, bad weather*

χείρ, χειρός f *hand* (βάλλω

χειραγωγέω - χρεία

χ. ἐπί *arrest, seize); power, authority; activity; finger* (Lk 15.22)

χειραγωγέω *lead by the hand*

χειραγωγός, οῦ m *one who leads another by the hand*

χειρόγραφον, ου n *record of one's debts*

χειροποίητος, ον *made by human hands* (i. e. *by men*)

χειροτονέω *appoint; choose*

χείρων, ον gen. **ονος** *worse, more severe* (εἰς τὸ χ. ἔρχομαι *grow worse* Mk 5.26; ἐπὶ τὸ χ. *from bad to worse* 2 Tm 3.13)

Χερούβ pl. **Χερουβείν** n *cherub, winged creature over the covenant box*

χήρα, ας f *widow*

χιλίαρχος, ου m *tribune* (a high ranking military officer generally in charge of 600–1000 men), *officer, high ranking officer*

χιλιάς, άδος f (group of) *a thousand*

χίλιοι, αι, α *thousand*

Χίος, ου f *Chios* (4 D–2)

χιτών, ῶνος m *tunic, shirt* (generally of the garment worn next to the skin under the ἱμάτιον); pl. *clothes*

χιών, όνος f *snow*

χλαμύς, ύδος f *cloak* (as worn by Roman soldiers)

χλευάζω *sneer, make fun of*

χλιαρός, ά, όν *lukewarm*

Χλόη, ης f *Chloe* (1 Cor 1.11)

χλωρός, ά, όν *green* (*pale* Re 6.8); τὸ χ. *green plant* (Re 9.4)

χοϊκός, ή, όν *made of earth or dust*

χοῖνιξ, ικος f *quart* (a dry measure)

χοῖρος, ου m *pig, hog, swine*

χολάω *be angry*

χολή, ῆς f *gall* (of something bitter)

Χοραζίν f *Chorazin* (2 D–3)

χορηγέω *supply, provide*

χορός, οῦ m *dancing*

χορτάζω *feed, satisfy;* pass. *be satisfied, eat one's fill*

χόρτασμα, τος n *food*

χόρτος, ου m *grass, vegetation; blade, shoot, sprout; hay* (1 Cor 3.12)

Χουζᾶς, ᾶ m *Chuza* (Lk 8.3)

χοῦς, χοός acc. **χοῦν** m *dust*

χράομαι (impv. **χρῶ**; aor. impv. **χρῆσαι**) *use, make use of, make the most of* (*make the most of the opportunity to get free* or perhaps *make the most of the existing situation* 1 Cor 7.21); *act, behave* (ἐλαφρίᾳ χ. *be fickle* 2 Cor 1.17; πολλῇ παρρησίᾳ χ. *be very bold* or *frank* 2 Cor 3.12)

χρεία, ας f *need, necessity* (ἔχω χ. τινός *have need of something* or *somebody); need, want, lack* (ἔχω χ. *be in need, lack;* πρὸς οἰκοδομὴν τῆς χ. *to build up as the occasion* *requires* Eph 4.29); *duty, task, function* (Ac 6.3)

χρεοφειλέτης, ου m *debtor*

χρή impers. verb *it ought, it should*

χρήζω *need, have need of*

χρῆμα, τος n mostly pl. *possessions, wealth, means; money;* sg. *money, proceeds* (Ac 4.37)

χρηματίζω *warn; direct, instruct; reveal, disclose; be called, have the name of* (Ac 11.26; Ro 7.3)

χρηματισμός, οῦ m *oracle, reply from God*

χρῆσαι aor. impv. of **χράομαι**

χρήσιμον, ου n *good, value, profit*

χρῆσις, εως f *function* (of sexual intercourse)

χρῆσον aor. impv. of **κίχρημι**

χρηστεύομαι *be kind*

χρηστολογία, ας f *smooth talk, plausible talk*

χρηστός, ή, όν *kind, loving, good, merciful* (τὸ χ. *kindness* Ro 2.4); *morally good, upright* (1 Cor 15.33); *easy to bear* (Mt 11.30); *good* (wine); comp. χρηστότερος *better* (Lk 5.39)

χρηστότης, ητος f *kindness, goodness, mercy; what is right*

χρῖσμα, τος n *anointing*

Χριστιανός, οῦ m *Christian* (Ac 11.26; 26.28; 1 Pe 4.16)

Χριστός, οῦ m *Christ* (lit. *the Anointed One,* equivalent to the Hebrew *Messiah*)

χρίω *anoint*

χρονίζω *delay, be long coming; stay a long while* (Lk 1.21)

χρόνος, ου m *time, extension or period of time* (ἐφ' ὅσον χ. or ὅσον χ. *as long as, while;* ἐπὶ χ. or χρόνον τινά *for a while* Lk 18.4; 1 Cor 16.7; πρὸ χ. αἰωνίων or χ. αἰωνίοις *before time began, from all eternity* 2 Tm 1.9; Tt 1.2; Ro 16.25; πόσος χ. *how long?* Mk 9.21); *time, moment of time, occasion; delay* (Re 10.6)

χρονοτριβέω *spend time*

χρύσεος see **χρυσοῦς**

χρυσίον, ου n *gold; gold coin, money; gold ornamentation, (costly) jewelry*

χρυσοδακτύλιος, ον *wearing a gold ring*

χρυσόλιθος, ου m *chrysolite, yellow topaz* (a precious stone, golden-yellow in color and more valuable than other topazes)

χρυσόπρασος, ου m *chrysoprase, green quartz* (a semi-precious stone, a greenish variety of quartz)

χρυσός, οῦ m *gold; gold coin; gold image* (Ac 17.29)

χρυσοῦς, ῆ, οῦν (from **εος, εα, εον**) *made of gold, golden* χρυσόω *cover* or *adorn with gold*

χρῶ impv. of χράομαι

χρώς, χρωτός m *skin, surface of the body*

χωλός, ή, όν *lame, crippled;* τὸ χ. *what is lame, lame leg* (He 12.13)

χώρα, ας f *country, region, territory; neighborhood, countryside; land, field* (of crops); *dry land* (Ac 27.27); *people* or *inhabitants of a region* (Mk 1.5)

χωρέω trans. *make room for, have room for* (χ. ἡμᾶς *make room for us in your hearts* 2 Cor 7.2); *accept, practice* (the celibate life); *hold, contain* (Jn 2.6; 21.25); intrans. *be room* (Mk 2.2); *go into* (of food into the stomach); *make headway, take hold* (Jn 8.37); εἰς μετάνοιαν χ. *repent* (2 Pe 3.9)

χωρίζω *separate;* pass. *separate oneself, be separated* (of divorce); *leave, depart; be taken away, be away* (Phm 15); κεχωρισμένος ἀπό *set apart from* (He 7.26)

χωρίον, ου n *piece of land, field; place*

χωρίς: (1) prep. with gen. *without, apart from, without relation to* (occurs postpositive in He 12.14 οὗ χ. *without which*); *besides, in addition to;* (2) adv. *separately, by itself* (Jn 20.7)

χῶρος, ου m *northwest wind* (κατὰ χ. *facing northwest* Ac 27.12)

Ψ

ψάλλω (fut. ψαλῶ) *sing, sing a hymn of praise, sing praise*

ψαλμός, οῦ m *psalm* (of the OT); *hymn of praise, hymn*

ψευδάδελφος, ου m *false brother, one who pretends to be a believer*

ψευδαπόστολος, ου m *false apostle, one who claims to be an apostle*

ψευδής, ές *false, lying;* ὁ ψ. *liar*

ψευδοδιδάσκαλος, ου m *false teacher, one who teaches what is not true*

ψευδολόγος, ου m *liar*

ψεύδομαι *lie, speak untruth; be false, live a lie*

ψευδομαρτυρέω *give false evidence* or *testimony*

ψευδομαρτυρία, ας f *false evidence* or *testimony, perjury*

ψευδόμαρτυς, υρος m *false witness, one who gives false testimony*

ψευδοπροφήτης, ου m *false prophet*

ψεῦδος, ους n *lie, untruth; lying; that which is unreal, imitation*

ψευδόχριστος, ου m *false-Christ, one who falsely claims to be the Christ*

ψευδώνυμος, ον *falsely called, so-called*

ψεῦσμα, τος n *untruthfulness, deceitfulness*

ψεύστης, ου m *liar*

ψηλαφάω (aor. opt. 3 sg. **ψηλαφήσειεν,** 3 pl. **-σειαν, -σαιεν, -σαισαν**) *touch, feel* (pass. ptc. *able to be touched* He 12.18); *feel around for* (Ac 17.27)

ψηφίζω *figure out* (a secret number); *figure out, count* (the cost)

ψῆφος, ου f *pebble, stone; vote* (καταφέρω ψ. *cast one's vote against* Ac 26.10)

ψιθυρισμός, οῦ m *harmful gossip, tale-bearing*

ψιθυριστής, οῦ m *one who bears harmful gossip against another, tale-bearer*

ψίξ, ψιχός f *crumb, scrap* (of bread)

ψιχίον, ου n *small crumb, scrap* (of food)

ψυχή, ῆς f *self, inner life, one's inmost being; (physical) life; that which has life, living creature, person, human being*

ψυχικός, ή, όν *unspiritual, not possessing the Spirit of God; non-spiritual, physical, material*

ψύχομαι (fut. **ψυγήσομαι**) *grow cold, die out* (of love)

ψῦχος, ους n *cold*

ψυχρός, ά, όν *cold;* τὸ ψ. *cold water* (Mt 10.42)

ψωμίζω *feed, give food to; give away*

ψωμίον, ου n *piece of bread*

ψώχω *rub* (the husk from grain)

Ω

Ω *omega* (last letter of the Greek alphabet)

ὦ interjection *O!* (used both in address and emotion)

ὧδε adv. *here, in this place* (πάντα τὰ ὧδε *all that is happening here* Col 4.9); *here, to this place* (ἕως ὧδε *here, to this place* Lk 23.5); *under these circumstances, in this case* (ὧδε λοιπόν *moreover, in this connection* 1 Cor 4.2)

ᾠδή, ῆς f *song, song of praise*

ὠδίν, ῖνος f *birth-pains; pain, suffering*

ὠδίνω *suffer birth-pains*

ὦμος, ου m *shoulder*

ὤμοσα aor. of **ὀμνύω**

ὠνειδίζομαι alt. pres. pass. 1 sg. of **ὀνειδίζω**

ὠνέομαι *buy, purchase*

ᾠόν, οῦ n *egg*

ὥρα, ας f *moment, instant, occasion; time, short indefinite period of time; hour of the day* (i. e. a twelfth part of the period between sunrise and sunset, sometimes longer and sometimes shorter than 60 minutes); ὥρα πολλή *late* (Mk 6.35)

ὡραῖος, α, ον *beautiful, attractive; welcome, pleasant* (Ro 10.15)

ὤρυξα aor. of **ὀρύσσω**

ὠρύομαι *roar* (of lions)

ὡς: (1) particle of comparison *as, like* (ὡς ἔπος εἰπεῖν *so to speak* He 7.9); *as though, as if, on the grounds that, on the pretext of;* with numerals *about* (ὡς ἀπὸ σταδίων δεκαπέντε *about fifteen stades away* Jn 11.18; cf. 21.8; ὡς ἐπὶ ὥρας δύο *for about two hours* Ac 19.34); introducing discourse *how, that* (ὡς ὅτι *how, that*); intensifying an adv. or adj. *very, how* (ὡς τάχιστα *as soon as possible* Ac 17.15; ὡς ὡραῖοι *how welcome* Ro 10.15; cf. Ro 11.33; Ac 17.22); *as* in the sense *to be* (e. g. ὡς προφήτην αὐτὸν εἶχον *they held him to be a prophet* Mt 14.5); (2) temporal and consequential particle *as, as long as, while, when* (with pres. or impf.); *when, after* (with aor.); *so that, in order that, because;* ὡς ἄν (ἐάν) *when, as soon as*

ὡσαννά *hosanna* (in Aramaic), an exclamation of praise

literally meaning, *"Save, I pray"*

ὡσαύτως adv. *in the same way, likewise*

ὡσεί *like, as; about, approximately*

Ὡσηέ m *Hosea* (Ro 9.25)

ὡσί dat. pl. of **οὖς**

ὥσπερ *as, just as, even as; like*

ὡσπερεί *as, as though*

ὥστε *that, so that, with the result that; in order that, for the purpose of; therefore, thus, so, accordingly*

ὦτα nom. and acc. pl. of **οὖς**

ὠτάριον, ου n *ear*

ὠτίον, ου n *ear*

ὠφέλεια, ας f *advantage, benefit*

ὠφελέω *gain, profit, achieve (something); help, benefit, aid, be useful (to)*

ὠφέλιμος, ον *valuable, useful, beneficial*

ὤφθην aor. pass. of **ὁράω**